The Feeling's Unmutual

The Feeling's Unmutual

Growing Up with Asperger Syndrome (Undiagnosed)

Will Hadcroft

Jessica Kingsley Publishers
London and Philadelphia

Extract on page 8 from Romans 12:2, *New Testament in Modern English*
by J.B. Phillips. Touchstone: New York.
Extract on page 8 from *Berserker* by Gary Numan © 1984 Numa Records Ltd. Line reproduced
by kind permission of Tony Webb, Machine Music Ltd.
Extract on pages 10 and 152 from *The Prisoner* TV series © 1967 ITC. Line reproduced
by kind permission of Carlton International Media Ltd.

The right of Will Hadcroft to be identified as author of this work has been asserted by him in
accordance with the Copyright, Designs and Patents Act 1988.

First published in 2005
by Jessica Kingsley Publishers
116 Pentonville Road
London N1 9JB, UK
and
400 Market Street, Suite 400
Philadelphia, PA 19106, USA
www.jkp.com

Copyright © Will Hadcroft 2005

Library of Congress Cataloging in Publication Data
Hadcroft, Will, 1970-
    The feeling's unmutual : growing up with asperger syndrome (undiagnosed) / Will Hadcroft.--
1st American pbk. ed.
        p. cm.
    ISBN 1-84310-264-1 (pbk.)
    1. Hadcroft, Will, 1970---Mental health. 2. Asperger's syndrome--Patients--Biography. I.
Title.
    RC553.A88H33 2004
    616.85'88'0092--dc22

2004015334

British Library Cataloguing in Publication Data
A CIP catalogue record for this book is available from the British Library

ISBN-13: 978 1 84310 264 9
ISBN-10: 1 84310 264 1

Printed and Bound in Great Britain by
Athenaeum Press, Gateshead, Tyne and Wear

For my mother
who taught me how to think

And in memory of my father
who showed me how to dream

Bernard Dominic Hadcroft
1940–2003

Contents

Don't let the world around you squeeze you into its own mould.

Romans 12:2

I'll question everything, I'll trade new dreams for old.

"Berserker" by Gary Numan

A Day at the Office
(with Asperger Syndrome)

As soon as the alarm clock goes off I feel it, running deep, like tremors before an earthquake, waiting to spark something bigger.

I'm happy to be working again after a four-year period of unemployment, and I can't believe I'm working in an office as opposed to a factory. Six pounds an hour rather than the minimum wage. It's what I've been dreaming of for such a long time: a job I actually like that pays reasonably well. Blended in with these positive emotions are other feelings, uneasy disturbing feelings, with which I have been doing battle for as long as I can remember.

As I get dressed and eat my breakfast I think about the day ahead: the eyes burning into the back of my skull, the uncertain looks on the faces of my peers as I do or say something not in keeping with the job or conversation. I feel nervous and apprehensive, and it's only the thought of six pounds an hour, the family car, the holiday we've booked at Center Parcs, the DVDs I like to buy, and the utter dread of going back on the dole that prevents me from throwing in the towel.

> I'm feeling sickly. I'm Gary Numan. I'm staring with those intense piercing blue eyes. "I may commit suicide or I may one day be completely all right."

I kiss Carol gently and wish her a good day before darting off down the stairs of our flat to the car. "See you later, Alligator!" she calls, and I, as is my custom, call back, "In a while, Crocodile!"

Strange custom.

There are many customs and norms in this world that I find strange. A lot of them are completely pointless to my mind, some are just plain ridiculous. I'm not sure where having to leave the person I love all day to go to work comes on the scale, but I wish there was another way of making a living.

When I arrive at work I'm fairly cheery. I like the wide open space of the car park. I smile and wave to other staff members as they trundle in. Things change, though, when I get inside the building. One of the office girls might trail behind me. "Morning, Will," she'll say and I'll open the door for her. As she comes near me, and especially if she's pretty, I'll look at the floor rather than look her in the eye. Pretty girls make me feel awkward and nervous, they always have. Even now, even though I'm married and know all about sex and have enjoyed it for ten years, I still blush and avoid eye contact with pretty girls. Carol thinks it's sweet and boyish. I think it's embarrassing.

Between the break room and the call centre there is an open space, a sort of ancillary warehouse where various items are stored on pallets. As I approach the call centre and see through the windows my fellow executives moving about, butterflies flutter in my tummy and, just before entering, I take a deep breath and brace myself.

> I am The Prisoner, tall and lean, with a serious expression on my face. I have Patrick McGoohan's rasping voice. "I will not be pushed, filed, stamped, indexed, briefed, debriefed or numbered."

The signing-in book lies in a little corner and out of sight from most of the office workers. I scribble in my hours: 9–5. Then I turn slowly, smile, take another breath, and walk with an air of well-rehearsed confidence to my desk, bidding everyone a hearty "Good morning!" as I go.

Most reply without even looking up. Suits me very well, does that. But Gabby actually watches me for a moment. She watches me walk to my desk. Her half smile unsettles me – if it *is* a half smile – I can't really tell. And if it is a half smile, what does it mean? That she doesn't really like me?

That she's not happy with me? That she thinks I've got the job on false pretences? That she secretly hates me?

> STOP IT! Stop! It! Stop it now! You're catastrophizing again. What did Stephanie say? "Tell yourself, 'You're catastrophizing again.'" Take a deep breath. Count to ten.

My manager Megan has caught my eye. She offers a smile. It is warm and welcoming, almost motherly. She's a bit older than the others, but still very attractive, pretty. She's like a favourite aunt, and yet she must be ten years younger than my wife. Who cares? Age is irrelevant to me. It's just another stupid distinction that the world makes.

I sometimes wonder if Megan regrets taking me on. During the interview I was well turned out, smart, eloquently spoken, warm and very natural. That was because I only had to cope with talking to one person at a time, Gabby or Megan, separated in the management office from the rest. I could answer their questions with ease and I knew, I just *knew*, that I could take those incoming calls and use the track-and-trace computer – and pretty much said so. Three months on, I can take the calls and use the track-and-trace with relative ease. I can do the job they interviewed me for. But I'm now worrying that they've noticed the things I *can't* do.

I sense Megan watching me set up my computer. I can't actually see Gabby and Megan once I've sat down because I have my back to them. But I *sense* them, their eyes on the back of my neck, scrutinizing my every move.

> Stop it. You're being ridiculous again.

Checking the clock to see if I will have set up and be ready before nine.

> They're not watching. They have *proper* things to worry about, like managing a call centre, for one.

Gabby shouts over the room, "Can everyone who starts at nine log on, please. There are calls waiting." She doesn't mean me, of course, because I'm already logged on – and yet it feels like *she does mean me*.

> She doesn't mean you. Get a grip.

The phone bursts into life. I put on my headset and hit the answer button. My delivery is up-tempo and cheerful: "Secular Deliveries, William speaking. How can I help?" It's someone from BJ Robert and Son wanting

to trace a parcel for their customer. They begin reading out the tracking
number: "It's 8-DKR…" I'm frowning as I type in the letters and I struggle
to concentrate on the remaining numbers in the sequence.

Something's wrong, but I can't tell what. It's those letters, I don't
remember ever typing DKR in the past. I pause, aware that the silence will
provoke a response from the girl at the other end of the line. I hit the
"Query Parcel History" button knowing it will throw up a "No Trace Of
This Parcel" blurb. It does.

"It's not bringing anything up," I say, stalling. Then a thought occurs to
me: both Megan and Gabby can listen in to calls to monitor how their staff
are performing. I swallow hard and stare at the incorrect code. DKR.

What's wrong?

DKR.

Why can't I see what's wrong?

"Can I just read that number back to you?"

Brace yourself.

Very deliberately. "8–D–K–R…"

The girl cuts me off. "No," she says resolutely. "It's not DKR, it's DKR."

"Right." I stare at the screen nonplussed. I know she didn't say DKR
the second time, she can't have; and yet that's what it sounds like to me.

"Not DKR," I say, hoping to stall again.

"No," says the girl. "*DKR*."

I burn holes in the screen, wanting the answer to miraculously appear
before me. My heart is pounding. I don't know what to do. Is Megan or
Gabby listening? What do I do? I don't know what to do.

I might commit suicide or I might be completely all right.

I daren't ask her again, she'll get angry. I feel like crying, I don't know
what to do.

I'm Dr David Banner. It's night-time and I'm crouching by the wheel
of my car, soaked to the skin with the rain, my clothes sticking to my
back, my hair matted and water trickling down my face into my eyes.
I'm trying to undo a wheel nut with the lug wrench. The steel is hard
and cold to the touch. I'm trying to twist the nut round but it won't

budge. There's a flash of lightning and a crack of thunder. The lug wrench slips and I smash my hand. Nothing really, but it's the final straw. I yell and cry in frustration. "Aarrgghh!!"

DKR. I'm staring. I can't breathe. My chest is tight. I don't know what to do.

> My adrenalin is flowing fast. My DNA helix floats in a solution, one of its cells flickering emerald green. A high pitched blend of synthesizers, strings and distorted voices accompany my eyes, which have changed colour from brown to white. My forehead becomes more pronounced and my hair grows thick and wild. Muscles swell and my clothes burst under the impact, revealing green skin underneath.

A voice. "For BJ Robert and Son."

> Immediate relief. Synthesizers, strings, voices. Gentler. Lou Ferrigno with full Hulk make-up, to Bill Bixby with prosthetic forehead and nose. Green colour fades to normal skin. Forehead and nose blur to Bill Bixby with just the white contacts. Eyes revert from white to brown. Dr David Banner exhales, so tired, so completely drained.

Of course, that's it. It's not DKR, it's BJR – for BJ Robert and Son. Rather obvious really. I've never in my life had to deal with a code that has DKR in it, but I'm always doing BJR. It is BJ Robert and Son after all.

Most of the calls are straightforward, standard, and my way of handling them is almost robotic. But every now and then my brain freezes and I literally cannot think. And the more anxious I get about it, the worse it goes. Sometimes I can see people puzzling over something I've said or not said. I often don't realize until I get the reaction – or non-reaction – that I've had an Asperger moment. They make me want to burst into tears and cower in a corner.

Sometimes, if he's on Lates, Julian, my deputy supervisor, will come in at midday. I like Julian, he's about to turn 30. I like everybody in the place, actually, but Julian makes me laugh. His observations are witty. I smile when he walks in, but he always seems distant, as though he doesn't really want to catch my eye.

He might be remembering what I said when his dog was ill. She's old and prone to being very poorly, and when I first learned of this it reminded me of our pet dog Ben. He was so ill, his back legs gave out when he was going down the stairs at home. I told Julian this. "Is he all right now?" he asked. My reply was nearly casual. "No," I said. "I had to have him put to sleep after that."

> Death. Let's be honest, here. You had him put to *death*. You heartless killer.

And I didn't stop there. I went on at some length about how awful it was, how I felt like a murderer, and how I would never own a dog again. Julian's eyes just got wider and wider, and his complexion changed as he began thinking of his own pet. It was only when he walked off, very subdued, that it dawned on me how tactless I had been. I recognized the signs in his face when it was far too late to do anything about it.

Every time I look at Julian I remember that conversation, and because of it, I find him more difficult to read. I can't tell whether he likes me or not. Sometimes I get paranoid and try to figure out what he thinks I'm thinking about him.

> Don't obsess. Forget it. He's just a man doing his job.

A song comes on the radio. It's one of ten that Tiresome FM play over and over. I'm sick of hearing it. The really catchy ones can stay with me for a whole day. I try not to think of them. TV jingles have a similar effect. I once had the BBC One continuity music – you know, the one where they dance the tango in the rain – in my head for a solid eight hours. Adverts are the worst, though. Short little jingles that my brain likes to put on a continuous loop, usually at night when I want to go to sleep.

> I can do it too with Kan-doo. I can do it too with Kan-doo. I can do it too with Kan-doo. I can do it too… SHUT UUUUPPPP!!!

Another call. This time the girl wants me to phone a depot and ask why a parcel has deadlocked. Sounds reasonable enough. She's put three fax enquiries through and no one has answered yet. And my trainer Ashley said we can do them a favour like that now and then. It's good customer care. "OK," I say breezily, "I'll phone the depot and then I'll phone you back."

I call the depot, then I call the customer. I call the depot a second time to give the customer's response, and then *vice versa* with the depot's; then finally again with the verdict for the customer. I smile to myself having pleased the caller and done the job well. I feel good about myself. I feel confident. I can do this. It's the best job I've ever had. Six pounds an hour, a car, a holiday booked at Center Parcs, a trip to Grasmere, the latest *Doctor Who* DVD. All thanks to this. All thanks to Megan and Gabby taking me on. I recall Becky at Just One saying I'm always cheerful on the phones, and Ruth at Harness Products, who would rather have me deal with her queries than any of the others. "Just think of all the positive things," Carol tells me when I'm plagued with doubt, and she's right. The positive things. Think about them.

Julian comes over. "Can I just have a word with you outside, Will?"

> What is it? What does he want? Are they having cutbacks and want to get rid of me? Are they concerned that I can't input data very quickly? That wasn't the job I came for anyway, I'm a front-liner, that's all I was interviewed for and I do it pretty well.

"We've been listening to your calls," says Julian.

"Right."

"And you've just made five outgoing calls in as many minutes."

"Right." I frown. I can tell by his face and tone of voice, and the way he seems to be choosing his words carefully (and the fact that I've been taken out!), that I've done something wrong. But what?

"What did we say about making outgoing calls?"

I can't for the life of me remember any instructions about making outgoing calls, but I take a guess. "We're not to do them."

"Everyone was sent an e-mail. Haven't you read it?"

> Oh yeah, the e-mail. And I *have* read it.

"And I did tell you the other week to ask a member of management before phoning out."

> Oh yeah, you did. In fact you took me out of the call centre to have a word discreetly like you are doing again now. I remember the conversation now.

I sink into my shoes. I feel embarrassed and ridiculous. Julian looks at me as if he's trying to fathom me out. He might not be doing anything of the sort, of course, because I'm hopeless at reading his body language. I decide to offer an explanation. It's the truth: "I'm still operating on the training

Ashley gave me. I'm sorry. I'd completely forgotten that I'm not supposed to call out."

Julian just stares at me, trying to figure out whether I'm lying, whether I'm telling the truth, or whether I'm just completely numb as a brick. This I *am* reading correctly, I've seen it in people so many times before; wondering how someone so articulate and confident can be so scatter-brained.

He doesn't believe me. He thinks I'm taking the Mick.

"If you do it again, it will have to go on your record, OK?" This is not a threat, it's a simple truth. I nod, shamed. I feel like crying. I feel sick to the pit of my stomach. I feel like an idiot. I want the ground to swallow me up. I want to hide in a corner, curl up and weep, sucking my thumb. I want the TARDIS to appear and take me away.

> A strange unearthly grinding noise interrupts the conversation, and Julian looks on in amazement as an old battered blue police box materializes in a clearing. I shake his hand, smile, and enter the box. Julian stares, speechless, as the TARDIS disappears, taking me with it.

I want Carol to nurse me. I want my mum.

I might commit suicide or I might be completely all right.

I go back into the office. I can feel everybody's eyes burning through me. I keep my own cast to the ground and make my way to my desk.

I might commit suicide or I might be completely all right.

I sit at the desk and log back in to the phone. There is a lull in calls. The silence crushes me. Because the silence isn't silence, it's just that I'm not speaking. My throat is dry and I keep swallowing.

> The lug wrench slips and I smash my hand. I yell and cry in frustration. "Aarrgghh!!" A high-pitched sound accompanies my eyes changing colour from brown to white. My forehead becomes more pronounced and my hair grows thick and wild. Muscles swell and my clothes burst under the impact, revealing green skin underneath.

I can't breathe. I'm dizzy. Everyone is watching me. Everyone. The spot-light's on Will.

The fax tray is full. I can go to the fax room. My eyes flick to the empty room straight away. I'm staring with ferocity. It's the answer. The way out. The Zero Room. Sanctuary. I put the phone on Make Busy, pick up the faxes and head for the fax room.

> Relief. Lou Ferrigno back to Bill Bixby. Green colour fades to normal skin. Eyes revert from white to brown. I exhale, so tired, so completely drained.

Five minutes' solitary brings me back. I'm cut off from everybody, the way I like it. I'm focused on my job, sending the faxes to the depots. I dream of our friends' house in the middle of nowhere in Anglesey. So isolated, so free. I wish that I lived and worked in a place like that. Just me and Carol. Just me and my writing. Just nature, the Creator, the Doctor, Gary, David, Patrick, John Christopher, Ken Freeman, Kenneth Johnson, Anthony, my family, Carol and me. Yes, that would be bliss.

My faxing complete, I take a deep breath, about turn, and join my colleagues in the office.

Most days at work are bearable, some are a joy, but even now, even after the counselling and treatment, I still get days like the one described above. But at one time, it was worse than that. Can you imagine it? Worse than that? At one time I had no idea what was wrong with me; why I was like every-body else and yet so different; why I had no problem with people but found it almost impossible to socialize; why I was desperate to give so much, but tended to be self-absorbed and reclusive; why I was sensitive and shy, yet labelled arrogant and bombastic.

I figured the answers out for myself gradually, by observing and analysing the world around me, by taking what I needed mentally and emotionally from the thinkers in our bizarre society. The writers, the storytellers, the dreamers, whose worlds and heroes I had become so fond of, would in the end release me and reveal me for who and what I am. They would define me.

This is the story of the working-class child who succeeds against the odds. The youngster who emerges from school with average grades but dreams of being something more. A loner and a geek, who marries a beautiful woman and pens a well-received children's novel. It's the story of a boy who grows up to be a man, all the while contending unknowingly with the secondary traits of Asperger Syndrome.

It is my story.

A Slight Cerebral Pause, 1970–74

W E LIVED AT GRANDMA AND Grandad Churchill's for a while, my mother's parents. I distinctly remember the Eastwood Avenue house in Little Hulton. Details like that are vivid memories, the house, the garden, the way the high brick wall rose up by the side passage. I had a keen eye for detail even then.

Shortly afterwards, my mother, father and I moved into an upstairs two-bedroom flat on Briar Hill Avenue on the Kenyon Way estate.

Life on Briar Hill was good. Our flat stuck out at an angle, creating a triangular shape with the row of houses to the left. The pavement on that section was dominated by a piece of grass, and I used to ride round and round it on my tricycle pretending to be the number 90 bus. Like all young boys I was fascinated with buses and, even as a toddler, I was noting the differences in design and style, the way the seats were arranged inside, where the door was situated, and so on.

Lancashire Transport buses were similar to the traditional London type; big and red, with the passenger door at the back. Some of them, though, had the door at the front: a single oblong panel which slid back on a compressed air mechanism. I was mesmerized by it. A lot of young children get a thrill out of going upstairs on a bus and sitting right at the front, but for me, sitting downstairs and at a vantage point where I could watch the door slide back and forth, well, that was bliss. Greater Manchester Transport ruined everything by bringing in their orange-

and-white buses with the now conventional concertina doors. It took me quite a while to get over it.

I was a shy and quiet child but, whenever the subject of buses came up, I would talk about the different types. When I wasn't talking about them I was thinking about them. Thanks to my mum, a rather impressive collection of toy buses was amassed. My parents didn't think anything of it, of course. All boys had phases like this. Terms like "obsessed" were not readily bandied about – because a bus fixation at that age was normal.

Reflecting on those years of my life, I now see evidence of "Aspie" behaviour in great abundance. The traits were not as severe as they are in children with full-blown Asperger Syndrome, but they *were* there: the seeds of what was to come.

My mother had noticed a curious thing in my hand-to-eye co-ordination. She discerned that whenever I was handed a biscuit or a rusk, I would grasp it firmly and then drop it. She knew it wasn't deliberate, that I wasn't rejecting the item or throwing it away. She would hold the biscuit in my hand for a couple of seconds, making sure I'd got it, and then leave go for me to get on happily with devouring it.

Mum was perplexed by this, but her mentioning it to staff at the children's clinic brought no joy. Her observations were dismissed. But she knew she was right. Even my primary-school headmaster Mr Brooks had noticed it. Something odd. Something he couldn't quite put his finger on. Something…

…different.

It wouldn't be until my arrival at secondary school that Mum would have a chance meeting with the president of a dyslexia association. Syndromes like dyslexia, dyspraxia and Asperger Syndrome were not really acknowledged at that time, but after Mum had described the behaviour she had witnessed in me, the man told her, "It sounds like your son has a slight cerebral pause." That is, a pause between the brain giving its commands and the body acting upon them. Very slight, almost unnoticeable, but it would make all the difference. Other Aspie traits, such as a preference for bland food as opposed to food with "bits" in (and my hatred for peas and beans because I couldn't stand the feel of their shells cracking when they hit the roof of my mouth), were passed off as just me being picky.

I'm getting ahead of myself.

The year 1972 brought a memorable trip to Whitby, that famous seaside town on the Yorkshire coast. We, that is Mum, Dad, Grandma and Grandad Churchill along with cousin Tracy, spent a week in that lovely fishing village. We adored it: the sun, the sea, the smell of freshly caught fish, and the town.

There was also a miniature railway line. Like most boys, I was fascinated by trains. The track of this miniature railway line went round in a large circle, with a straight piece veering off into the centre where a couple of sheds housed the carriages and the engine. Such was my fascination that every morning at eight o'clock, I was escorted from the hotel by Grandad or my father to "help" the driver set up the carriages and bring them out of their shed. He let me sit with him in the engine free of charge as he tested the track, and then rewarded me with a lollipop for my invaluable help. I loved that train, and would spend most of the time, when I wasn't actually on it, looking forward to the next time that I would be.

Again, words like "obsessed" and "fixated" were never used by adults at this stage, probably because no one had come to appreciate just how obsessed with it I actually was. They just thought it was cute.

Other fixations which were beginning to develop in my early life involved household appliances such as washing machines and vacuum cleaners. I'm not entirely sure why this came about, but I can only think that the family was very much a matriarchal one. Grandma and Mum ran everything. I was in their presence more than I was with the menfolk, my best friend at that time was cousin Tracy, and my brothers had not yet been born.

I would often draw comparisons between Grandma's washing machine and Mum's. For a time they both had the old fashion Hotpoint machine where one would throw the clothes in through a lid in the top and a large plastic paddle would then drag them back and forth. At the back of the machine was a pair of rollers which would wring the water from the clothes as they were fed through them. After that the clothes would go into the spin dryer and then be pegged out on the line to dry. Grandma's machine was better than Mum's because the wringers could be swivelled over the draining board of the sink. I marvelled when Grandma swung the wringers across. After a while she went upmarket and bought a front-loader machine, which, of course, made Mum's look even more rubbish.

Then there was the washing machine that belonged to my mother's friend Margaret. That was quite a strange one because the window-door sat on an angle. The shape of the machine had me staring at it for a good while. Her vacuum cleaner, however, was a different story. I didn't like Margaret's vacuum cleaner at all. It wasn't the way it looked that bothered me, but rather the noise it made. It was very loud. I'm told that I used to go into a screaming frenzy whenever the cleaner was switched on, and that no one could understand it, because I only ever reacted in such a way to that particular cleaner.

Another peculiarity reserved only for visits to Aunty Margaret's was something called Bungy. Not as in bungy-jumping, but with the "g" as hard: Bung-ie. No one, myself included, has the slightest clue what Bungy is or was. Apparently I would point to various parts of Margaret's living room ceiling and exclaim, "Bungy!" I was clearly seeing *something*, but nobody could work out what. The two adults would smile and ask, "What is it, William? What's Bungy?" I'm afraid they never got an answer.

Then there was the grid near the shop a few doors up from Aunty Pat's house. It was quite small and round, and was sunk down into the ground more than was normal. I was convinced that the grid had something horrible down it, maybe a monster of some sort. Why I believed this remains a mystery. No one ever told me that a monster lived in it, and I don't recall seeing anything like it on TV or having a story like it read to me. It might simply have been the gurgling sound grids sometimes make. But I was terrified of it.

I was perpetually nervous, frightened of everything. I hated trains going over railway bridges whilst I was underneath, I was frightened of balloons bursting, the suddenness of party poppers and the crack made by Christmas crackers. I was very cautious of anything that might make an unexpected loud noise. It goes without saying that I was terrified of thunder; even later, when I knew that it was the lightning which was the dangerous part, I always feared the thunder more. Guy Fawkes Night also made me tense, although I loved watching the fireworks.

Until I was six years old, Mum attended the meetings of Jehovah's Witnesses down at the local Kingdom Hall. This in itself made her "odd" and "different" to her family and peers. I can remember going to the Hall with her. It was a nicely decorated but functional building, a cross between a modest church and a classroom. While there were hymn-like songs and prayerful approaches made to Jehovah God on behalf of the congregation, traditional aspects such as chanting and repeating prayers by rote were exchanged in favour of study and question-and-answer discussions. All of this was to have an impact.

When Mum left the organization in the mid-1970s she maintained friendships forged there. She also kept all her books, which I would occasionally flick through. At a very early age I came to appreciate that society derides minority groups. If something isn't trendy or fashionable it is rejected as odd, even dangerous. Although Mum wasn't practising the doctrine any more, I regarded it as my religion, and so would be prone to talking about it. Other children would be fascinated – their parents less so. Some would go very quiet, others would change the subject.

It served as preparation for what was to come.

My crippling shyness often got in the way of progress. For example, when the rag-and-bone man visited the street, he always gave a balloon to children who brought rubbish out to him. I remember running up the stairs of our flat excitedly, "Mum, Mum, the rag-and-bone man's here. Can I have a balloon?"

"Go down and ask for one," she replied, and I swayed to and fro nervously.

> I can't do that. I can't go downstairs and ask him for one. I can't do it.
> What am I supposed to say to him? I can't do it. I can't do it.

Then I mumbled, "I want you to get it." I procrastinated so much that by the time we got downstairs, the rag-and-bone man had gone. Frustrated and angry with myself, I burst into tears. This was a trend which would haunt me for a couple of decades, and I would miss out a lot because of it.

While we were living in Briar Hill Avenue, Mum became firm friends with a neighbour called Doreen. She had two children at that time, Angela and Karl. Karl was to be my first non-family best friend. We had quite a bit in common. We both had overactive imaginations, and both suffered from a dose of shyness. Our time spent together would always involve outlandish fantasies inspired by various science-fiction programmes on television. The more out-of-this-world it was, the more we loved it.

On 7 May 1974, my mother gave birth to her second son, Jonathan George. I'm told that I was amazed when the baby was brought home, and innocently asked, "Can we keep him?"

It was around this time that we left Briar Hill Avenue to live in our first "proper" house: a semi-detached in a quiet street lined with oak trees. Number 28 Worsley Avenue would be our address for the next ten years and would see in me the development of some rather unorthodox personality traits. A deep thinker prone to questioning the status quo, I would always be on the outside looking in.

Steve Austin, Jaime Sommers, David Banner, Blake's Seven, the Doctor and Me (Oh, and Primary School), 1974–80

D AD DESIGNED AND CONSTRUCTED the gardens. He put a path up the centre of the back garden, grew vegetables on one side, and sowed grass on the other. He also built his own greenhouse from old railway sleepers he found on a local wasteland, and tacked polythene all over it, putting in a door and a hinged window, which he propped open with a stick. And it worked too! I always admired my dad's ability to make things like that. It was far more interesting than buying stuff from shops. Other kids marvelled at his handiwork and I felt proud.

Your dad doesn't make things like that, does he?

When he came into some money he bought a proper aluminium greenhouse. Jonathan and I were sad to see the old one go, and we watched, somewhat crestfallen, as he pulled it apart. He was inspiring.

Mum was forever baking. There was always an abundant supply of homemade cakes and buns, jellies and blancmange. One year, when we had a party, some youths came over from across the street and sampled Mum's cakes. Her baking was only ever second to Grandma's.

I started Nursery around 1974. It was situated in a converted house and was run by a married couple. Like most children I cried my eyes out when my mother left me there on the first day.

Once the panic had subsided, I adjusted.

By this time, I had become quite an avid fan of certain kiddies' TV series. In fact, one might say I was a tad obsessed. I absorbed myself in *Rainbow*, the show where a young man named Geoffrey lived in a house with a bear (that is, a man dressed as a bear) called Bungle, as well as two puppets by the names of Zippy and George. The latter was a dozy hippopotamus, while Zippy was a loud, talkative thing with a zip for lips. I loved it when Geoffrey used to zip up his mouth to stop him talking!

My earliest memory of taking things too literally involves *Rainbow*. It was customary for Geoffrey to end each instalment by saying, "That's all we have time for now, boys and girls, but we'll see you again soon." One afternoon I got it into my head that "soon" meant soon the same day. As the afternoon progressed I kept approaching my mother to ask, "Is *Rainbow* coming back on yet?" To which she would absent-mindedly reply, "I don't know, love." It was only when I approached with an alarm clock in my hand, and pointing at the fingers, that she realized I was very anxious about *Rainbow* coming back. This time she sought clarification. I explained, "Geoffrey said he would see us soon." Mum smiled, "No, love. He doesn't mean soon today. He means the next episode in a few days."

Oh... Why did he say "soon", then?

Play School was usually presented by two adults. They read stories and showed the viewers how to make things out of cardboard and old washing-up liquid bottles. They sang songs and told the time with a big clock full of moving cogs.

Then there were the animation shows. *Bagpuss* told the story of a young girl named Emily who would bring a damaged or lost item to her shop. She would say a magic rhyme to her cloth cat, Bagpuss, and he would come to life along with a selection of other toys to restore the broken item.

Other animations, such as *Chigley*, *Camberwick Green* and, best of all, *Trumpton*, were set in fictional towns and villages populated by all manner of characters.

I knew by heart the times and days when each of these programmes were on, and at Nursery on that first day, as we neared 1:45 p.m., I kept saying to the lady in charge, "You won't forget *Trumpton*, will you?"

> The long hand is on the eight and they still haven't put the telly on. They're just rushing about doing jobs. None of the other children seem bothered. They've still not put the telly on.

I was quite concerned that they might not watch it there, and this was a source of considerable anxiety for me. I was only settled when the opening credits rolled.

The day went splendidly, and I was a bit miffed when I had to stop playing with their slide and inflatable swimming pool. In fact when Mum came to pick me up, I burst into tears again, this time because I didn't want to go home!

Mum had her hands full with Jonathan. He was always crying and needed constant supervision. I have vivid memories of her telling people that he was hyperactive and that she was watching his intake of substances in soft drinks, the ingredients of which might be contributing. She may have been quite glad when September 1975 arrived, because now I was starting junior school, and she could concentrate exclusively on watching out for my brother.

On my first day at St Andrews West, Mum sat me in my chair and knelt by my side. She knew I didn't take to new situations well. She whispered into my ear, "You can't see them, but the angels are watching over you, looking after you." I glanced about the windows after she had gone…

> Huge with big folded wings on their backs, luminous white, their faces barely visible, two to each of the tall windows.

…and felt pleased that the angels were looking after me.

Our teacher was called Mrs Leach, and it didn't take long for us to start calling her "Mrs Bleach" behind her back. I found this kind of thing highly amusing. The day would consist of lessons in the morning and "activities" in the afternoon. (Activities was just playing with toys.)

The caretaker, Mr Mulligan, had constructed a hardboard three-fold entrance with a door in it, which was pulled over a room containing a mock-up house interior. The "house corner", as it was called, was everybody's favourite place. My obsession with household appliances often got the better of me and I would end up pretending to do the ironing or vacuuming. The then traditional male role simply did not interest me. I adored hoovers and washing machines!

I once saw an episode of *Play School* where they made a washing machine out of a cardboard box. It had a Sellotape window and a Dairylea cheese box for the dial. A coat hanger was stuck in the back to turn the clothes round. I made one and showed it off to my friend Karl, who went on to make one of his own.

At school, if anybody did not complete their assigned work in the morning, their punishment was to miss Activities. One day, I knew I was not going to finish in time. Panic seized me as I anticipated telling Mrs Leach I hadn't met the deadline. This must have been one of my earliest experiences of having to deal with that sort of anxiety, the memory is so clear.

I stuttered and stammered, "I'll finish my work instead of Activities, Miss." She seemed to resent my pre-empting her chastisement. "You're right, William Hadcroft, you will."

One of the highlights of my time in the infants was having a day off to ride with Uncle John Hadcroft in his lorry. He picked me up early in the morning while it was still dark, and I thought it was the middle of the night. It all seemed so daring because my dad had always frightened us with stories of what happens when children stay up past midnight. "Quick, get in bed," he'd say, "Midnight's coming." His tone implied something threatening and awful, or at least that's how *I* interpreted it. I actually thought "Midnight" was some sort of monster.

It was great in Uncle John's lorry, I really enjoyed myself. But I was very aware that I was missing school and thought I was engaging in something wrong. The word "illegal" had not entered my vocabulary by that time, but the feeling of guilt whenever an adult saw me crippled me. I have very distinct memories of sliding myself down the passenger seat of Uncle John's car for fear of someone telling the authorities.

By the end of the first term, I had come to the conclusion that Mrs Leach didn't really like me. Looking back it's very obvious to me now that she made no distinction between me and the other children whatsoever, but even at that tender age it would seem that some sort of neurological problem akin to paranoia was beginning to set in.

My peers on the whole were quite a friendly bunch, though. Jason Innes and Sean Flowers were particularly pally with me. Graham Hodgeson was quite shy, as was Kay Lancaster. I admired and envied the confidence demonstrated by some of the others. Jason Jarrett and Gary Smeaton were nice.

One playtime, we had a discussion as to whether we would smoke when we grew up. Everybody but Sean Flowers and Graham Hodgeson said they would. I didn't rate those Park Drive things my mother smoked, because they smelled like burning wood, but I did like the look of the longer, tipped cigarettes smoked by my Aunty Glenda. She always drew hard on her cigarette and looked like she really enjoyed it. So I decided I would smoke that kind when I grew up.

Unbeknown to the adults in my life, the 100-millimetre cigarettes, enjoyed by Mum's friend Jackie, were a source of fascination to me. I would hang around and wait for her to flip open the packet and slide one out.

They're so long!

And like Aunty Glenda, Jackie drew hard and savoured the act. I was completely obsessed with the 100-millimetre cigarette.

After the Christmas break, Cousin Tracy's brother, Anthony, joined us at Mrs Bleach's. We got on like a house on fire. Leach had an expression which she always said when the children got too rowdy: "Er, the noise is growing." I would get a certain degree of enjoyment out of imagining a visible form of noise growing larger and larger, and I told Anthony about it. We would glance at one another across the room and do a rising motion with our hands – and then burst into manic laughter. Leach would then frown at us for a moment. I don't think she ever got to the bottom of that one!

Being eccentric at that age was not a problem.

The summer of 1976 brought scorching heat and a drought. It also brought our second trip to Whitby, only this time Grandma and Grandad stayed at home and Tracy's place was filled by my brother Jonathan. We had a great time, and now both of us were "helping" the train driver test his carriages at eight o'clock each morning!

September 1976 saw me moving up into Mrs Craggs's class. I liked her, and so did most of the adults. Grandma would often comment on what a lovely smile she had.

I once had to deliver a message to the staff room. It was like entering the Holy of Holies in Heaven: the teachers' own room, and there they all were. And when the door opened I noted that both Leach and Craggs smoked those longer cigarettes with the filter.

> They look like they are really enjoying it. That's the kind of cigarette I'm going to smoke when I grow up.

One of the most exciting things we did in Mrs Craggs's was going to the theatre to see *Dick Whittington*. It starred *Play School* presenter Derek Griffiths. I knew he was going to be in it, but when he came on stage dressed as a mouse, I was awestruck. I mean, *Derek Griffiths!* I was more impressed by that one fact than any other aspect of the show, and to this day it's all I remember about it. He was my favourite of the *Play School* presenters. He also composed and sang all the songs for an eccentric animated series called *Bod*. A few years later I saw him on *Saturday Superstore* playing the very tricky *Bod* theme on a piccolo. Derek Griffiths was my first television hero.

Another trip saw us going to bird sanctuary Martin Mere. It poured down with rain all day, but that didn't mar my enjoyment. On returning home, I lectured my parents at length about mallards, flamingos and the like, and they smiled fondly at my enthusiasm.

Shopping was always a highlight. We would go with Anthony and Tracy's mum Aunty Linda. She had multiple sclerosis and was confined to a wheelchair. Her car was one of those old-fashioned blue three-wheeled vehicles for the disabled. There was only one seat – the driver's. But that didn't stop Linda, Mum, me, Jon, Anthony and Tracy all piling in and speeding off to Kwik Save. On one trip the tight squeeze became unbearable and I started to sob. After a while, Aunty Linda bellowed, "Oh, stop your shrieking!" Needless to say I did. Embarrassment silenced me, followed by one deep-seated emotion: rage.

As well as vacuum cleaners, washing machines, *Rainbow, Play School, Trumpton* and 100-millimetre cigarettes, I had an obsession with Aunty Linda's wheelchair, and on one occasion made the mistake of asking my mother if I could have one. "But Aunty Linda can't walk, can she? That's why she has a wheelchair." I couldn't see what that had to do with anything. "Well, can't I have one anyway?" I asked. She shot me one of her piercing looks and I knew not to push it any further.

One of my earliest Christmas presents was a toy hoover which I had specifically requested. Friends Colin and Steven, who lived in my street, found this behaviour very strange indeed. "You're not queer, are you?" they would ask, and I would just smile and say no. Of course, I had little comprehension of what they meant by "queer". My friends took great delight in telling others about my toy vacuum cleaner, but whenever they came round to play, they always had a quick go on it. It was strange to them, but irresistible nonetheless.

I had strange fixations like that, and they didn't do my reputation any good at all.

Colin was totally obsessed with sport, football in particular. If he couldn't find any of his other friends to play it with him, he would nag me into it. I would always buckle and play the game, all the while hating it because of my poor coordination. I couldn't kick a ball in a straight line, couldn't catch, couldn't do anything that required precision. Colin had a great time playing football against me because he always won. I'd half walk, half run to tackle him but, because I was terrified of falling over in the middle of the road, never really took him on. All I could see was aggression. I hated the way he pretended to do the commentary: "It's Hadcroft now, Hadcroft's approaching. Wilson's tackling. Oh! He's got the ball! Hadcroft can't get back. What a goal for Wilson!"

I hated the tackling, I hated the commentary, I hated the aggression, I hated the competitive spirit, I hated football, I hated sport. Full stop. My father never played footie in the back garden like other dads, and as a result my brothers and I were never really exposed to it, apart from helping to choose Dad's potential winners on the football coupon.

Sometimes Colin would beg me to go up to his back bedroom to play snooker with him. Once or twice I had waited until I had got near the door, and then I'd made a run for it. After a while Colin got wise to this and scrutinized my every move. Any signs of me making a getaway and he would dart towards the door.

His obsessive nature was similar to mine in its intensity, but the difference lay in his wanting others to join in. He could not enjoy periods of solitude, whereas I could quite easily get lost in a world of my own, and frequently did. Later I would prefer it.

Every generation of children, it seems, find something to get hooked on. Nowadays it's computer software; in my parents' day it was Elvis Presley and the Beatles. The mid-1970s saw a fascination with cult television series. The programmes in question usually had a science-fiction slant or some fantastical notion about them. And like many other kids in my generation, I was well and truly absorbed by them. Unlike the others, I thought about them excessively and my interest never died, not even when the series in question were discontinued.

One evening, when Dad was getting ready to do his twelve-hour night shift at the plastics factory, he came into the living room and said, "There's a new programme on tonight, Bill. It's on at [whatever time] and you'll love it. Tell me all about it when I come home in the morning." Instructions like these were given periodically, because we were a long way from the advent of home video. If you weren't available to see a programme, you missed it. Simple as that.

My appetite whetted sufficiently, I watched as instructed. The series was entitled *The Six Million Dollar Man*, and told the story of Steve Austin, an astronaut who had been testing a new space plane. The plane had crashed, resulting in the amputation of both legs and the right arm. The accident also rendered him blind in one eye. The opening titles show the crash and then Steve Austin on the operating table. An arm is brought into view. As the camera pulls back, we see wires and circuitry emerging at the elbow. Another scientist/doctor holds up an electronic eye. Finally we see a fit and healthy Steve Austin running on a treadmill exerciser. The speedometer clocks up 60 miles per hour.

Dad was right – I did love it! Every child at that time wished they too could jump off high buildings and remain unharmed, or bend steel bars with one hand. An eye with a zoom lens would also have proven very useful. Whenever Steve used his bionics, he would move in slow motion to a metallic, grinding, sound effect. At school, we copied the sound vocally and mimed the movements. We were all wishing that we'd had a six million dollar re-fit.

Jonathan was completely taken in by it and, on one occasion, informed Grandad that when the horses ran in slow motion on the action replays it was because they were running so fast the people at the *Grandstand* studio had to slow them down in order for us to see them.

After a couple of series, actor Lee Majors was joined by a female counterpart, Lindsay Wagner, who starred as Jaime Sommers, *The Bionic Woman*, ending up in a series of her own. After that, there was a bionic teenager, and even a bionic dog! Not surprisingly, bionic action figures were on the list for Christmas.

September 1977 saw me move up to Mrs Skinner's class. I liked her a lot too. She encouraged creativity. We all had to bring egg boxes in over a few weeks, and I marvelled as they were slowly constructed into the form of a large dragon. I thought it was amazing, and wished that I had room enough in my bedroom to make one of my own.

On another occasion, she told us the story of Shadrach, Meshach and Abednego from the Bible. We were then asked to write as much of the story as we could remember. When I took my story out to Mrs Skinner, she chuckled as she read through it, impressed that I had remembered the story right down to the dialogue and had put it in.

Knowing things no one else knew often went against me. Like the time the headmaster, Mr Brooks, played the *1812 Overture* in assembly. "Who knows what that music is called?"

I raised my hand and everyone gawped at me as Brooks looked across the hall. "Yes, William?"

"It's the *1812*, Sir."

There was a smile of approval. "And do you know who composed it?"

"No, Sir."

Mum and Dad showed little interest in the pop music of the day. Mum liked BBC Radio Two, so I was exposed to the more wholesome side of it. The only single she ever bought that I can remember is *Money, Money, Money* by Abba. Dad loathed *Top of the Pops*, and in particular the "bloody puffs" of Glam Rock, who were very theatrical and wore make-up. This hatred would later extend to the New Romantics and the pioneers of electronic pop. The only exposure I had to musicians like David Bowie and Marc Bolan was when I visited Colin. His parents appreciated modern music. Mine tended to play *The William Tell Overture* and Ravel's *Bolero* when the desire to put on a record seized them. I look back on these days and, although I later grew to appreciate the likes of Bowie and Bolan, I'm grateful that my family were different.

We are different. I am different.

My knowing classical music titles did little to endear me to the rest of my class, nor did my "scientific" experiments. Mr Brooks took me up on my idea of sticking a sewing needle through the end of a paper cone in order to demonstrate how record players work. Getting rewarded for being curious meant being a swot in the eyes of my peers, which in turn meant being disliked.

Mrs Skinner was the first teacher to read us Clive King's classic tale *Stig of the Dump*, which tells the charming story of a boy who befriends a caveman living in a rubbish tip. At first one is never sure whether Stig is a pretend friend or whether he really has somehow been left over from the Stone Age. I loved it. Again it was about being different.

Another TV series which captivated me was the BBC's low-budget phenomenon *Doctor Who*. Each season was split into five four-part serials, and a six-parter to close the run. Twenty-six half-hour episodes a year were enjoyed by millions of children. The starting point for the series tended to be the beginning of autumn, September thereabouts, which meant that it lasted the whole of the winter, taking a well-earned rest the following March.

The programme was placed just after the football results on a Saturday teatime. The distinctive "gothic" theme music and the blue-and-white vortex signalled 25 minutes of pure unadulterated adventure.

The lead character, known only as "the Doctor", travels in a bizarre time and space vehicle called the TARDIS (Mum informed me that TARDIS stands for Time And Relative Dimensions In Space), which is bigger on the inside than it is on the outside. The TARDIS is also stuck in the guise of an old-fashioned police telephone box.

The enigmatic Doctor, played by eccentric actor Tom Baker, would land sometimes in British history, perhaps to help find a cure to a disease or something equally life threatening; and then in another story would land on an alien planet to try to stop megalomaniacs from taking over the universe. There was a great wonderment permeating the whole thing, and a tremendous sense of freedom, since the Doctor had little control over his bizarre ship and could not predict where he would land next. He didn't seem to care much either. I remember lamenting to a school friend: "It's all right for the Doctor. He doesn't have to go to school or to work or anything."

Who invented work and school anyway? Who thought up all these rules? Who says it's so important? Who are the Government? Why do people do everything they say? Anyone can make up rules. We're all the same.

It was the character of the Doctor, the variety of the storytelling and the whole strangeness of the thing that captured my imagination. There really wasn't anything else like it.

His deadliest enemies, the Nazi-like machine creatures the Daleks, were the big favourites. My classmates and I would march around the playground, arms outstretched, chanting, "Exterminate, exterminate." Everyone loved the programme. It was a family affair in many households.

Mrs Skinner had to take some time off in order to look after her poorly husband. Her temporary replacement, Mrs Woodward, encouraged me even more. I took a cardboard model of the TARDIS in to show her. She was suitably impressed and displayed it to the class. I was very proud of it, and of myself, I suppose. Again my inventiveness split the class. Some marvelled at my ingenuity, others resented me for it.

After showing off the model, I took it into the playground and imagined myself to be the Doctor arriving in some barren wilderness aboard the police box shaped time machine, ready to do battle with the evils of the universe. Suddenly, a hand reached down and picked up the TARDIS. It was Barry Nesbitt, son of the local lollipop lady. "What's this supposed to be?" he jeered. I looked sheepish and stammered, "It's Doctor Who's TARDIS."

"Haaa!" yelled the bully and rolled up the model in his hands until it looked like a mass of swirling cardboard and sellotape. "It'd make a good football, wouldn't it?" I looked on helplessly as he and his friends kicked the box from one end of the playground to the other. I said nothing, but inside I was seething with anger and hate.

On returning to my class, I burst into tears and presented the squashed remains to Mrs Woodward, who reacted immediately. "Who has done this?" she demanded.

Though delighted that she was as equally horrified by the event, I still had trouble asserting myself. I mumbled very shyly, "It was Barry Nesbitt, Miss." The hour of justice arrived and Barry Nesbitt was dragged from his class and given a good telling off. For once, someone had come down on my side.

This was not the only run-in with Barry Nesbitt, though. One lunch-time, we were sitting at the same table, and somehow ended up talking about God. Influenced by the books I had been leafing through at home, I casually asked, "Do you know what God's name is?" To which he replied confidently, "Of course. It's Jesus."

I found this most incomprehensible. "No, it's not," I said. "He's called Jehovah."

Barry returned the dumbfounded look. "God is called Jesus. Everyone knows that."

I shook my head, "No. Jesus is God's son."

"I know he is," said Barry.

I paused, and then pointed out, "Well if Jesus is God's son, how can he be God as well?"

At that moment, the chief dinner lady Mrs Mather passed by. Barry called her attention. "Miss, isn't God called Jesus?"

"Yes, of course he is," came the assertive response.

Barry smiled, vindicated, and announced, "He says he's called Jehovah."

I squirmed as Mrs Mather glared at me reprovingly. "No," she said in a stern voice, no doubt realizing where I had got my information from, "God is called Jesus." I looked up, believing for a certainty that I was right, but dared not say a word back.

This argument played on my mind for the rest of the day. Of course, nowadays, in Britain's multicultural society, a child might get confused over the identity of God even more than I had. An Asian boy with Asperger Syndrome will insist that Allah is God's name, while a child brought up in an atheist household would declare to one and all that God doesn't actually exist.

The serialized film *Jesus of Nazareth*, starring Robert Powell, had me spellbound. The personality of Jesus as depicted in the series was a potent one. I was struck by his charisma and the way he taught. Most of the time he was gentle and loving, but on occasion he would get angry and shout, most notably at the hypocritical religious leaders. The final episode affected me very deeply. I had always known that Jesus died nailed to a cross or stake, but I had not fully appreciated why until now.

His rivals in the religious world hated him so much that they plotted to have him executed. One of his own followers betrayed him for money, and

Jesus was put on trial for declaring himself the Son of God. My mother explained to me that the Romans ruled Israel at that time, so the religious leaders had to charge him with a crime against Rome if they wanted him dead. When the governor Pontius Pilate dismissed the charge of blasphemy for claiming to be God's son, they switched it to treason, since Jesus had been hailed a king.

Jesus made it crystal clear to Pilate that his kingship was not of this earthly realm, and so therefore he was not a rival to Caesar, and in turn not a traitor to Rome. Pilate accepted this reasoning, but because of his fear of the people, he had Jesus executed in a fashion reserved for hardened criminals.

The death in this film is depicted in a realistic fashion, and the overall message of the story hit home: *If you're going to be different and go against the tide, the world will hate and reject you.*

I took the principle to heart because deep down I knew I was different to my peers. It wasn't just my religious ideas, but my interests and obsessions. I had quite a lot of friends during this period of my life but sensed I was slightly at odds with them. I felt like an alien, as though I had come to earth from somewhere else. *Jesus of Nazareth* reached so far into my psyche that, at the age of seven, I began to wonder if I too had been sent by God for some special purpose and that it would be revealed to me in my adult life. This wasn't something I announced to the world (thankfully!), but it was a concept I found very attractive and I entertained it privately.

October 1977 saw the third addition to our family, as my brother Matthew was born into the world. While Jonathan and me didn't always see eye to eye, neither of us ever had a problem with Matt. He was naturally very easy going.

Anthony and Tracy visited regularly, as did my mother's friend Doreen. Her son Karl was the closest I'd got to having a best mate. We had so much in common. Same temperament, same outlook; we both loved *Doctor Who*.

As I mentioned before, my two local friends were Steven and Colin. Steven was a big fan of the Christopher Reeve *Superman* films and enjoyed the superhero genre in general. We used to invent our own characters and dress up as them. Colin, on the other hand, was very much a fan of *The*

Beano. He often likened himself to Dennis the Menace and said that I was like the cowardly Walter, who was the butt of Dennis's pranks. Yet despite these comparisons, Colin was a good pal.

At Christmas I was granted my request of a tape recorder, and I hit upon the idea of making our own "radio" programme. It started as Radio Worsley and then was reinvented as the TBC (Taping Broadcasting Company!). Once we had made our first recording, Colin was hooked on the idea. We did a Top Ten show which consisted of our favourite records and an "outside broadcast" whereby we approached members of the public and asked them questions. We asked a gentleman in the street what he thought of Little Hulton. "Bloody awful!" came his brisk reply. We kept playing it back and laughing. We thought it was hilarious. On another occasion we experimented with recording television broadcasts, including the theme music from the *BBC News.* We were astounded by our own ingenuity and forced our parents and friends to listen to what we had done.

Being quite shy and timid often proved to be traumatic. The bullies would home in on these traits and take advantage of them. I was very easy to wind up because I believed absolutely everything I was told. Often when children innocently asked me questions I would be unable to discern whether they were being sincere or were in fact setting me up.

On rare occasions they would provoke a response which left them in shock.

The trouble with bottling up your feelings is that sooner or later you reach the end of your tether. And when you *do* blow, you let off steam that has taken months to accumulate. Very often the final straw is something quite trivial.

One afternoon Mr Brooks, the headmaster, took over the class for our weekly science lesson. This involved listening to Brooks's fascinating discussions and colouring in pictures. This particular afternoon, however, proved to be quite an ordeal. The class bully had decided that he was having all the crayons. I politely asked for a particular colour, and he decided that, whichever colour I wanted, he would want it at the same time. This went on for a few minutes.

I was consumed with rage. "I'm sick of you," I said, seething.

"Well," he smirked. "I'm sick of you too." He pushed me back in mock retaliation.

His characteristic smirk was not well received. I pushed him hard. He smirked again. I pushed him harder. He pushed me back and then resumed his colouring, grinning and chuckling to himself. My fury peaked and I pushed him so hard he fell off his chair. He landed on his rotund backside and just stared at me in total shock.

The whole class turned to face us. Silence swept through the room. Mr Brooks raised his eyebrows and took off his spectacles. "What's the matter, William?" he said slowly.

Embarrassed and shaken, I immediately burst into tears. "It's him, Sir. He always has to have all the crayons, and I'm sick of him."

Gary Smeaton quickly came to my defence. "He's right, Sir."

I gained the bully's respect that day, but it didn't really change his demeanour beyond that.

This bully often picked on a sensitive girl called Kay. She had a round pretty face and long brown hair. She also had what my mother termed "puppy fat". Mum would comment that Kay was destined to grow up to be a very attractive girl.

"You're fat, you are," the bully would jibe. He'd go on and on and never tire. The irritating thing was that if anyone was overweight, it was him! On this particular day he got her to the point where she was going to cry. I could see the eyes turning glassy and the bottom lip starting to quiver. The glee on Bully's face enraged me.

"Why don't you just leave her alone!" I shouted.

I remember the relief on Kay's face, that someone had finally come to her rescue. Bully wore his smirk again. "Why?" he teased. "Do you fancy her, or something?" I blushed at once and lowered my head. "No," I said sheepishly, hoping that the way I said it hadn't made Kay feel worse. It hadn't, and on 14 February I received what was to be my one and only Valentine's card. All because I stuck up for her that day.

Capitalizing on the success of *The Six Million Dollar Man* became the job of a certain Kenneth Johnson. Universal Television commissioned him to adapt the Marvel Comics character the Incredible Hulk into a TV series. The only comic I followed at that time was *Nutty*, which told the story of schoolboy Eric who, after eating a banana, would become the superhero send-up Banana Man. I knew little of *The Incredible Hulk* comic. However, with the television adaptation, I found myself identifying with the quiet-natured Dr David Banner as he lived the life of a fugitive, all the time trying to "control the raging spirit that dwelt within him". The opening titles would cast a spell upon me. Taken from the pilot film, which I would not see for a good few years hence, the titles depict David Banner crouching by the wheel of his car during a night-time thunder storm. He is cold and wet and getting to the end of his tether. He is trying to undo a wheel nut and change his flat tyre. There's a flash of lightning and a crack of thunder, and the lug wrench slips. He yells out in frustration. Actor Bill Bixby conveys real emotion here. The lug wrench slipping under any other circumstances would not provoke such a reaction, but here it is the final straw.

> It's like me trying to undo the wheel nuts on my bike, or attempting to screw something together with a screwdriver. It slips, and the frustration – oh, it's so deep. It's like me pouring myself a cup of tea from the teapot and missing the cup; it's like me trying to tackle in football and tripping over the other boy's feet; it's like me saying the wrong thing at the wrong time and feeling so embarrassed. IT'S LIKE ME!

We get a shot of David's rushing adrenalin and then a close-up of his DNA helix, with one of its cells flickering green. He shivers in his fury, his brown eyes having turned white. His clothes burst around his swelling body, his skin turns green, his hair grows wild, and his face takes on a beast-like quality. Ex-body-builder Lou Ferrigno becomes the personification of Banner's rage.

The lug wrench slipping, the yell of frustration, the adrenalin rush, the glowing DNA: these images rooted themselves deep into my mind and, whenever I was faced with frustration, anger or fury, I would immediately recall Dr David Banner. I'd watch as the gentle scientist faced the bullies of his world, getting beaten up in some back street – only to transform into the huge green-skinned man–beast. The white eyes, accompanied by a high-pitched sound effect and tense music, signified the start of the transformation and, as I absorbed the Incredible Hulk into my own persona, I would often be found impersonating the sound vocally during moments of stress.

Strange behaviour, perhaps, but a coping strategy that helped alleviate frustration. In my mind's eye, bullies were sent flying by my raging alter ego. Oh, how I longed for an overdose of gamma radiation! As I got older, I identified with the loneliness and isolation of the character of David Banner, and took to heart the scenes where he broke down crying, unable to cope with his bizarre illness.

Starring in the Christmas play was exhilarating. The show revolved around a dragon-type character who had a line that cracked me up every time the boy playing the part said it: "Great, walloping, jungle bonks." It was meant to be funny, but I tended to laugh at it more than anyone else. I would get fits of chuckling to myself about it and, when asked what I was laughing at, would be met with blank faces after explaining.

We all had a part to play. The school borrowed some costumes and I had a little skip and dance routine dressed as a Womble. What a Womble was doing in it beats me! But that tiny role gave me a taste of performing in front of an audience.

The late 1970s were full of union strikes, and this led to great shortages of food. I distinctly remember the bare shelves of the local mini-market. That particular shop was run by an Asian chap who used to keep certain items of food on one side for my mum. She would come home feeling very pleased with herself and hold up a bag of sugar, and say, "Look what he's saved for me."

These favours were sent our way on the grounds that we were "different" to his regular customers. We were honest and nice, and used his real name, rather than calling him "Sam" (Sambo, or perhaps a shortened form of the surname Zaman) or some other ignorant substitute. Mum treated all persons as equal, and as a result I did too. I didn't really "see" the skin colour. I judged people on whether they were nice or not nice.

The year 1978 went well, until September, when nerves ran high; for the time had come to move up into the next class, Mrs Lees's. I was always a bit afraid of Mrs Lees. She did not suffer fools gladly, and I was never sure if I constituted one. Additionally I wasn't that sure what the procedure was supposed to be for moving up, and had spent most of the six-week summer break worrying about it.

On arriving at school, I swallowed hard and went to stand with Lees's regular pupils. There were no other children from Skinner's class present. Was I the only one moving up? No, there must have been some mistake. Lees stalked in confidently and spoke in a matter-of-fact manner. "Right you lot, single file, and no talking." She broke off and caught sight of me. I blushed immediately and looked at the floor.

"Who – are – you?" she said slowly and precisely.

"I'm William Hadcroft, Miss. I'm moving up from Mrs Skinner's."

She raised an eyebrow, and I was unsure what it meant. "OK," she announced. "All of you, follow me."

I found a seat in the class and looked about nervously. I felt vulnerable and alone. Where were the others who were supposed to be moving up with me?

> The lug wrench slips, I cry out in frustration. "Aarrgghh!" Adrenalin rush, glowing DNA helix, white eyes, high-pitched strings. Me shivering.

Then a familiar face made a welcome appearance. "I'm sorry to disturb you, Mrs Lees," said Skinner. "But has William Hadcroft come in here?"

I put up my hand. "I'm here, Miss."

Skinner laughed and said that I wasn't moving up just yet, as I had a few things to collect from her class. On returning, I was more than relieved to see a number of others preparing to make the transfer.

It was hard settling in to Mrs Lees's class. She rarely smiled and I could never be sure if she liked me. Others, like Helen Jardine and Catherine Whiley, didn't seem to have any problem and enjoyed being in her class. But for the shy ones, such as myself and Kay, it took longer to adjust.

Helen Jardine. Now there's a girl I liked. She caught me holding a Crayola crayon between my fingers and smiled. "Are you pretending it's a cigarette?"

"Yes," I replied. "I like those longer ones with the orange bit at the end."

"That's called a filter," said Helen. I remained fascinated with smoking.

Christmas was round again, and this year was special. I'd begged my mother to knit me a long multicoloured *Doctor Who* scarf. She declined, since the actor playing the Doctor wore a scarf so long that it looped round his neck several times and still touched the floor! However, Aunty Ethel took me up on the challenge. There were great arguments between me and Mum as to how long the scarf should be. I wanted it to be as long as the real thing.

"No," insisted Mum. "You'll break your neck!"

Trips to Aunty Ethel's and Uncle Bob's were made all the more exciting by glimpses of the scarf. "How are you getting along with it, Ethel?" Mum would ask. "Oh, it's harder than I thought," would be the reply.

"I know," Mum would laugh with a hint of mischief. "That's why I wouldn't do it!"

The Denys Fisher company brought out a range of *Doctor Who* toys that year, including a Dalek which issued threats of extermination at the touch of a button, a Tom Baker doll, and a TARDIS made from plastic and stiff cardboard. When Christmas morning came, I was in paradise! I hung the scarf around my blue pyjamas and unravelled the wrappings from my new toys. Truly one of the best Christmases ever.

Aside from *Doctor Who* and *The Incredible Hulk*, there was another science-fiction drama which came near the top of my favourite programmes list. *Blake's Seven* told the story of Roj Blake, a principled man who lives in a time when space travel is as common as airflight, and Earth's totalitarian Federation runs hundreds of colonized worlds. Blake discovers to his cost that the Federation is completely corrupt, and so leads a band of convicts to escape their exile. After boarding the abandoned alien space ship *Liberator*, Blake's Seven become freedom fighters against the oppressive regime.

The external design of the *Liberator* fascinated me. The chandelier shape could be made from Fairy Liquid bottles and toilet rolls – a small football would serve as the engine on the back. I loved the ship's hexagonal corridors, the main navigation computer Zen, and the teleport system which was employed for "beaming down". Members of the crew would put on a special wrist bracelet for this activity, and absolutely I hated it when Blake actor Gareth Thomas gave away a real teleport bracelet as a prize on the Saturday morning show *Multi-Coloured Swap Shop*. I was so jealous!

Thankfully, *Blue Peter* presenter Lesley Judd showed us how to make bracelets from the rings of orange squash bottles. Of course, *Blue Peter*'s looked like the real thing, mine looked like orange squash bottles. I made several and took them to school. Again, as in the case of the homemade TARDIS, I was both admired and hated.

Someone who shared my love of *Doctor Who* and *Blake's Seven* in 1979 was a boy called Carl Tandy. One day, whilst engaging in PE, Carl and I stood on opposite sides of the hall-cum-gym, pretending to talk to one another through imaginary wrist communicators.

Mrs Lees noticed this and stopped the lesson. "William Hadcroft and Carl Tandy," she bellowed. "Please stop talking to your wrists."

As usual, I had to speak up. "We're not talking to our wrists, Miss. We're pretending to have teleport bracelets like on *Blake's Seven*."

"Oh," said Lees, a little flummoxed. "Well stop it anyway."

I don't think she really knew what to make of me.

Doctor Who was becoming increasingly popular, and I've since learned that 1979 saw its biggest audience. Over 13 million viewers were tuning in every Saturday teatime. The Daleks had returned that year, causing hysteria to break out in every junior school playground across the country. My friends from up the road, Lawrence and David, joined me and my friends at playing Daleks. David was superb as the Dalek creator Davros!

With these friends I would go "down the fields", to an area that can only be described as wasteland, to play at *Doctor Who*. The old coal slag heaps bore an uncanny resemblance to the alien environments presented in the programme.

It was through *Doctor Who* that I met David Broadhurst, a very good pal with a similar emotional disposition to myself. He also owned a Denys Fisher TARDIS and we enjoyed many imaginary adventures together.

Such was the Doctor's appeal in 1979 that Marvel Comics debuted their new title *Doctor Who Weekly* that year. I collected the issues religiously: 12p every Thursday. One issue featured a competition to win the *Doctor Who Sound Effects* LP. All the readers had to do was think of a new gun "sound" for their comic strip. Harder than it seems, believe me! Mum came up with the word "Zzweeeessk", which impressed me no end. We posted it off and forgot all about it.

Then one day, after returning home from a school trip to York, my mum and grandma asked me to look at a page in the *Doctor Who Weekly*. It contained the names of sound effects album winners. I nearly fell off my chair when I saw "William Hadcroft" about half way down. I was then led to the mantelpiece upon which sat a square brown envelope. My name was on the label. I ripped the paper off in a frenzy. The LP. It was the first time I had ever won anything. Of course, sound effects records are produced for amateur film makers and the like, but that day we played it as a conventional album. Grandma was completely baffled by it!

As I didn't own that many records, I treasured the sound effects album. Later, Mum bought me the Geoff Love and his Orchestra album *Themes For Super Heroes* for my birthday. All the themes I had grown to love were orchestrated on it. And with the sound effects record, the *Doctor Who* theme and a tape recorder to hand, I began making my own little audio plays.

The great thing about *Doctor Who Weekly* was that it taught me so much about the series' past. I became acquainted with the notion of regeneration: when the Doctor's body wore out or was damaged beyond repair, an automatic process of physical renewal would kick in. Hence the different actors who'd played him over the years.

One picture strip had the Doctor being regressed back through his previous incarnations. From Tom Baker to Jon Pertwee, from Pertwee to Patrick Troughton, and finally to the original characterization as played by William Hartnell. Also, the comic continued when the series was off the air during the summer months. Little did I know it, but an unhealthy obsession was beginning to fester. The comic acquired a large enough following to go monthly, and today it exists as the adult-styled *Doctor Who Magazine*.

The end of the school year was marked by Sports Day. I loathed it. In addition to the general nervousness suffered by most of the class, I was actually frightened of the pistol which was used to start each race. I thought there were real bullets in it! I remember getting ready for the sack race and expecting to be accidentally killed as the others were cheered on. Once the race began, I soon found myself drifting to the back of the crowd, and thinking, *What on earth are we all running in sacks for?* The egg-and-spoon race seemed even more pointless. I felt nothing but relief when the event was over.

Then came the announcement of who was to move up into the final class. I feared this transition because the final class was the only one taught by a male teacher, Mr Davies. I didn't like the idea of this at all. Moving into a new environment was always traumatic for me, but having a male teacher doubled the tension and so, after relentless pleading, Mum paid Lees a visit and explained that it had taken me a long time to settle in, and would she hold me back for another year?

Lees was persuaded against her better judgement and I felt relief again at knowing that I could stay with her for another year. When, in September 1980, I finally did move up, I deeply regretted not having done it the previous year! Mr Davies was superb. Everyone liked him. It had been my shyness and fear of new situations which had prompted my begging to stay in the lower class; and now I hated myself again for being such a coward.

A giddy moment at Chester Zoo. Me, Jon, Dad and Matt, circa 1980.

Birth of an Obsession, 1980–81

I REALLY ENJOYED MY TIME in the final year. Mr Davies was good fun. He had a training shoe called "Fred" which he would fetch out periodically, and walk about the class slamming it down on various desks to make us jump. All part of the grand plan to keep us in line, and it worked too. That's what's wrong with children today: no Fred.

For PE all the girls went off with a female teacher to play rounders, while us boys played football and cricket. Need I say I was rubbish at both? Giving up after a while, Mr Davies let me stand on the edge of the field to watch. He knew I hated it.

Davies also read *Stig of the Dump* to us. It was great having a repetition of this story. My favourite chapter was "The Snargets", which told of a bunch of unruly city kids who infiltrated Stig's chalkpit den. They were typical bullies and I identified with Barney's dilemma – and loved Stig's solution.

The year 1980 also marked a change of direction for *Doctor Who*. A new producer had taken it over and had decided that it was time the programme had a facelift. Excitement filled our house that Saturday evening as my brothers and I noted the new titles sequence and theme music. The blue vortex and diamond logo had gone in favour of a moving galaxy which formed the Doctor's face and the new neon title. The theme was a rearrangement of the original tune.

The Doctor's costume had been subtly changed too and had now acquired a question mark motif on the shirt collar. Tom Baker's wisecracks were lessened, his character becoming darker and doom laden. And the stories themselves were spattered with real scientific theory. The whole momentum of the programme had changed. I was terribly excited.

Afterwards, I went up to Carl Tandy's to see if he'd seen it. I walked at a pace, singing the *Doctor Who* theme to myself over and over. Initially Carl appeared equally excited. "Have you seen it?" I piped. "The new music and everything?"

He frowned. "Has it been on?" I was appalled that he could have missed it. He invited me in. "We're watching this new programme. *Buck Rogers in the Twenty-Fifth Century*. It's brilliant and miles better than *Doctor Who*."

Deflated, I turned down the invitation and sloped off home. That week at school, *Buck Rogers in the Twenty-Fifth Century* was the talk of the playground. Everyone commented on the special effects and how superior they were to *Doctor Who*. The ITV channels were at last providing some good competition to the BBC, and I was beginning to feel distinctly isolated and alone.

Christmas came round again, and we all prepared for the school fancy-dress party. Guess who I went as! Mum borrowed a top hat from Grandma's friend Mr Waring (it was the nearest we could get to a broad-brimmed floppy hat!). I draped my scarf over the cardboard K9 robot I'd made, and then Aunty Doreen remembered something. "What about the question marks, Margaret?" she said.

"What question marks?" Mum quizzed.

"He has question marks on his shirt collar."

"Oh yes," said Mum and drew two large coils on my collar with black mascara.

The photographer quite liked my homemade outfit and got me to stand with a few of the other children. Every time he said "Smile" I did the wide-eyed Doctor stare. Mr Brooks tried to discourage this. "Come on, William, *smile*." But I was adamant. In the end they gave up and took the picture. I was as pleased as Punch when the photos came back. I pointed out my bulging eyes to my mother and said proudly, "I'm staring like Doctor Who."

My mum studied the picture and bit her lip. "I know."

Christmas Fancy Dress, 1980. I'm Doctor Who, complete with home-made K9, long scarf (courtesy of Aunty Ethel), and doing the Tom Baker stare. Birth of an obsession.

January 1981 brought the fourth and final series of *Blake's Seven*. For the last two years the crew had been in search of their great leader, and in the final episode they find him. But he is a shadow of his former self, obsessive and thriving on past glories. In a misunderstanding, the new lead character, Avon, shoots him dead. The others are then systematically gunned down by Federation guards, leaving Avon standing alone. This was a real shock ending, and it left vivid images in my mind for years after.

The next shock came around February when the robot dog K9 was written out of *Doctor Who*. The tabloid press ran a "Save K9" campaign, but the programme's new producer John Nathan-Turner was determined to get rid of the motorized mutt. His reason? That the writers were all too often using him as a plot device to get the Doctor out of a sticky situation. The character was also loathed by those who had watched the series from its inception with William Hartnell. While I was heartbroken by K9's departure, I soon adjusted to him not being there.

Following this came the announcement that Tom Baker was set to leave at the end of the current series. His penultimate story, *The Keeper of Traken*, saw the return of his arch enemy the Master. I can remember running into the kitchen with tremendous excitement shouting, "It's the Master! It's the Master!" Mum and Dad laughed at my hysteria and encouraged, "Quick, go back in before you miss the rest!"

Then one night, as I was tucked up in bed, my mother quietly walked into the room and whispered, "The new Doctor Who has just been on the *Nine O'Clock News*. It's that vet out of *All Creatures Great and Small*. You know, that Peter Davison."

The anticipation for the new Doctor was unbearable. When the final episode of *Logopolis* was screened, silence fell over the living room. Mum, Jon and Matt sat huddled up on the couch. I sat directly opposite the television.

I sat on the edge of my seat as Tom Baker struggled to maintain his grasp of the cable amidst the gantry of the radio telescope. My heart missed a beat when his strength gave out and he fell, apparently, to his death. The final sequence culminated with his familiar features metamorphosing into those of a young Peter Davison.

As the closing theme blasted into our living room, we sat there, stunned. I was affected quite profoundly. The new Doctor was here at last. But once the transformation had completed, I was overwhelmed with sadness.

That particular series had got a hold on me stronger than anything else. The stand-in teacher, Mrs Woodward, had done a few lessons with us around the Easter period when Mr Davies was away. We were doing a special project about our favourite celebrity. It could be an actor or a pop star, anything really; just so long as we researched our subject well and illustrated the text with pictures and photographs. I decimated my collection of *Doctor Who Weeklies* for photos and background information.

The best ten were given prizes on the final day before the Easter break. I felt really down-hearted when my project didn't feature among the nine runners-up. They each received a Cadbury's Creme Egg. It never occurred to me that my project would be considered the best. Since mine was the most thorough and detailed, I won first prize: an Easter egg.

My interest in writing was probably kindled by this experience. I was a keen follower of the *Doctor Who Weekly* strip *Tales from the TARDIS*. Each instalment told a classic tale, the most memorable being a comic strip rendition of *Dr Jekyll and Mr Hyde*. So I decided to write some stories based around a character called Doctor Bill (!). Doctor Bill traversed time and space in an American telephone box named the SHATM (as "TARDIS" is an acronym for Time And Relative Dimensions In Space; so "SHATM" stood for Space Hyperspace And Time Machine). I called the series *Tales from the SHATM*. Naturally, other children called it something slightly different.

One afternoon, Mr Davies had us pick a book from the school library. A boy named Adam asked if he could read one of my books instead. Davies granted his request, and before I knew it, William Knights had taken one of the others, and then I was inundated with pleas. "Can I read it next, Bill?" Although I enjoyed the attention a lot, it never occurred to me that I could deliberately cultivate such appreciation.

In 1981 I fell in love. I'd had crushes on the likes of TV personalities Dana and Twiggy, but this was different. This was a person in my real life. Tina was by far the prettiest girl in all the land. She was sweet and gentle, and had a countenance similar to the aforementioned Twiggy. She was a year or two my junior and I couldn't look at her without feeling lightheaded.

It was no secret that I adored Tina, and she blushed as I tried to tell her how much in love with her I was. Funnily enough, I bumped into her years later in Bolton. I was dumbstruck at what a beautiful woman she had become. The gentleness had not diminished. She smiled and asked me how I was. Almost as if 17 years had not really passed by, I stuttered and stammered a simple response, and went away feeling quite ill.

As a child I used to go home in a trance and my mother would smile at my bewildered expression. Oh, how my heart ached! Especially when Tina found another boy much more attractive. I think he was called Carl. There were a lot of Carls in those days.

"Go and ask Carl if he'll go out with me," she'd say. I so desperately wanted to go out with her myself. We had something in common: she listened to the school radio programme *Singing Together with Johnny Morris*, and her favourite song was *Here Come the Navvies*. That was *my* favourite! I wrote Tina into my Doctor Bill stories as the companion, who then spent every adventure getting rescued from the clutches of the evil Carl.

The final term drew to a close. *Singing Together with Johnny Morris* finished its run, and *Here Come the Navvies* was voted the best of the songs. I asked Mr Davies if I could keep the recording, and to my surprise he said yes. Everyone hated me because they hadn't thought to ask. That particular trend was now set in concrete: a lot of what others took for granted baffled me, and conversely, I thought of ideas no one else had.

I spent the last month dreading senior school. I'd seen too many episodes of *Grange Hill* to be convinced that it was going to be OK. One play time, Mr Brooks and Mr Davies stood reminiscing about old times. It wasn't only the end of my time at the school, it was also the end of the school itself. St Andrews West was in dire need of repair, and the authorities had decided to shut it down. I went over to the two men, feeling somewhat distraught. "Sir, they won't make me play football at the new school, will they?"

Davies smiled and nodded. "Oh yes, you'll have to join in when you go there."

My heart sank as I envisioned running about with those aggressive yobs. I often watched the teenage boys as they walked from their school, shouting and swearing. I was quite determined even then that I wasn't going to be like them. I deplored that uncivilized demeanour.

The six-week holidays went very quickly. My most dearest friends were either going to a different school, or were a year or two younger than I and would not be joining me the following month.

A certain amount of excitement was to be had picking up the new school uniform, with its black trousers, grey v-neck pullover, burgundy tie and maroon blazer. But, by and large, I just became more and more terrified of the whole idea.

My first best friend and neighbour Karl, whom I'd known from infancy, started his senior school a week in advance of me. He was so ill with nerves that his mother had to go in and explain how shy and bashful he was. He was taken to see the headteacher and was gradually settled in. Reports came back that Karl was loving every minute of his new school and had made a full recovery.

I took comfort from this and assumed that I would have a similar sort of experience. Yes, I told myself, I'll probably go in all worked up and frightened, and then come home wondering what all the fuss was about.

Alas, it was not to be.

"I Hope It's Not Like *Grange Hill*", 1981–82

EXCITEMENT MINGLED WITH FEAR. THAT'S how I'd describe my feelings on anticipating my first day at secondary school. In this respect I was no different to all the other 11-year-olds embarking of this new phase of life.

I'd heard all the usual stories of how kids put your head down the toilet and flush the chain, but I had also been assured that life at "Joeys" (Joseph Eastham High School) was not as bad as all that.

My friend David was also starting his first day there, and his older brothers escorted us. We were joined by Colin, who galloped across the road in frenzied excitement. He was as thrilled as I was nervous.

My stomach churned as our fivesome became part of the swarm moving up the school's main drive. I observed the yobbish aggression displayed by many of the boys, and the bitchiness in a few of the girls; traits only a year or so earlier I had vowed never to adopt. I renewed my determination. I saw no logical reason why anyone should want to behave like that. Some of the older ones were smoking, and the language was appalling. I had never experienced such behaviour en masse before. The odd "f" word at primary school, yes, a bit of a vulgar joke, maybe; but here the "f" word featured after every other and sexual references were frequent.

On arriving at the entrance, we were directed to the hall by kindly prefects. It was exactly as I'd remembered from a few months earlier, when I'd been forced to miss the repeat of the climax to *Blake's Seven*'s third series in order to acquaint myself with my future. The spacious room was packed. We took our seats and waited for the assembly to begin.

Teachers lined the aisles and silence fell over the great room as the terrifying figure of Mr Livesey marched to the podium, complete with ceremonial cap and gown. This headmaster was nothing like the gentle Mr Brooks from my St Andrews days. I don't recall a single word of what he said. All I remember is being terrified by his sharp intelligent glare and his authoritative voice. Most children were awestruck by him, he was such an imposing figure.

After the speech, we were separated into our various "houses" and forms. I was in the first form of Windsor House One, or 1W1 (the other Windsor first form was designated 1WA). As I began to soak in my surroundings, I noticed familiar faces, some from St Andrews, others from Worsley Avenue's neighbouring streets, all being segregated off into their various classes. I was relieved to find that David was going to be in my form. A young, medium-sized man with a long fair fringe stepped forward to call out the names of 1W1. This was Mr Davenport, my form tutor.

On arriving at our classroom, I noted that every other child had paired themselves up with a friend. Even David found a pal. This put me out a bit because I had assumed I would be sitting next to him, and now I was friendless, just observing the others all chatting away. I sat at the back. Alone. Alone and frightened.

After a few minutes, a blond-haired boy entered the room and apologized for his being late. He scanned the classroom swiftly and spotted the empty chair next to me. I was immediately relieved. He introduced himself as Chris Millard and said that his mother was a lab assistant in the science department. I was quite taken by his talkative cheerful approach. It made life much easier for me. I didn't have to rack my brain trying to think of things to say, and I didn't have to worry about saying stupid things in an attempt to keep a conversation going.

I clicked with Chris straight away, and took advantage of his perky, confident nature. He knew what he was doing, where all the classrooms were, and wasn't afraid of asking prefects and teachers for help when he got stuck. Brilliant. I figured that so long as Chris was about, I would be OK. The trouble was, and it hit me like a bombshell, he was only going to be with us until April, after which he and his mother were moving to another area. This prospect haunted me for the next six months. What would I do when Chris had gone?

Mr Davenport was great. He was very jovial and made us laugh. His humorous approach defused any tension quite considerably, and he always had time to talk. The only downer was that he tended to gravitate towards the more confident, expressive children; but I felt comfortable in his presence nonetheless.

We were all given a map of the school. It was a pretty basic layout, really, with most of the corridors linking up in a big square. Odd bits jutted off here and there, but generally it was easy to fathom: all you did was look at the door number nearest to where you were, check it on the map, and then make your way to the next class. Except I didn't. For me it was as though the map presented a detailed and complicated maze, and the directions were written in hieroglyphics.

The school seemed awe inspiring in size. Even after several weeks had passed by, I still couldn't find my way to certain rooms. I would just look at the nearest door number and then at the piece of paper in my hand.

I don't know what to do.

I would just look at the nearest door number and then at the piece of paper in my hand.

There's the number, now which way do I go?

I would just look at the nearest door number and then at the piece of paper in my hand.

What do you do?

I would just look at the nearest door number and then at the piece of paper in my hand.

I DON'T KNOW WHAT TO DO!!

On one occasion a female teacher approached as she witnessed me poring over the document in silent terrified panic. "What's the matter, William?"

I looked up and felt pathetic. "I don't know where to go, Miss."

The teacher gave a warm smile, a reassuring smile. A smile that made me feel suddenly at ease. She was going to help me. "Oh William," she said. "Do you *still* not know your way around?"

Break-time was absolutely horrible. If I wasn't with Chris, I just stood in a corner of the play court watching the masses enjoy themselves. I was desperately lonely and afraid. I prayed that no one would come over and start making fun of me, but sadly my face had my request to the Divine written all over it – and it attracted undesirables.

I hated them.

> A strange grinding and tearing noise shatters the moment. The merciless clan about turn to see what is making such an unearthly noise. I grin a broad toothy grin as the time machine materializes, square and blue, in a clearing. "Well," I announce casually. "It's been fascinating listening to you all, but it really is time I was off." They look on, flabbergasted, as I board the box, and in seconds fade away…

The lowest point of my first day was the science class. Miss Stephenson was deadly serious and determined to establish a no-nonsense approach from the start. As I've intimated, Chris was quite a talkative chap, and all the while Miss Stephenson was addressing the class, he was chattering on with great zeal. I turned to ask him to be quiet while Stephenson was speaking. She immediately picked up on my movement. "You," she said. "What's your name?"

> The class zoom out. It's just me, sitting at a desk. Me, sitting at a desk, with Miss Stephenson glaring. My throat is tight and dry. The pulses in my ears are pounding. I can't breathe.

"William," I stammered.

"Why are you talking in my lesson?" demanded the teacher. As I started to reply, she cut in. "Oh, I've heard every excuse a thousand times before. I've heard them all." And then she added, just for formality's sake, to complete the standard teacher–pupil exchange, "But go on."

> It wasn't me talking. Chris was talking. I was listening. Chris was talking and I was asking him not to.

"I wasn't talking, Miss," I said sheepishly. "Chris was talking and I was telling him to stop so I could listen to you."

Stephenson raised an eyebrow and paused. "Well, I must admit I've never heard that one before."

Chris was told to stand outside, and I felt awful. My friend had been disciplined because of me.

All eyes on me as Chris leaves the room. You grass. That's what you
are. Grass on a mate. Snake in the grass. Told on him to save yourself.
But it's the truth. He was talking and I was asking him to stop. Grass.
I was just telling the truth, that's all. He was talking and I was asking
him to stop. He was talking, I was trying to listen. Grass, grass, grass.

I hated the school and I hated myself.

I had so hoped my first day was not going to be like Karl's: arrive in a
panic, feeling sick, with a face as white as a sheet, and then go home
grinning like mad and wondering what all the fuss had been about.

When I got home, I looked at my mother, who smiled in nervous
anticipation. "Well?" she said. "How was it?" I think she had been dwelling
on the Karl episode too. He and I were alike in so many ways.

I burst into uncontrollable sobbing. "It was horrible," I kept saying. "It
was horrible."

Sadness and disappointment in my mother's eyes. Nothing she can
do to change it. She looks so frustrated. I feel so guilty. I've let her
down.

As time went by, I did make a couple of almost-friends. I say "almost"
because while they were friendly towards me, I didn't really click with
them, partly due to my shyness, but mostly because I refused to compromise on what was deemed by the popular majority to be socially acceptable
speech and conduct.

These almost-friends were good friends of Chris's and, in turn, tolerant
of me. Craig and Duncan were his bosom buddies. Craig was a pleasant lad
who bore the nickname "Doggy" (presumably because of the shape of his
head), while his smaller, more casual pal just went by his own name,
Duncan, and sometimes Dunc.

My enthusiasm for *Doctor Who* earned me the nickname "Doc" from
those who liked me. Those who didn't called me "Bog-eyed Billy". Oh,
and there was a brief phase of addressing me as Isaac, which I rather liked
because I had assumed it was due to my fascination with all things Biblical.
"No," one of my classmates advised nonchalantly, "it's because you've got
big eyes. Isaac: Eyes-ak. Geddit?"

Looking in the mirror. Bog-eyed Billy. Frog eyes. Goggle eyes. Just
blank, staring. "Smiler" because I never smile. Nothing to smile

about. Greasy long hair cut like a basin. Rubber lips and goggle eyes. Ugly. Repulsive.

After a few months had gone by, Duncan noticed that I hadn't uttered a single oath all the time I'd been there. This simple truth made me stand out from the crowd. "Hey Bill," he breezed. "How come you've not started swearing yet?"

I shrugged my shoulders and gave an honest reply. "I don't want to."

Another reason was I had been completely shell shocked by the transference to secondary school. It was much worse than I had imagined. Towards the end of primary school and throughout the six-week break I had been thinking, *I hope it's not like* Grange Hill, and now to my horror I was discovering the reality to be much worse. The yobbish behaviour was only one aspect. There were many others I had not anticipated.

I now had to come to terms with more subtle stuff. Wind-ups, for example. "Hey, Bill, you know that John? He had sex with his girlfriend last night." / "Did he? Really?" / "Haaa! You fell for it! I can't believe you fell for that."

> I believe everyone unless they're obviously lying. It's called trusting people.

That's what I used to tell myself anyway. Of course, the real reason I was an easy target for wind-ups was because I couldn't read the social cues. Even when other youngsters were grinning away as they waited for my reply, I couldn't tell that I was being set up. Or I could tell, but I failed to discern what the joke was going to be.

Packs of girls used to approach me and ask me if I was a virgin, knowing full well that I didn't know what a virgin is. I recall as clear as day their jeering and laughter as I stood silently trying to guess what answer I should give. "I don't know what a virgin is" would have been the safest bet, looking back, but at the time the mockery crushed me.

The instant change in speech and behaviour completely baffled me. I would puzzle over the way my peers could be so polite and helpful in the presence of a teacher, and then seconds later be "effing and jeffing" with the best of them. I simply could not get over how easily they turned it on and off. One minute they were in primary-school mode, the next they had metamorphosed into pseudo-teenagers.

Their views and opinions radically altered depending on whose company they were in too. If a group were talking about football, absolutely everybody would join in, even the ones who weren't really bothered about it.

> But you never talk about it normally when you're with your own friends!

Sometimes I would find myself in the company of just one person, maybe Chris or Duncan or Craig, and they would talk with great enthusiasm about the things I liked. "Tom Baker was the best Doctor Who." / "That TARDIS is weird, isn't it? I love the way it's a little phone box on the outside, but inside it's dead big." / "What's happened to *Blake's Seven?* Is it not coming back? Blake isn't really dead, is he?"

But when a bigger group was talking about my things, everyone tended to just laugh at the cheap special effects and the ham acting, including the ones who had expressed their appreciation of the programmes privately.

> They're all false.

In adult life I learned that this changing to fit in with one's peers has an official designation.

> Superficial and shallow.

Social skills.

> Fake.

Adaptability.

> Two-faced.

Compromise.

And now they had noticed that I wasn't swearing. Not swearing every other word like some, not even swearing a bit like the majority. Not even saying the milder swear words just to fit in.

> Fit in? I'd rather die.

Why couldn't they all just be themselves? Not one of them would make a stand for who they really were in the face of popular opinion. So, Duncan asked, "Hey Bill, how come you've not started swearing yet?"

I shrugged my shoulders and gave an honest reply. "I don't want to."

Craig softened my countenance with a gentle fatherly smile. "Don't worry, you will in time."

They had interpreted my resolve as shyness, and assumed it would subside as I gained confidence.

I WILL NOT.

And I didn't.

Every so often, a group of first formers would encircle me and try to prompt a swear word. "Say 'shit'." Why? "It sounds funny when you say it."

These confrontations deeply angered me. I abhorred the kids who did this. That said, my affection for Chris, Duncan, Craig and some of the others was also deep. I *did* like them. I liked them a lot. But I wasn't the same as them. Not better, don't get me wrong. Often, because of my aloof tone of voice and precise speech, I would be challenged and asked if I thought I was superior. The great irony was, of course, that I believed I was *inferior*. Looking back, I see that I was neither. I was just different.

The canteen always proved to be tricky. My family were on a low budget, and because of that I was allocated a "free dinner" ticket. When the others in the queue approached the servers, they would quickly calculate what they could afford with their predetermined expenditure.

All those prices. All those prices on the board. What's David having?
I'll watch him and have the same.

I panicked every time. I couldn't, and still can't, do mental arithmetic. If I was separated from David or one of the others on free dinners, I had to rely on trying to figure out the prices for myself, and as a result ended up having a pie or something equally boring, in fear of over-stretching the prescribed budget. If Chris was with me, I would ask, "Can I have chips with this too?" And he would reply, "Of course you can! You'll probably manage apple pie and custard as well."

But if no one was there to do the adding up for me, it was back to a simple pie, and maybe a bowl of rice pudding.

Can't work it out. Too afraid to ask. They'll all laugh at me.

My whole approach to school was governed by one emotion: morbid fear. My enjoyment of the actual lessons varied depending on who was teaching. Mr Davenport doubled as our Religious Knowledge teacher. He was quite funny.

As already stated, Davenport took registration for my form. One morning, Chris was playing with that now famous 1980s icon, the Rubik Cube, and Davenport challenged him to complete it in under a minute. Everyone held their breath as the colours swiftly reorganized themselves. Even the window cleaner stopped outside to watch. And he did it too! Chris completed the puzzle in under a minute. Everyone clapped and cheered. Chris was very popular with everyone. I wished I was. This was not jealousy, you understand. I never resented his popularity. I just wished that I was as articulate and funny and likable too. But I enjoyed him enjoying being popular.

Davenport also liked to indulge the unusual. He encouraged all of us to bring in potted plants with which to line the bare window sills. One girl named Andrea brought in a plant and told the form tutor it lived on cold tea. At first Mr Davenport was sceptical, but after a brief exchange, he agreed to water the soil with the dregs of the staffroom teapot. The plant really thrived too!

The deputy head, Mr Comrie, took History. I enjoyed this subject, and Comrie always made it fun by saying things like, "So let's go back in time in our TARDIS to the year 1066." Of course, as soon as he said "TARDIS", everyone would look round at me and grin.

I also liked English with Mrs Morris, not least because she had procured a long list of *Doctor Who* novelizations (that is, television stories which have been adapted into children's books) for the school library. Most of these books were written by the series' ex-script editor Terrance Dicks. I would examine the cover art and check his name on the front and spine and inside, and dream of having my own name on the front of a *Doctor Who* book. It's what I wanted to be when I grew up: a *Doctor Who* novelist or, better still, have my name on the opening titles of the programme itself.

While I was very shy, I did have a flare for Drama, in spite of the no-nonsense Mrs Hatfield. My shyness held me back from joining in a lot of things. I loved the idea of being an actor and fantasized about being in productions and being admired for my talent, but when it came to it I was terrified of doing anything where the spotlight would be upon me.

It goes without saying that I disliked Maths a great deal, though the gentle Mr Robinson was very kindly towards me and made allowances. On one occasion, we had to create a dartboard using pieces of measuring equipment. We were told that if we didn't finish it by home time, we would be kept behind. I stared at the instructions, and then I stared at the paper. Then I watched the rest of the class quietly getting on with it.

They all know how to do it. I don't know what to do.

They were swishing their compasses to make the outer perimeter and then adjusting them to create the inner rings, measuring the distance between their pencils and the points on their rulers. Then they drew lines out from the centre according to the measurements.

I don't understand it. I don't know what to do.

The class had all pretty much finished by home time.

I don't understand it.

They were putting the finishing touches to their work. Some of them looked pretty stunning too.

I don't know what to do.

I suddenly burst into tears and endured the crushing embarrassment, sensing the class all whispering to one another as Robinson kindly brought me to the front and took me through it. In the end he just did it for me. I can remember the tears and sweat vividly. And the exhaustion too. I was *exhausted* by the stress of it.

The worst lesson of all, though, was PE. Mr Griffiths was very nice, but as I had never played a game of football for real, I found the whole business highly traumatic. I was frightened of the other boys, and this was very apparent to them. Tackling was a nightmare, and I let the ball go without much of a fight, to the fury of my fellow team members.

Griffiths was convinced that I would improve with practice. I never did, and by the fourth year, the teacher had given up.

On one occasion, I was put in the goal. "I can't do this, Sir," I protested. "I can't catch, you see." In fact, I couldn't do anything that required hand-to-eye coordination. I was tall and lanky and very clumsy. I couldn't even kick the ball in a straight line! After I'd let a few balls in, my team members begged that I be taken out. Griffiths complied and I remember feeling completely overwhelmed with anger, and trembling, "I *told* you I couldn't do it."

Embarrassment, frustration and anger are quite closely linked in my psyche.

Breaking my shoulder during the half-term holiday proved most fortuitous. The doctor at the hospital said, "Well, I've got some good news and some bad news. The good news is that it'll take about six weeks to heal. The bad news is that you won't be able to do anything physically demanding. So, no football, I'm afraid."

I smiled at my mother as she corrected the doctor on his diagnosis. "I think in William's case, it's good news and good news."

Too right.

At home, I maintained my friendship with David Broadhurst, and continued to adore the lovely Tina. She couldn't wait to go to secondary school. This depressed me no end. "You'll change, like all the others," I said. Images of Tina swearing and laughing at vulgar jokes swirled about my head. I felt sick at the thought of it, because I knew it was inevitable. And I really loved her too.

After a very welcome half-term break, the need to endure school up to the Christmas break was eased by BBC Two's special repeat run *The Five Faces of Doctor Who*. For those few weeks, each school day was lightened by the knowledge that an old *Doctor Who* episode was going to be screened when I got home. The black-and-white stories fascinated me and I came to fully grasp the series' legacy. For the first time I saw William Hartnell, Patrick Troughton and Jon Pertwee in the title role, and the closing week showed Tom Baker's grand finale, with another chance to watch him "regenerate" into his successor, Peter Davison.

Video was still in its infancy and very expensive. In fact it would be another three years before my family would take the plunge with the craze.

While we waited, I hit upon another way of preserving and enjoying my favourite programme. Inspired by a TV adventure soundtrack released as an LP (*Genesis of the Daleks*) I decided to set up a tape recorder by the television and record the programmes on audio tape. This way I could listen to the episodes as though they were on the radio and, because I'd already seen the adventure unfold on television, I could play the pictures back in my head.

My fanaticism was being fed regularly, with the series on TV, releases of *Doctor Who Monthly* every four weeks, and now my growing collection of audio tapes. I listened to an episode of *Doctor Who* every night in bed before going to sleep. The escapism the show provided helped me deal with the hostile world around me, and boy, did I indulge. At school, I would imagine the place being over-run with Daleks. Various teachers would be exterminated, and the whole class would look to me for salvation. I was a hero in these imaginary situations. In real life I was "weird", and as a result, a very lonely soul; but in my imagination I was the protector and overcame the aggressors with wisdom.

Before the Christmas break, Mrs Morris set us the task of writing and presenting a talk about our favourite subject. I knew already what my topic would be. Christmas was another source of relief. Any chance to get away from school was welcome, though I never once played truant. Again that was repugnant to my inbuilt sense of principle. I hated school with a passion and would have preferred a jaunt around town instead, but disregarding the law in such a way never entered my head.

January 1982 saw the first full appearance of Peter Davison as the Doctor in *Doctor Who*. The programme was now being shown twice weekly on Mondays and Tuesdays (and not on Saturdays, as was the tradition). I had mixed feelings about this. *Doctor Who* twice a week was, of course, a wondrous thing to behold; but it also meant that the 26 episodes were over and done with by the end of the thirteenth week. The series, which used to run from September through to March – the whole of the winter – now only ran from January to March. A very short season indeed.

While the Fifth Doctor was an instant success in terms of viewing figures, the tabloid press did not respond well to Peter Davison's "vulnerable aristocrat" portrayal of the Time Lord. I think it was the *Daily*

Mirror that referred to him as "the wet vet", which was a reference to his Tristram character in *All Creatures Great And Small*. My mother picked up on this and I grimaced whenever she said it.

What had become a nuisance to her personally was serving as a lifeline for me. Therefore, any criticism of *Doctor Who* was a criticism of me too, as far as I was concerned. He was like a father figure to me. Like Tom Baker before him, Peter Davison was my hero, but on a more human level because of his youth.

My obsession with the programme peaked with the broadcast of the story *Earthshock*. It marked the triumphant return of one of the Doctor's classic adversaries, the Cybermen, which provoked great excitement even among my peers – and the death of the Doctor's young companion Adric.

Over the last year I had seen elements of myself in the boy Adric. He was isolated from his family and friends. He spoke in such a way that tended to make him sound pompous and over-confident. With Tom Baker he had been like a son for the Doctor, but with Peter Davison he was more akin to the Time Lord's younger, immature brother. This change in their relationship's dynamics made him unlikable in the eyes of many (especially my dad, who would exclaim, "I hate that kid!"). But to my mind, the boy's perceived arrogance was really a side effect of being disenchanted with his life aboard the TARDIS, particularly since the Doctor's regeneration.

In the final moments of *Earthshock*, the Cyber freighter is drifting in and out of different time zones as it hurtles towards prehistoric Earth. Adric is still on board and the TARDIS can't get a lock on the ship in order to materialize inside. With the Doctor and companions looking on helplessly, the ship acquires a bright silver glow and then explodes. Adric's death is followed by silent closing credits.

I sobbed my heart out that night. I was deeply traumatized, as though someone real had passed away. Of course, this sort of reaction is common in children. They blur the line between fact and fiction. And some adults are moved to tears when they watch a "weepy" film. So my reaction in that context was not so out of the ordinary.

What *was* out of the ordinary, perhaps, was the length of time it took for me to get over the "bereavement". When David met me the following morning to go to school, I said, "Did you watch *Doctor Who* last night?"

He said, "No. Why, what happened?"

"Adric died," I replied solemnly. Then, within seconds of stating that simple fact, I burst into tears. No doubt reports of this spread far and wide that day. Whenever I thought of the scene my bottom lip started to quiver and, when the episode was repeated the following year, I walked out of the room during the final moments.

In Mrs Morris's English class my talk on *Doctor Who* went down very well. I played an excerpt from my homemade drama and took along my cardboard K9 model. The audience marvelled at his illuminated "eye screen". Mrs Morris came to me after that, whenever she was expanding the school library, in order to determine which *Doctor Who* books should be included. Of course, any treatment like this makes one unpopular with the others. "Why does she always come and ask *you*?" they would sneer.

April arrived, and the time I had been dreading was upon me. Christopher Millard left the school. I was *so* alone. I can't describe the emptiness I felt for the remainder of that term.

The end of the first year was marked by the retirement of the headmaster, Mr Livesey. I remember the deputy headmistress, Mrs Bramwell, crying when he made his final speech. My History teacher and deputy head, Mr Comrie, was to succeed Livesey in the position the following year.

The summer holidays were finally upon us. Six weeks of relief. And it hadn't come soon enough.

"William's a Bit Slow", 1982–83

SEPTEMBER 1982 MARKED THE BEGINNING of my second year at Joey's. I trudged up the main drive, inwardly scowling, as the hordes around me swore and cursed and smoked. I say *inwardly* scowling, because outwardly I looked either blank or frightened. Most probably the latter, which attracted the bullies.

I tended to get on well with younger children, and famously with adults. Children didn't have any preconceptions and adults talked about proper sensible things. I felt safe with adults. They didn't laugh when I made philosophical observations. They would just say things like, "Oh, that's a very interesting way of seeing it. I hadn't thought of it like that before," or, "You've got an old head on young shoulders." Whereas many of my peers were extremely superficial, and as a result, difficult for me to warm to.

I had made the mistake in the previous term of bringing this superficiality to the attention of odd individuals. "Have you noticed how false everyone is?" I would start. "The way they change depending on whose company they are in? They talk one way when they are on their own, and a completely different way when they're with their friends – sometimes even altering their feelings and beliefs to suit. It's because they're scared of being themselves, you see." I didn't win friends by talking like this. Individuals would either change the subject or just walk away. They didn't like me asking questions and making observations, and I lacked the insight to discern that many would think I was making a judgement about them personally. I slowly but surely gave up this line of conversation, although inside it still infuriated me.

As I approached the main door of the school, I noted a group of girls teasing some poor lad sitting on the grassy bank of the playing field. He was clutching his satchel and shouting: "Stop it! Leave me alone!"

The ringleader was a girl who lived in my street. She was only in the first year herself, and yet she had the confidence to persecute this older boy. I was astounded by her guile as I remembered how timid and nervous I had been on my first day.

I loathe you and all your kind.

Once the crowd had dispersed, I sat beside the boy and said, "I know how you feel. They pick on me too." He looked round, red faced, his eyes full of worry and anger. It seemed to me he wasn't sure if I was just another bully playing a psychological game. He was reluctant to talk, but I managed to get his name: Ian. He seemed like the sort of person I could be friends with. We had one single attribute in common: we were both very much alone.

At break times, Ian would seek out a secluded spot or hide in a corner, and then he would be set upon by cruel predators. He had a reputation for being easy to intimidate which had followed him from primary school. This and a tendency to react in rage. His face would go blood red with fury and he would shout, "Stop it! *Stop it!*" But there was something about his countenance or his voice that just made his persecutors laugh with hysteria. He was only 11 or 12 years old, and yet he shouted like a teacher, which the bullies loved.

We were different in other ways too. I was shy and reclusive; he had the courage to speak up. I would be devastated by episodes with the bullies; he, while he would be upset, would bounce back. He was quite resilient. I was slow on the uptake; he was sharp, quick with his mind. He knew what to do, where to go, what he wanted and where he was going in life. I didn't. I was almost always overwhelmed. Ian was a great stabilizer for me. After some persistence I succeeded in demonstrating how we were very much in the same boat, and we became firm friends after that.

The French teacher, Miss Sharman, became my form tutor for the second year. I rather liked her, and was impressed no end when she said she'd met Tom Baker after watching him in a play at the theatre.

During my time in 2W1 I continued to feel vulnerable and anxious, like being rolled up inside a giant carpet and left to find my own way out. Whenever I panicked or froze, the bullies were always ready to set upon me. In the play court, if I hadn't managed to hook up with Ian, the vultures would descend upon me. The worst were girls, who delighted in asking me embarrassing questions.

"Are you a virgin, William?"

> Oh…er…what do I say? I can't tell them that I don't know what a virgin is. If I say yes I am one, they might all laugh at me because it's something bad or rude; but if I say no I'm not, they could also laugh because it's something I should be. What do I say? What do I say?

My throat dried up, my heart was pounding. "Why?" I stuttered. "Are you one?"

The girls laughed. One of them gestured towards the ringleader. "She's definitely not one!" They all laughed again. "Bitch!" roared the ringleader. "And *you'll* always be one!" I still had no idea what they were talking about.

"Come on, William," teased the ringleader. "Are you a virgin?"

I took a guess.

> Oh, please God. Let this be the right answer.

"No," I said, barely able to look them in the eye. "I'm not a virgin."

The reaction was immediate. Group hysteria. "Haaa!! He's not a virgin! Why, how many girls have you been with, William?"

> What? What are they talking about now?

"Come on. How many girls have you been with?"

I shrugged. "I haven't been with any girls."

"Well you *must* have if you're not a virgin."

> Ah, so that's what a virgin is. My throat is tight, my heart is a rock. I'm tearful. Please, please, leave me alone.

The second girl raised her hands. "William," she began, "which one of these are you?" She made a circle with her forefinger and thumb, and then with her other hand pointed through the hole. "One of these?" Then she extended the forefingers of both hands and pointed the ends together. "One of these?" Finally she made the circle again, but this time with both hands, and tapped them against one another. "Or one of these?"

They tried to stifle their giggling as they registered the look on my face. I had no idea what they were talking about. "I don't know," I stammered, and the girl offered to run me through the choices again. In the end I decided to get it over with and chose one at random. I put my two hands into circles and tapped them together. "I'm that one."

Their reaction confused me even more. "Haaa! He's a lesbian!"

What's a lesbian?

Later, my worldly-wise friend David explained it to me. "The finger pointing out is a man's penis. The circle is a vagina. So the penis and the vagina going together mean you're straight, the penis on the penis means you're queer, and the vagina on the vagina means you're a lesbian."

I was none the wiser. "What's a lesbian?"

David was astounded. "You don't know what a lesbian is? Have you never seen a blue movie?" He enjoyed being my educator. "Lesbians are women who sleep together like your mum and dad do."

I've never heard of that before.

"And queers are men who sleep with other men."

I found this difficult to believe. "You're not winding me up, are you?"

David laughed and shook his head.

"Do they kiss each other and all that?"

David nodded. "Yeah. They're disgusting." He went on to make a show of being disgusted, screwing up his face and putting his finger in his mouth as if to make himself vomit. "You should have said the first one. That means you're straight, you're normal."

Normal. I have problems with that word. "Normal" means "like them". I am not normal.

My fear of others, what they might think or say, had descended into the realm of paranoia. On one occasion, having just had my hair cut, I waited outside the form room right up to the time for registration. I was so scared of the ridicule. A boy called Mark approached me as he was entering the room. "How come you're stood out here, Bill?" he inquired. I was staggered by the question. He hadn't even noticed that I'd had my hair cut, and now I was going to have to draw his attention to it. Others would have made up a story: "Oh, I just want to be on my own for a bit," or "I'm just warming myself on the radiator." But not me. I couldn't do that because it was a lie.

I swallowed hard, knowing my truthful answer would induce the ridicule I had been trying to avoid. "I had my hair cut on Saturday, and I don't want them to laugh at me."

Mark's eyes radiated with glee and he was barely able to contain himself. He couldn't wait to tell the others. After he'd gone in, I waited a few seconds, held my breath and then followed.

As soon as I made my entrance, the jeering started. "Hair cut! Hair cut!" And all the usual jokes. "When are you gonna go back and get it finished?" Followed by hysteria. The comments themselves meant nothing, of course. It was the fact that they *knew* they were hurting me. They knew I couldn't handle it. And they were right, I couldn't. And so for that moment I despised them with all my soul.

> My voice electronically treated, my eyes burning with rage. "Des-troy them!" Shards of bright blue energy and searing heat. Piercing sound and purest light, the classroom shimmering white and blue, like a film negative held up at the window, the faces of my classmates twisting and contorting with agony. Girls screaming, boys clutching their tummies and writhing. They, all of them, drop to the floor – dead.

They never seemed to get bored with saying the same old predictable pap. *I* got bored with it, though. And I got very bored with *them*, quickly.

Ian was very interested in horticulture and agriculture. After a little chat with the Maths teacher, Mr Tonge, we got ourselves into the Gardening Club. Tonge wrote out special 'passes' to show to the prefects. For me, this was a Godsend. We now had a way of avoiding the play courts at break-time. For Ian, though, it was more than that. He had a genuine love of gardening.

Kids would mock and shout as we walked through the corridors, watering the school plants. They might call us "Bill and Ben the Flowerpot Men" if they were nice. Unfortunately a proportionate number of them had thought of something else.

"You're not gay, are you?"

This, I learned, was a reference to homosexuality, the same-sex relationship previously described as queer. In retrospect, I can see how it might have looked as if Ian and I were gay. We didn't mix with the other boys much, except during class, and neither of us had girlfriends. The crazy thing about this was that both Ian and I suffered terrible crushes on television actresses and girls at school. I had a soft spot for a girl called Natalie, while Ian talked regularly about the character Jody, a stunning blonde girl in the American TV series *The Fall Guy*. But, because we never mixed much with the others, they didn't hear us discussing such things.

The first major school trip was a holiday in France. Many of us had never been abroad before and the excitement was tangible, but I looked at my peers and considered what a lot of them were like when the teachers were not around and instantly dismissed the idea. The effect of seeing primary-school friends suddenly change their personalities upon arriving at Joseph Eastham had not even begun to wear off at this stage. I balked at the suggestion of how fun it would be to go to France with them for a week.

Another issue was Mr Davenport, who often spotlighted individuals for a dollop of good old-fashioned tawdry embarrassment. Most of my peers had no problem with this and just laughed it off. "Well," they would smile dismissively, "it's just a laugh, isn't it?"

No it isn't. It's humiliating.

The holiday would have been a whole week of feeling homesick and lonely, a whole week of people saying, "Oh, you don't have to join in/dance/whatever, you can just watch," and then later changing their minds and putting on the pressure. Mum thought me going to France with the school was a lovely idea, and although she would struggle to pay for it, she was quite prepared to do it. Maybe she thought the experience would help me ease up. I think she was disappointed when I insisted on staying behind.

Teachers scrunched their faces, baffled, when they realized it wasn't a question of my parents not being able to afford it, as it was for some of the others. I just did not *want* to go.

The second year, or Year 8 as people now call it, also marked our preliminary education on the matter of sexual intercourse. Fairly graphic diagrams
portrayed the inner workings of the sex organs, and I finally realized the
meaning behind the vulgarities uttered by my classmates.

Earlier on, when I had been teased about being straight, gay or lesbian,
I had not been entirely sure about things, even after David's gentle
explanation, because I hadn't comprehended what men and women
actually do when they sleep together.

It was also during Year 8 that I suffered a particularly traumatic episode
with one of the school nasties, a predator three years my senior whom we
will call Bully. It was one dinner-time, I found myself alone in the play
court and hiding away in the shadows hoping no one would find me. I
don't know why I wasn't gardening. Maybe this incident occurred before
the Gardening Club was inaugurated. Unfortunately, Bully could see me
only too clearly. He seemed to appear out of nowhere and grabbed my arm.
I jumped and glared up into his menacing eyes, terror struck.

Bully looked around and checked for teachers, and then snarled
through gritted teeth. "You have got a face like a slapped arse," he said. (I'll
forgive you if you can't help laughing.)

The youth tightened his grip and lowered his voice. "*Say* it."

I just kept looking at his hideous expression. I was terrified.

"Say it!" he sneered.

I gulped. Then: "I have got a face like a slapped arse."

The reaction was immediate. He threw his head back and roared with
the kind of insane laughter one expects from megalomaniacs like Emperor
Ming in the old *Flash Gordon* movies. "Excellent!" he shouted.

With a yank of the arm, he dragged my thin frame around the court,
stopping at various groups of friends. "Hey, hey, listen to this," he'd call,
and then his peers would look at me in expectation. He tightened his grip.
"Say it."

I could barely face the jury, knowing what their only judgement could
be.

"I have got a face like a slapped arse."

The group collapsed, many of them holding their tummies and
gasping for breath. Bully dragged me to another little congregation on the
far side. An overweight fifth year with masses of blond curly hair led the
group. I recognized him as one of Colin's friends.

"Hey, Spring Head!" Bully shouted. "Listen to this."

Spring Head and his gang waited to see what I had to say. I felt the tightened grip once more, and delivered my humiliating line. "I have got a face like a slapped arse."

The peal of the school bell released me from the anguish and I headed for afternoon registration, embarrassed, humiliated and traumatized. I sat at my desk as the register was called out, and then after a few minutes of silence, I broke down in tears. A visit to Mr Davenport (now acting deputy head) ensued. Bully was summoned, and I was forced to repeat the scenario in front of the teacher.

I'll give him his due: Davenport kept a controlled expression when Bully burst out laughing as I delivered my report. Apparently, Bully had a history of this kind of thing, and was given a few strokes of the cane as punishment.

I went home feeling frustrated and angry. The episode had confirmed to me what I already believed: I was unpopular, a subject for ridicule and persecution, an oddball, and most crushing of all, ugly. I was ugly. The sort of boy that teachers found dependable, the sort of boy girls felt sorry for – but not the sort that girls wanted to go out with, not the sort they fancied.

UGLY.

School. The best days of my life? I think not.

My mother paid a number of visits to the school in order to discuss my problems, in particular my inability to settle. Mum had little time for teachers and social workers because they didn't listen. "They think the world revolves around school," she'd say. "Someone should tell them, the world doesn't end at half-past three!" She was more than a little aggravated when the social worker said it would be better for me to remain in school at lunch-times rather than go to Grandma's. But Grandma was my lifeline, my respite to stop me from going mad. She was also very encouraging when it came to my dream of being a writer.

I had a meeting with the head of the Windsor house, Mrs Wray. She asked me some questions, but because I felt nervous about my being quizzed, I struggled to give her anything meaningful to work with.

My answers were generic, they were about feeling different. When asked what exactly *was* different, I couldn't explain. I didn't really understand it myself, and I lacked the nerve to say what I really believed;

that my peers were false and changed personality depending on whose company they were in, that they used the most appalling language, that I felt like I'd fallen to earth from somewhere else, that I was an alien trapped on this awful planet, that I was like Jesus – I spoke the truth while everyone else preferred the lie. I could hardly tell her *that*, could I? So I just kept shrugging and saying, "I don't know."

After discussions with teachers and headmaster Mr Comrie, the assigned social worker concluded by telling my mother, "You'll just have to accept it, Mrs Hadcroft. William's a bit slow."

My problems with school, and life in general, were worsened by my realization that the planet Earth and the people on it are only a minuscule cog in an awesome, vast universal machine. A single lesson in basic Physics opened my eyes to these facts. The teacher, a young woman called Mrs Stevens, would never know what a profound effect her lesson was to have on me.

She explained that the earth rotated on its axis and performed a complete cycle in 24 hours. While it was doing this, it travelled through space on a fixed orbit around the sun, completing its path every 12 months. Eight other planets, some several times larger than Earth, some smaller, also made orbits round the sun at varying speeds. This arrangement was called a solar system.

It boggled me to realize that our sun was just one of billions in our galaxy, the Milky Way, and that the Milky Way was one of about 50 billion galaxies hanging like a bunch of grapes in a cluster. Clusters too hung together in their thousands in super clusters. And even super clusters were arranged in complex groups. My realization? The universe is a colossally large place, and we are so very insignificant. We were also taught that in a few million years' time the sun would burn itself out and expand, destroying the first three planets in the process (including Earth) and then implode, sucking the remaining planets in, and then turn supernova.

> There's no point to our existence. On this scale, nothing we do matters. The love we show, the wars we fight, the causes we champion – it's all irrelevant – *we are irrelevant*. Why strive to pass exams? Why make a name for myself? Why should I want to be

remembered when I'm dead? When the Earth has gone, no one will be remembered, no one will matter. Nothing matters.

Doreen's son Karl had become hooked on Douglas Adams's novel *The Hitch-Hiker's Guide to the Galaxy*. While taking the form of a comedy, the big universal issues mentioned above are explored by Adams in some detail, especially the question of life's meaning and the fact that Man is so small and yet so full of himself. One of my favourite sequences exposes Man's tendency to rationalize away the things he wishes to debunk, regardless of their validity. In the sequence, Man employs some dodgy reasoning and proves that God doesn't exist – to the Almighty's face! Feeling triumphant, he then proves that black is white and meets a timely end on a zebra crossing.

Reading a proper adult novel was a daunting prospect for me, but I enjoyed listening to Karl as he read bits of it out. I recalled the BBC TV series, which I had enjoyed very much, and later took the plunge with the books and the original BBC radio series. Author Douglas Adams was not a religious person and entertained many notions put forth by scientists, but in his writing he was not afraid to acknowledge the absurdities and contradictions present in speculative science. He laughed at religious belief, the concept of God, the theory of evolution, philosophy, bureaucracy, and Man's arrogance. It's not without reason that thinking people love *Hitch-Hiker's*.

Though no longer being one of Jehovah's Witnesses, my mother received regular visits from her Witness friends Carole and Joan. They would pop round for a chat every fortnight, fill Mum in on all the latest gossip and leave *The Watchtower* and *Awake!* magazines for her to read. And she appreciated this.

I had reached the age where one wonders about God and the Bible, and I recalled some of the things I had been taught: that the world is in its last days and God will remove Man's rulerships, and return the world and the human race to how he originally meant it to be. We'd had our go at ruling ourselves, got it wrong big time, ruined everything – now it was time for him to reestablish his sovereignty and put things right. God's Kingdom had been inaugurated in heaven, now it was time for his will to be done on Earth.

One Saturday I rode my bike up to Old Lane where the Kingdom Hall was situated, and I just sat on the saddle and looked at the building. It had been built in 1972 and my mum had helped out with providing sandwiches for the workers, all skilled but unpaid, as was the Witness custom. Everything they did was purely for love of God and Christ.

I gazed at the legend "Kingdom Hall of Jehovah's Witnesses" and then at the meeting times listed below. I suddenly felt very holy and special, not because of any supernatural occurrence, but because it seemed perfectly right. I didn't experience a blinding light or hear any disembodied voices calling to me. What I *did* see, though, was a sense of security, a place and a people that were "safe", somewhere warm and welcoming, ready-made friends.

When I arrived back home I approached my mother. "Mum, can we go to the Kingdom Hall tomorrow?" Mum's response was less than encouraging. "You've been to the Kingdom Hall before and you didn't like it. In fact you cried, as I remember."

I decided not to press the subject any further, as it was clear she didn't really want to go.

I'll go on my own, then.

And so, on a bright and sunny Sunday morning, I picked up a Bible and songbook, put them in a carrier bag, and rode back up to Old Lane. Feeling extremely nervous, I took a deep breath, plucked up courage and entered the Hall. It was exactly the way I remembered it: well-dressed people chattering and laughing, hanging up their coats in the foyer. Others queued up at a counter to pick up literature for distribution to the public. A voice, not from heaven, but from the sound system, descended upon us, advising that we take our seats. I did so. The meeting opened with a song, someone approached Jehovah in prayer, and then a speaker took the platform to deliver a talk.

It lasted a whole hour. Admittedly, I found most of it incomprehensible, and when the speaker encouraged the audience to turn up scriptures in their Bibles I didn't have a clue where any of the verses were. After the Public Talk, for the second hour, a different speaker chaired a question-and-answer discussion based on a lesson in *The Watchtower* magazine. This was easier to follow because it was more like a class. A designated person read the paragraphs, the chairman asked the questions provided, and then members of the audience offered their comments down a microphone.

Thrilled to see me, Joan approached afterwards and asked, "Where's your mum, love?"

"Oh," I said airily. "She's at home."

She frowned. "Then, who brought you?"

I took great delight in telling her, "No one brought me. I came on my own." She marvelled at my resolve, and it wasn't before long that a sizeable crowd had surrounded me. They kept smiling and telling one another, "Look, he's come on his own."

> I feel normal. They like me. They accept me. I'm important. I'm popular. They know what it's like to be hated for being different. Everybody hates them. Everybody in the world. We're all weird, but in here it doesn't matter.

After a couple more Sunday meetings, I was approached by one of the elders, a very warm-hearted and gentle man called David. "Are you having a Study, William?" he asked. I didn't know what "a Study" was. David explained, "It's where someone spends about an hour a week teaching you the Bible."

I adopted my usual "vague" look and shook my head. David squeezed my shoulders, as was his custom with children, and turned me to face the sea of adults. "Who would you like to study with?" Inside I desperately wanted to say, "Can I study with you?" He was my favourite of all the elders, so warm and kindly. I really loved him. But I was just too shy. So I homed in on the only other person I felt comfortable with. "I want to study with Aunty Joan, please."

And so, every week, Aunty Joan visited my house with the Bible and the beautifully illustrated study aid *You Can Live Forever in Paradise on Earth*. I learned about Jehovah's purpose for the Earth and mankind; about Man's rebellion at the dawn of time; about the influence of Satan; and about how orthodox Christianity had woven in with Bible doctrine concepts adopted from ancient pagan religions. The term "witness" was taken from a number of Bible passages which referred to individuals who publicly testified to the truth as they saw it: the prophets of pre-Christian times, Jesus Christ, and the first-century apostles.

I *loved* it. I loved their lines of reasoning, I loved the way they quoted verses in the Bible that blatantly contradicted church dogma, and I adored the quotes from secular history books and encyclopaedias which highlighted the origins of such ideas.

The organization of Jehovah's Witnesses were concerned only with establishing the Bible's truth as they saw it and declaring it in a manner reminiscent of the work done by Jesus and the apostles. Their motive was entirely born from a desire to please the God of the Bible. They were not deliberately rocking the boat, nor were they anti-society. They promoted obedience to the laws of the land and respect for government.

But the appeal for me at the age of 12 was the pure defiance they showed in the face of orthodoxy. I despised and loathed the system of the world, with its fashions and trends and flimsy ideas and philosophies, its media and its social conditioning.

The idea of a heavenly father watching over me was also potent. It put paid to the notion that we were so small in the universe, that we were insignificant. It also helped me cope with the bullies. Joan encouraged me to pray for the strength to endure, and she gave me a Bible text to meditate upon as a means of comfort.

In the summer, I attended the big district convention at Bolton Wanderers' Burnden Park stadium. Tens of thousands turned up and I found the whole extravaganza overwhelming. The following year, the congregation was assigned the Manchester City Maine Road stadium. I felt a bit better about it, but my problem with crowds, even very nice crowds where nobody swore and everyone was polite, still posed a problem. Yet I felt at home with them. They were my people. I was safe with them.

My new-found spirituality caused a few problems at school. I was eager to tell the world about "the truth" as my mentors did on local doorsteps, but I had absolutely no sense of tact or balance. The evangelical zeal was there, but not the social skills to make my message more reasonable and palatable. As a result, I tended to bring the subject up at the wrong moment and then suffer great ridicule. I also got terribly flustered if someone openly disagreed with me, and angry if they put forth a line of reasoning that challenged my belief.

Why can't they see it?

Of course, there was another reason behind people disagreeing with me, but I could not accept or even comprehend it: people have a right to believe what they wish, and might be genuinely convinced by their perception of truth.

My friend Ian was a churchgoer. He and his mother attended a local Methodist chapel. Our religious discussions swiftly descended into arguments, mostly because I was attacking the whole fabric of his faith, which in turn put him on the defensive.

If I started talking about the Kingdom Hall, he would try to match what I was saying by quoting something his minister had said, or maybe quote a psalm. Conversely, if he mentioned anything that had its roots in pagan religion, I would immediately declare, "That's pagan. It doesn't come from the Bible. In fact God finds it offensive."

I once made the statement that Christ could not have been born in the winter, since the sheep were out at night. He argued and argued, stating over and over again that sheep can withstand cold temperatures. On rechecking my literature, I realized I should have said that the *shepherds* would not have been out at night in the winter. "Oh I know that," he announced. "But you said it was the sheep."

We were sniping at one another all the time.

What was to be my last severe episode with the school bullies was almost entirely orchestrated by my paranoia. I feel angry with myself now when I look back to this incident: I was so frightened of everyone, such a coward. It was the weekend and my brothers and I were playing on the old disused railway embankment, when we saw some lads from my year coming the other way. As soon as I caught sight of them I was terrified.

> They'll start picking on us. They'll push us about. They might beat us up.

Eye contact was made and I was petrified. "Oh," I laughed nervously. "Here are those lads from my school."

> Try to think of something, try to think of something. Pre-empt whatever they're going to do.

"I know, why don't you get us by the arms and legs and throw us down the embankment?"

The boys rubbed their hands, delighted by the suggestion. My brothers, utterly dumbstruck, just looked at me. "Just throw yourself into a roll," I advised. "Like when we've been doing stunts." They, being nine and five years of age respectively, and following my lead, nodded and prepared themselves for the assault.

The boys took me first, as I'd suggested, by the arms and legs, and swung me back and forth to gain momentum. "One, ar, two, ar, three." I went flying, hurled myself onto my side, and connected with the steep slope of grass hard. I rolled down to the bottom and landed in a muddy ditch. Absolutely terror struck, I scrambled towards the adjacent slope. Matthew landed behind me, I heard the wind knock out of him. He burst into tears, "Wait for me, Bill. Wait for me."

We got half way up the adjacent slope and stopped to see how Jonathan was faring. He was rolling down the embankment and the boys were running and skidding down after him. He landed in the mud, but before he could get to his feet, the boys were stood over him. I watched on helplessly as they started to kick him. I could see his pained face and hear him yelping.

If I go back, they'll get me. They'll get me.

One of them picked up a big white stone with both hands, lifted it above his head, and dropped it onto Jonathan's stomach. He stifled a cry. It was like watching Jesus being nailed. The evil tormentors ran off.

I'm a coward. I should have gone back. I should have helped him.
I'm a coward. I'm a coward. I HATE MYSELF.

The three of us made our way home, sobbing and nursing our wounds. Mum and Grandma were absolutely outraged. "Who did it?" Mum shouted.

"I don't know," I lied. "Some boys from another form."

Mum paid a visit to the school and vented her rage upon the headmaster and the boys' parents. I felt wretched inside. It had been my idea for them to do what they did. They probably wouldn't have thought to do it if I hadn't suggested it. I kept recalling the images of baby Matthew tumbling down the grass and landing with a thud in the ditch, his face twisted with pain and fear. Then Jonathan writhing in agony as they dropped the boulder on him.

I hate them. I hate them. I HATE THEM!!

But I hated myself the most.

My friendship with David Broadhurst, my fellow *Doctor Who* fan, was brought to an abrupt end. His parents were splitting up, and his mother had decided to move right away from Little Hulton and start again. The day he came to tell us was awful. He was so traumatized. I can still see the tears streaming down his face. "We're moving away," he kept saying. "We're moving away." It was terrible. We were like brothers.

I was devastated. My only true peer friends now were Karl, Ian at school, and one or two boys in my street. They used to come and call for my mum in winter time and have snowball fights with her. "Is Margaret coming out?" they'd say. I think this activity was looked upon with some scorn by the other parents in the street. I think, looking back, my family was generally regarded as eccentric.

There was also a good friend with whom I spent quite a portion of my time, who seemed to be everything I wasn't. He was very popular and attractive, he was handsome, his blue eyes had a sparkle of intelligence, and girls would swoon around him. He was amusing and quick with his comments, but at the same time kindly and thoughtful. He had it all. I admired him so much, he was the sort of boy I wished I could be.

One day he came round to my house to play and, as I watched him, I became overwhelmed with feelings of affection. His smile and his eyes, the sound of his voice as he talked – everything. I had what can only be described as a schoolboy crush on him. Me, a boy, had fallen in love, with a boy.

I love you. I really love you. I want to tell you. I want you to know.

"I love you," I said. Instantly the smile fell from his face. He could not look me in the eye. He coughed and then gave a nervous chuckle. "Yeah, as a mate."

"No," I replied honestly. "I *really* love you. I love the way you do things and the way you talk. And I love your eyes and your smile."

He cleared his throat again. Then he looked right at me. "You're not queer, are you, Bill?"

I frowned. I was stunned and frightened. "No," I said sheepishly, but I knew he wasn't convinced.

Christmas arrived, and the break from school was greatly appreciated by both Ian and me. I felt nothing but relief. However, another kind of trauma was just ahead: the break-up of my parents' marriage. It had been struggling for some time, and the older I'd got, the more aware of it I had become. Dad was asked to leave shortly after Christmas. It was an awful time, but after a while my brothers and I adjusted to staying over at his bedsit in Bolton and it became normal. In fact we very much looked forward to our weekend trips to places like Buxton and the Jodrell Bank radio telescope.

A period of peace followed and my mother resumed her studies at college. Our relationship became quite strong during those months, and Mum would often proudly announce to her peers, "My best friend is my eldest lad." And she was right. In fact I was on good terms with most adults. I enjoyed their company and conversation. They were just so much more mature. If I wanted to voice my ideas on the universe or science, they didn't laugh. In fact, they indulged me. And if I drew conclusions that were not quite in line with current theory, they would praise my individuality and call me "a thinker", a term I greatly appreciated.

It was the same at the Kingdom Hall too. Some of the youngsters I came in contact with were eager to talk – so long as it wasn't about the Bible and Jehovah. Their interests tended to lie in the secular world, the fashions, the trends, the cars and the damned football. All the boys loved football, and I loathed it.

Parents urged their children to befriend me. "Go and talk to William, he's here on his own." A number of sincere ones would approach and try to make conversation.

"Hiya."

"Hiya."

"Is it William?"

"Yes."

"We're all having a game of footie later this afternoon. Fancy coming?"

"No. Don't like football."

"It's good once you get into it. I can understand you not wanting to watch it on telly, 'cos I'm like that. But once you meet everyone, you'll enjoy it."

He's trying to talk me round. What do I say?

"I won't enjoy it."

"You *will*, just give it a try."

I'm feeling anxious now, my throat's drying up. And he's so nice too. He's smiling.

"I won't. I'm no good at it."

"Well I'm not either."

Beginning to stammer.

"No, I mean, I really am rubbish… I hate football. I think it's pointless."

He's not smiling now. I've upset him. He's shrugging. He's giving up. No! Don't give up! Please! I like you. I think you'd be great to have as a friend. Stop him walking off. Try to salvage it. Say something.

"I like *Doctor Who*."

Nothing.

"A lot of people wonder why the TARDIS is a police telephone box. It's because it has a device called the Chameleon Circuit, and it's supposed to disguise itself wherever it goes; but in the first episode, when it took the form of a police box, the Chameleon Circuit broke, and it's been stuck like that ever since. You see, if people understood these things, they wouldn't think it's daft."

No, gone… Failed again.

As far as the religion was concerned, some of these children at Kingdom Hall were unsure of their convictions, while others were completely indifferent about it. Maybe my problem lay in the fact that I had *chosen* to be with Jehovah's Witnesses, and at the age of twelve wanted to talk about Bible prophecies. I *wanted* to discuss the *Watchtower* lesson we'd had the previous Sunday. And so, I started to feel like an oddball among my "own" people. There was a set of youths who looked like they had it all sorted out, but they were just that bit older. Pity. Those whom I saw as my friends in the congregation were the adults – adults with commitments, adults with families to care for.

The loneliness was creeping in again.

As the summer term rolled on, I sensed that I was, at long last, beginning to settle. Maybe having a regular friend in Ian had helped stabilize me. At the same time, though, it felt as if some of the teachers had formed a particular opinion about me following my mother's meetings with the social worker. Either that, or I was becoming increasingly paranoid – which is wholly possible. I was all too aware of the impact me and my mother had made. For example, a teacher whom I later grew to admire, when he caught sight of my name on a library book card, purred, "Ah. So *you're* William Hadcroft."

Mr Davenport now had less patience with me. During his Religious Knowledge lesson the class played a game where he would ask a question, and then we had to find the answer in a cited scripture. It was simply a race to turn up the text (presumably to get us used to the chapters and verses, and the whereabouts of the 66 books of the Bible).

"Who was the first murderer?" he quizzed. "Genesis, Chapter Four, Verse Eight."

Due to my Bible Study with Jehovah's Witnesses, I already knew who the first murderer was. It was Cain. So I wrote the answer down and took it to the front. He looked at it and made a display of shaking his head. "Wrong," came his loud announcement.

"It's not," I challenged, feeling somewhat put out.

"Go and look it up," said Davenport.

It transpired that I had spelt the name wrong. I had written "Cane" instead of "Cain". A little commendation for knowing the answer without looking it up would have been nice.

On another occasion, we had to write an explanation of the fall of Jericho. Davenport relayed the "facts" as presented in his pamphlet, which tended to put it all down to natural elements rather than divine action, and then we read the Bible account and wrote our pieces. Privately, I had disagreed with the explanation presented for the curriculum, and so I put what the Bible actually said; namely, that God had reduced the city of

Jericho to rubble. Mr D made me stay behind to rewrite the piece after everyone else had gone home. In the end I just restated the same explanation, and walked out without showing it to him.

It bothered me greatly that the teachers of religion tended to rationalize away the supernatural elements of the Bible. OK, there were parts where it was being allegorical and symbolic, but much of the supernatural stuff had been recorded and presented as historical fact. What were cynics and doubters doing teaching religion?

Mum saved up enough money for a week's holiday at the Butlin's Holiday Camp in Pwlhelli, North Wales. She, Jonathan, Matthew and I went with Doreen and her children. The highlight for Karl and myself was a children's pantomime group called the Push Button Click. It was a fresh take on the age-old genre. The central character, a Fonz/John Travolta type nicknamed Push Button Pete, journeyed with his friends Keeley and IQ through time and space with the help of a unique robot. The Click (that's Clique, if we're being pedantic) would encourage the audience to put their hands on their heads and chant the magic words, "Hold on to your hats, 'cos here we go!" A low synthesizer drone would strike the theatre and a strobe light would indicate the act of time travel. The back curtains would then open to reveal the setting of their latest adventure, and Push Button, Keeley and IQ would assume regular panto roles (the hero, the best friend and the fool), along with three other cast members (the eccentric older female, the love interest and the villain).

The Push Button Click song was performed at the beginning and end of every show, affording plenty of audience participation, including an instrumental break which involved clapping and chanting "Oh yeah", and the three golden rules, the first of which was "Fun! Fun! Fun!", the second, "We don't like school!" As you can imagine, the children lifted the roof off shouting those.

Karl and I developed a very bad crush on the actress playing Keeley, and when we told her at the autograph session, she offered us a kiss on the cheek. We kissed her, and immediately went weak at the knees! This was the nearest either of us had come to kissing anyone other than our mums, grandmas and aunties. It took several weeks for me to recover, especially since I had taken photos of her.

The summer holidays did not come soon enough. On odd days, I accompanied Mum on her various college lectures. I found Dr Malcolm Pittock's media studies lesson on modern storytelling quite fascinating. He took us through the then recent Deirdre–Ken–Mike scandal of *Coronation Street*, and pointed out how the drama was punctuated by various close-ups and snappy dialogue. He even drew our attention to the rooftops title sequence and brass-band theme music.

My ears pricked up when he started talking about how television, when done well, can make the viewer suspend disbelief. He stood, cup of tea in hand, and recounted a particular example. "I remember an episode of *Doctor Who*," he began, "where Tom Baker fell off a radio telescope." He paused to take a sip of his tea before breaking into a wry smile. "And then changed into somebody quite *considerably* different!" His voice rose in pitch with the words "quite considerably", to hammer home the point that two entirely different-looking actors were supposed to be the same person. The class fell into unbridled laughter as they acknowledged the point.

I looked for the things Malcolm Pittock had highlighted in all television programmes after that. Consequently, my family found me hard to live with, as I talked through every TV show and film, drawing their attention to the direction, the acting, title sequences, even the music and sound effects! It was tiresome for them – but fascinating for me. It was my new obsession.

This picture is deceptive. On the first attempt the photographer
was appalled by my non-smile. On the second attempt I gave a sarcastic
over-exaggeration of a smile and he snapped it; circa 1983.

"Why are you Weird?", 1983–86

THE THIRD YEAR, OR YEAR 9 as it's known now, was very important as it saw the choosing of our "options" for O levels and CSEs. The teachers made a lot of fuss about which subjects we could take for our main exam courses over the last two years. I was undecided about most of what was on offer.

In order to make an accurate choice of the sciences, we covered each one for a few months at a time. Biology teacher Mrs Barton found me exasperating when I innocently asked her why people, when they are happy, smile, but dogs wag their tails instead. "Well, we no longer have tails, do we, William?" she declared (nice and loud for everyone to hear).

I frowned, and thought, *Well, when did the animals start smiling? And why aren't there some animals without tails who smile?* But I dared not say it.

It irritated me greatly that teachers, scientists and television presenters depicted the theory of evolution as though it had been proved conclusively. They often talked about the missing link between ape and Man, but they never spoke of the thousands of missing links between all the other species. Where were the giraffe skeletons with necks two thirds or half the present length? Where was the apeman? These latter creatures were supposedly superior to the regular ape, so why did the ape survive, but not the superior apeman? Then there was the question of actual fossil evidence. One of the earliest life forms, the dinosaur, had thousands of unearthed skeletons to represent it as having lived, as did all the other fully formed animals. But what of the intermediary links between ape and Man?

What evidence was there in the fossil record? A handful of skulls, most of which were incomplete.

My classmates, and some teachers, derided the idea of God or a greater intelligence on the grounds that there was no hard evidence. This infuriated me, not because I didn't want it to be true, but because *their* beliefs were hardly conclusive. They accepted an idea or a concept simply because a scientist said it was so. Not a very scientific approach, really. They only ever questioned the things that they didn't like the sound of.

It bothered me so much it became another obsession. I would spend hours going over the arguments in my mind, creation *versus* evolution. Very often I would be left mentally exhausted. The older I got, and the more I questioned the status quo, the more angry people seemed to become. The sense of being alien to this world had not left me, and I began to wonder if it ever would.

My mother had been telling me about her friend Stanley Warburton, who worked as chief engineer for the Merchant Navy. I realized after a while that Stan was some sort of boyfriend. It didn't bother me in the slightest that Mum had met someone. I mean, I knew she wasn't going to spend the rest of her life on her own, and in any case, I wanted her to be happy.

Stan and Mum on her Graduation Day, circa 1983.

One evening, Stan came to see us. Barrel shaped, with a shock of wiry ginger hair, he removed his glasses and mopped his brow. "I'm hot," he said, but I knew he was just nervous. My mother had told him that any future for them as a couple rested on my and my brothers' acceptance of him. Nowadays I feel quite touched about that. Most parents would have made their children adjust whether they liked it or not. Of course, we did accept him, and Stan being on the scene proved rather fortuitous. He treated Jonathan, Matthew and me as his adopted sons, and spent ridiculous amounts of money on the family as a whole.

Marriage was inevitable.

A special teacher came to the school to give us in-depth discussions on sex. There were two classes arranged, one for the bright kids and one for the others. Unfortunately, I was regarded as one of the others.

We were shown a film which demonstrated, in no uncertain terms, how the reproductive organs worked. The penny had finally dropped. Even though we'd had preliminary sex education the previous year, certain aspects had left me baffled – but not any more. The images presented on screen, while two dimensional, made it potently clear what was done and what the end result could be: a pregnant girlfriend. There was talk about contraception, and the word "condom" entered my vocabulary. A lot of kids found it amusing, some were embarrassed by it – I was overwhelmed. I was sexually aroused as never before, and had a bump in my trousers to prove it.

Sit closer to the desk. If anyone sees that, I'm dead.

Pupils were invited to drop questions anonymously into a box for the teacher to answer. I had several queries, but knew that if everyone laughed when my questions were read out, my blushing complexion would betray me as the author. So I just listened. The teacher was outraged by the lack of maturity she found in my class, and I was equally angered.

Ian and I were now well and truly settled at school. We had become part of its character and were notorious for trekking about watering the plants. On the first day of Year 9, we entered Geography teacher Mr Booth's room. He explained to his new (and nervous) first-year students, "Now, you'll see these two from time to time. They're harmless. Just ignore them. I do." We laughed a great deal about that one!

Ian even made it into the school magazine, *Profile*, edited by Art teacher Mr Bates. They took photographs of him, watering can in hand, and super-imposed them on a drawing of a winding road infested with Triffids. In another issue they had him starring in a picture strip spoof of the film *Gregory's Girl*, which was appropriately re-titled *Higgy's Girl*. We had progressed from laughing-stock status to boys others could laugh along with.

Even though life had become a lot easier and happier, I still had my days when I felt desperately alone, days when I just knew I wasn't rowing in the same direction as the other boats; rowing against the current, in fact. On these occasions I would revert back to type and stand in a corner of the play court, or hide in the shadows cast by the temporary science labs. It was on such a day that I turned a corner and bumped into Debbie. She was smallish, very pretty when she smiled, with a face framed by gorgeous long wavy black hair. Unfortunately, she was as spiteful as she was attractive. I froze and cast my eyes to the floor.

> I'm ugly. Who would want me?

She studied me momentarily. I felt her eyes burning into my face.

> Keep staring at the floor. That way she won't see how uncomfortable you feel.

The scrutiny was unbearable. I looked up, only to receive the full impact of her hateful eyes.

"Why are you *weird?*" It sounded more like an accusation than a question.

Now, the average person would simply respond, "I'm *not* weird." Or, perhaps they would just fire it back: "Why are *you* so ugly?" But not me. I couldn't do a thing like that. I couldn't deliberately wound another person with cruel words. There was something else playing on my mind too.

> I *am* weird. It's a fact. The evidence stares me in the face every morning when I look in the mirror.

I thought for a moment, considered her question, and then shrugged. "I don't know."

She snorted an almost-laugh and walked off.

> I want to be loved. I want a girlfriend. I want someone to just accept me as I am. Why are they so impressed with trendy boys? Why are they flattered by empty comments so obviously designed to win them over? They complain when they are treated badly, "All boys are the same." They're not! They're not all the same! I'M NOT THE SAME!! I might have goggle eyes and rubber lips, greasy hair and a few spots. But I can be funny, if you just give me a chance. I'll take you places they haven't even thought of. I'll treat you like a princess. I'll buy you flowers. I'll love you like no other could. I *want* to love.

Once I understood that Christmas was the fusion of a pagan festival (Saturnalia: held on 25 December by the Romans in honour of their sun god; involved the exchanging of gifts and over-indulgence at wild parties) with the Biblical account of Jesus' birth (designated Christ's Mass by the Roman Catholic Church), and that the Bible condemned the blending of Christianity with other philosophies, I believed that, to please God wholly, I would have to dispense with the festivities. Bravely, I took a stand against it in December 1983.

I informed the teachers that I would not be able to participate in the Christmas service, and was granted leave to go and water the plants instead. No soon as I had left the hall, Ian slipped out after me. I was very surprised. "What are you doing?" I said.

He grinned. "Mrs Wray said I could come with you."

"But it's the Christmas service," I said. "You *believe* that Christ was born on December the twenty-fifth."

"I know," he laughed. "But the service is *so* boring."

Mum was a little concerned that I might feel somewhat put out watching my brothers open their presents. But I was really quite pleased with myself, because I had taken a stand for what I believed was right.

The new year and the 7 January brought my mother's wedding day, which turned out to be very enjoyable. I remember liking the Swinton registry office and thinking that I would get married there when that special someone finally arrived. I also remember thinking how strange it was that my mother would now be called Margaret Warburton. I even briefy considered changing my own surname, but I couldn't hurt my father like that.

I decided that to drop the name Hadcroft would have been a despicable thing to do.

January 1984 also saw my return to school and, more important, the twenty-first series of *Doctor Who*. The Doctor was given a new companion, a young American brunette called Peri, played by Nicola Bryant. Typically, my peers only saw her breasts and legs. All I could see was how pretty she was. Her eyes, the shape of her face, her bob haircut: she really was lovely. I played her voice back on my tape-recorded episodes, and I acquired a big *Daily Express* picture of her, which Grandma had kindly cut out. "Oh, I saved you this article about *Doctor Who*," she said, not realizing I had a bit of a crush on the new girl assistant.

The penultimate story of that year, *The Caves of Androzani*, was Peter Davison's last. In it, he was shot at, blown up, he crash-landed a spaceship and was riddled with a lethal alien virus. Computer graphics enveloped the character, denoting the regeneration process, before exploding. The burly newcomer had an alertness, an edge to him. As the closing credits rolled, my mum decided that she quite liked Colin Baker, the Doctor's sixth incarnation, because he was more like the original character played by William Hartnell.

After the new Doctor had debuted, the children's points-of-view programme, *Take Two*, ran a feature on the series. With a little help (well, a *lot* actually) from my mum, I sent a letter into the show. Sadly, it did not appear in that particular instalment, and after I'd gone to the trouble of setting up my tape recorder as well. The following week, however, right out of the blue, my letter was read on TV. My heart thumped as I saw my name on the screen: "William Hadcroft, Worsley." Since I'd not managed to get on the previous week, I had assumed I'd missed my chance, and so failed to record it. But I did get a *Take Two* badge for my efforts, which I wasted no time displaying to my school friends.

That summer, my family took a trip to Blackpool and I, as was my custom, headed straight for the *Doctor Who* exhibition situated on the Golden Mile. As I approached I could hear the oh-so familiar theme music, and a large grin spread across my chops. In times past, Mum and Dad had tried to limit the amount of time I spent in the place, but after a while they realized I wasn't going to go wandering off...

Wander off? Wander off? I might *wander off*?! Are you mad, people?

…and so gave in and left me to talk *Who* with whoever might be in there. Now it was Stan's turn to admit defeat, and I left him and Mum on the beach while I followed the beat of my favourite tune. I turned the corner and my heart leaped at the sight of the oversized police box.

I bought my ticket, descended the steps, and strolled through the dark corridors, taking time to note the new exhibits from the latest series. Then I took in the mock TARDIS control room, and headed for the merchandise kiosk to chat with the girl that worked in it. She seemed all of a dither. The new Doctor, Colin Baker, was currently in Blackpool to open the latest roller-coaster, the Space Invader, on the Pleasure Beach, and there was a buzz going about that he would probably be coming to the exhibition soon after.

I was quite stunned by the prospect and started thinking of possible things I could say, or questions I could ask. The voice of my mother broke my concentration. "William! William!" I glanced round, confused, as Mum came running in through the exit door, still dressed in her bathing costume, dry sand stuck to her skin. "He's here," she kept saying. "Doctor Who is here."

And sure enough he was. A vaguely pompous but cheerful voice said, "Now you wouldn't want to meet *that* on a dark night, would you?" I just froze, absolutely awestruck. It was Colin Baker in full costume commenting on one of the exhibits. He turned and beamed at me, his green-blue eyes dazzling with keen alertness. "Hello."

It's, it's, it's the Doctor!

Fluffy fair hair, a slightly intimidating smile, a multicoloured patchwork coat, a green cravat, black and yellow humbug trousers, green shoes and red spats. I could not utter a single word in reply. Mum snatched the record I'd bought of the *Doctor Who* theme music. It didn't differ from the record that I had at home except for the fact that Colin Baker's face was on the sleeve art instead of Peter Davison's. She handed it to the Doctor. "Will you sign my lad's record, please?"

"Of course," said the Doctor. "Has anyone got a decent pen, mine's run out." The girl in the kiosk immediately began scrambling about for one. He took it. "Mm, it's felt tip. It might rub off, so be careful." He scribbled something on the record and handed it back to me. The inscription read: "To William, best wishes. Colin Baker – Who?"

Once back on the street, Colin arranged to have the police box doors on the exterior closed so youngsters could have their photograph taken with him. When Mum and Stan finally dragged me away, Mum kept saying, "That costume isn't cheap, you know. I had a good look at it. They've spent a few quid on that, it's good quality material. And I think he's going to be a good Doctor Who. He's sharp and intelligent. You can see it in his eyes."

Little did we know it then, but the days of the *Doctor Who* exhibition were numbered. It wasn't long after this experience that I returned to Blackpool only to find to my absolute horror and disappointment that it had gone. The Mecca for all true fans had been replaced by a shoe shop.

Leaning on a TARDIS, the entrance to the much-missed
Doctor Who Exhibition in Blackpool, 1985.

By this time, my favourite teacher was the tall, eccentric Mr Simpson. He had taken English in the second year, and marvelled at how I was able to turn any given subject into a science-fiction scenario. He wrote in a report that he liked my essays but wished I would set them in "the here and now rather than the there and then"!

Simpson took Religious Knowledge in the third year, and always made the lessons informative and interesting. When I told him of my plans to become one of Jehovah's Witnesses, he deliberately tailored each lesson so that it didn't conflict with Witness doctrine. At the end of the session, he would turn to me and ask, "Is that all right, William?" To which I would blush and reply, "Yes, Sir." This was a great source of annoyance to the other pupils.

Simpson had explained that the universe was constantly wearing away and winding down. The ageing process in plant and animal life, and the wear and tear of physical things like buildings and cars, was regarded as proof of this. Some scientists referred to this natural erosion of material things as entropy.

"Now, does anyone know what entropy is?" Simpson inquired.

I put up my hand and announced, "It's the second law of thermodynamics."

He glared at me with intense eyes. "Yes, it is."

"It's the rust on wheels, the mould on bricks," I continued, remembering the explanation from Tom Baker's final *Doctor Who* adventure. "The more you put things together, the more they keep falling apart." He just stood there boggling at me. And again this made me unpopular with the others.

At the end of the lesson, Simpson asked, "How do you know about entropy?"

"It was on *Doctor Who*, Sir."

His eyes widened. "They talk about entropy on *Doctor Who*?"

I nodded, both eager and grateful for an opportunity to relate the story. "The Master released entropy into the universe, you see, and it started to collapse. Then the Doctor stopped it by beaming out a message from Jodrell Bank to a special gateway in space, filtering out the excess entropy, and returning stability to the universe. The Master tipped the dish of the radio telescope round while the Doctor was on the gantry, and he fell off."

Simpson grinned, taken by my childlike zeal for the programme. "And how did he get out of that?"

"He changed into Peter Davison."

Mr Simpson roared with laughter. "You keep enjoying your *Doctor Who*, William," he said. "It sounds very interesting."

At the Kingdom Hall it was noted by David that my studies with Aunty Joan had fizzled out. A young man in his early twenties called Ken had just moved into the congregation from Broughton, and David decided that he would be perfect to take up my studies of the Bible. And he was right, Ken was spot on. We went through the book *Your Youth: Getting The Best Out Of It* first, each week covering a chapter of my choosing. Then we went back to the basic doctrine textbook *You Can Live Forever in Paradise on Earth*, and started from scratch.

I really loved Ken. He became a role model and father figure.

Towards the end of the school year, we were given forms to fill in, indicating which subjects we wished to study over the next two years. Maths and English were compulsory. I really liked the idea of Drama, as I'd been nurturing the desire of becoming an actor for some time. I watched others during class and knew that I had a flair for it. The actor's life was without any doubt for me. But my diminished self-confidence led me to turn it down.

I chose Science At Work, as opposed to any of the individual sciences, and History of the Twentieth Century rather than General History. I had enjoyed Social Studies with the humorous Mr Holden, so I plumped for that too. Writing was probably my greatest interest, and so I chose to do English Literature. Art was thrown in as a last resort.

After I had submitted my form, Windsor house mistress Mrs Wray pulled me to one side.

"William, can I have a word?"

Tight throat. Eyes cast to the floor. Nervous smile. Wobbly legs.

I had never quite got over our sterile chat about bullying the previous year. "I've been looking at your options, and I see that you've not chosen Religious Knowledge."

"No, Miss," I said sheepishly.

"Why not?" she pried.

I shrugged. "I don't want to, Miss."

The next sentence completely baffled me. "But, Ian's put it down. He wants to do it."

I said nothing, hoping my facial expression wasn't betraying my thoughts. I really wanted to say, "So? What's Ian got to do with it?" But I just looked at her and said nothing. After an awkward silence, I blurted, "I'm going to be a Jehovah's Witness. I don't believe in the churches. They're all pagan."

She looks angry. I've offended her. She will be religious herself, that's why she asked. I said her religion is pagan. What am I going to do? What do I say next? But it *is* pagan, they all are. Christmas, Easter, birthdays, the sign of the cross, hellfire, the immortality of the soul, the trinity – they were all adopted from ancient religions by the churches to popularize Christianity. It's true. What else could I have said? It's all true, Miss. Look it up in an encyclopaedia if you don't believe me. I'm hot now, I can't breathe, my face has gone bright red. My heart is coming through my chest. I can't breathe.

Mrs Wray frowned. "Who told you that, William?"

Don't speak, don't say anything.

After a very long pause she shook her head and went about her business, and I, as was my custom, went to a toilet cubicle to try to calm down. It later transpired that Ian was the only pupil in our year to choose Religious Education in his options.

My brothers and I went to Butlin's again that year, but this time with Mum and Stan. We loved it: the freedom, the fairground, the miniature railway, the beach, the Redcoats. But the main attraction for me was the pantomime group The Push Button Click. They occupied my every thought in the weeks leading up to the holiday. I loved them, and fed my new obsession by recording parts of their shows off-stage with a tape recorder. The group consisted of a different bunch of actors to that of the previous year, and I was a bit disappointed initially, as I was hoping to see the actress who had played Keeley the last time. But she had been replaced like all the others.

The most thrilling thing this time was the discovery that a Push Button Click single record had been produced. A man called Jimmy Jemain, who bore an uncanny resemblance to Cliff Richard, supplied the vocal for the theme song, as well as the B-side "The Name's Push". (He would go on to win his heat of the TV series *Stars In Their Eyes* as Cliff Richard a few years later.)

On returning home, Mum grimaced at the new obsession. I was giving her a brief break from the *Doctor Who* theme music and the BBC Radiophonic Workshop LP while I indulged in my tape recordings and the single. Every so often Mum would scream up the stairs: "I'm sick of hearing the Push Button Click! Turn it off, for God's sake!"

Ken encouraged me to attend the Thursday night Kingdom Hall meeting, which meant missing one of the two weekly *Doctor Who* episodes. I agreed, giving strict instructions to my brothers on how to tape-record the programme while I was out.

For the first hour, the meeting was something called "The Theocratic Ministry School", and featured various individuals presenting little five-minute talks. For weeks and weeks I resisted the invitation to join the school, but eventually gave in to Ken's pressure. And so, one Thursday night, having had some preparatory help from Ken, I debuted in the school. My natural instincts as an actor were released as I faced the welcoming audience. I gave my introduction, remembering the advice given to other students – make it conversational, try to pick out friendly faces in the audience and talk to them – then I read the prescribed Bible verses.

> Remember to breathe. Read slowly, but not like a robot. Put feeling into the dialogue parts, act it out. Keep the narrative bits varied, but restrained.

I left the platform to a rapturous applause and felt a glow unlike any other feeling I'd experienced. They loved it, said I was a natural. Ken gave me a hug when I sat back in my seat, and the school overseer, who just happened to be David again, piled on the praise.

I had, at last, found something I was good at.

My options began in earnest in September 1984. I wasn't particularly impressed with any of it, barring English Literature, which, despite the fact that once again I had been dropped in a class with the uninterested folk, turned out to be rather enjoyable.

The first book we did was Paul Zindel's *The Pigman*, which told the story of two teenagers who befriend an elderly eccentric. The so-called pig man (because he collected pot pigs) takes the kids deep into his confidence, allowing them in his house and so forth, only to have that confidence betrayed when their not-so-friendly peers have a drunken party and destroy his collection. The man is devastated, and the relationship with the two youths is lost.

I was very deeply touched by this story, and angered, since I could see some of my peers behaving in such a cruel fashion if they had been part of the tale. Instead of relating to the children in the story, as some in my class might have done, I saw myself as the pigman: solitary, lonely, with strange interests that nobody appreciated. The abuse heaped upon him, and the after-effects, troubled me very much, because I could see it being true.

Yes, they *would* do that. Because that's what *they* are like.

Mrs Morris was very pleased with my essay on that book, and she continued to consult me over the *Doctor Who* range in the library. She also suggested that I have a go at penning a novel myself in the future. I valued her encouragement.

History of the Twentieth Century was with the deputy head, Mr Rooke. He was quite a jovial chap. In one report, he made kind comments about my "humorous" and "individual" approach to the subject.

The worst subject (after Games, of course) was Social Studies. I saw absolutely no point in discussing the class system. It just annoyed me that different "types" of people were categorized and pigeon-holed depending on how much money they had or where in the country they lived. The concept of social hierarchy had always been meaningless to me. I saw people as individuals and, while I respected law and order, I did not see the need for special titles or for customs. Doing things because of etiquette or simply because "it's traditional" sorely bothered me.

For some reason, perhaps because of a vibe I thought I was picking up, I had become convinced that the teacher Mrs Stagg didn't really like me. By this time paranoia was flowing strong, and it was fed constantly by my knowledge of the discussions my mother had had with the school, by my tendency to question teachers (and the resulting baffled looks on their faces), by my peers telling me I was weird for obsessing about *Doctor Who*, and the prejudices held by those who openly disliked Jehovah's Witnesses.

Every so often, I would get severe attacks of paranoia and imagine all the teachers discussing how strange I seemed to be. I don't think the staff room scenes on *Grange Hill* helped much in this regard. At school I felt paranoid all the time. I was convinced that everybody thought I was weird, that the boys were bored with my company, that all girls thought I was repulsive to look at. I believed that every negative thing spoken about me was true, and that the compliments were just kind individuals being nice.

In retrospect, I see that this was not the case at all.

Autumn 1984 saw the debut of the BBC's new science-fiction series, based on John Christopher's successful trilogy of novels *The White Mountains*, *The City of Gold and Lead* and *The Pool of Fire*. Simply titled *The Tripods*, it turned out to be more of a coming-of-age tale than a sci-fi blockbuster, and heavily indulged in the issues of freedom: freedom of choice, freedom of thought – and the all-pervading air of conformity.

For the first couple of weeks, my peers were very impressed with the alien Tripod machines, which stalked future earth. In the story technology has been eradicated, and human life is reminiscent of that of the late eighteenth century. The Tripods are keeping humans subservient and docile by "capping" them at the school-leaving age of 16 (14 in the original 1967 novel). The capping process, achieved by implanting a wire mesh in the skull, signifies to the populace the child's crossing the threshold into adulthood. But, as young Will Parker discovers, the cap is really a conditioning device. He and two companions decide to avoid capping by joining the "free men", a community of uncapped principled thinkers who are hiding in the Austrian Alps, plotting to destroy the enemy. The journey to the mountains is fraught with danger and it's the everyday folk and the "normal" world who often pose the threat. Even something as innocent as falling in love with one of the Capped could jeopardize the mission.

I followed the series for all of its 13 episodes, absorbing myself in the serial's underlying back story, the state-of-the-art special effects and Ken Freeman's superb music. When the first series concluded I bought a copy of the theme music on record and played it relentlessly. It seemed to be a fusion of synthesizers and orchestra, and was similar in style to the great classical piece by Holst, "Mars", from his symphony *The Planets*. I later learned that Ken actually invented the synthesizer he played and that no orchestra was involved. This deepened my appreciation for electronic music. It also explained why there was no string section credited on *Jeff Wayne's Musical Version of The War of the Worlds*: Ken had played the synthesizers on that too.

To my dismay, most of my peers had grown weary with the series because it concentrated too much on the coming-of-age theme rather than the Tripods themselves, and promptly switched to watching *The A-Team* on the opposing channel. Even then, even though the subject of my new fascination was better than *Doctor Who* in terms of effects and presentation,

I was unable to find a group that appreciated it. Individuals like Andrew Massey, yes, but not my peers generally.

Andrew Massey was tall like me, thoughtful, and smiled a lot. When the class watched the children's TV series *Murphy's Mob* as part of our English lesson, he laughed out loud at the funny bits, whereas I just acknowledged to myself that they were funny. I can remember noting that particular difference and deciding I should laugh out loud a bit more than I tended to. Andrew had read the last book in *The Tripods* trilogy, *The Pool of Fire*, and had enthused at some length about a scene where the Free Men capture a Tripod. I couldn't wait to read it. In retrospect I see he would have been a really good friend.

There was one boy who watched *The Tripods* at the Kingdom Hall, and when one Sunday I overheard him talking about it to a friend, my heart leapt.

> He likes *The Tripods*. I don't believe it. Someone in here who likes what I like. It'll be brilliant!

"We'll watch *Tripods* first," I heard the boy say.

His friend pulled a face. "You don't like *that*, do you?"

"Yeah, it's great!" the boy enthused.

His friend's face was a picture as he contemplated the proposed viewing. "But it's so booooooring."

As soon as his friend had gone, I seized the chance and approached the boy, not an easy thing for me. "I like *The Tripods* too," I said. "It's so much like our world, isn't it? I hate it, don't you? The way everybody is so false and just puts on an act, and the way they change depending on whose company they're in. It's like everyone is capped, and we're the only ones who can see it."

He smiled politely and waited for my overly enthusiastic appraisal to cease. "Yes, it's good. Anyway, I'll see you on Thursday."

And that was that.

> They're all capped. Even here. I am so utterly and desperately alone. I've got to get out of this building or I'll burst into tears.

Towards the end of Series One, we got our first video recorder, and I taped the last two episodes and watched them more times than is healthy. *The Tripods* theme music replaced *Doctor Who* and the Push Button Click as the most-listened-to track in the house. Mum would scream, "Not again! If you don't play something else, I'll cut the plug off!"

I drove them all crazy. It was little wonder I had no friends. I was so absorbed in the fictional worlds presented on television, they were where I wanted to be. Even the loners in these stories had friends and a place in their world. I was also beginning to appreciate that script writers and novelists were not just telling stories for the sake of it, they were making observations about the real world, and in science-fiction I tended to agree with what they had observed.

Doctor Who Monthly was packed with interviews. The writers, the script editors, the producers, the sound-effects people, the musicians: they all had fascinating stories to tell. At one time my interest in series such as this would have revolved purely around the plot and characters, but now it was becoming more and more a question of what was being put across and the process by which it was achieved.

I had also come to appreciate the role of the allegory: that the setting, situation and characters in an adventure might be symbolic of issues and philosophies in the real world. I realized that *Doctor Who* and *Star Trek* were full of that kind of thing, and *The Tripods* was very obviously making points that I could agree with.

And so I found a new kind of hero: the writer. Clive King, who wrote *Stig of the Dump*; Terrance Dicks, author of the *Doctor Who* novelizations; Douglas Adams, the galactic hitch-hiker; and John Christopher, who wrote my all-time favourite trilogy *The Tripods* – these were my role models now.

Other television shows which struck a chord included *Heidi*, a dubbed adaptation of Johanna Spyri's classic novel broadcast on Children's BBC; and Anthony Read's adaptation of the John Wyndham story *Chocky* for Children's ITV.

The character in *Heidi* with whom the viewer was supposed to identify was the protagonist herself. However, I tended to reflect upon the character's grandfather. In the story he is ostracized by villagers because he prefers to live away from them in a log cabin up in the hills. I wished I could have joined him.

The adaptation of *Chocky* was very well realized. In Wyndham's book the story is told from the dad's point of view and we see him worrying about his son Matthew who appears to have acquired a "pretend friend", an invisible alien called Chocky. In the TV series, though, the emphasis is on Matthew, and we watch the relationship between him and his strange ethereal companion develop. Chocky herself is entirely alien and questions absolutely everything about our world and society. She concludes that much of it is pointless and ridiculous.

Hurrah! Someone who sees it the way I do.

My greatest heartbreak was having no one with whom to share my passion. Ian at school was only vaguely interested (he was heavily into the gardening scene by this stage), the adults at the Kingdom Hall gave me as much time as they could, and Mum would indulge my discussions to a point. But my interest in such things was more like an addiction. I didn't just enjoy them, I *needed* them.

One of the first movies we rented on video was *The Elephant Man*, a superb film which tells the true story of John Merrick, a man who was grossly disfigured and cruelly persecuted as a result. As with *The Pigman* this movie touched a raw nerve with me because, although I knew my own features were nowhere near as bad as his, I could empathize very strongly with the harassment and prejudice he experienced – all because he was "different" to the "norm". Yet he was so kind and gentle. I was deeply affected when he committed suicide at the end. I went on about it at length to my schoolmates, but they showed little compassion.

It shouldn't have surprised me. They laughed and made jokes about the most appalling tragedies, like that horrific space shuttle accident. When I saw the live news feature of *Challenger's* lift-off, and then the disbelief on the faces of the relatives as their family members were vaporized before their eyes, I grieved on their behalf. It was *so* awful. My gut wrenched inside and I wanted to cry but couldn't.

When I got back to school the following day I was asked, "What does NASA stand for?"

I shrugged, not really thinking. Someone offered the answer. "Need Another Seven Astronauts!"

Frustration becomes anger, anger becomes rage. I cry out. It's primal, it's coming from the abyss of my soul. The adrenalin rushes, the DNA helix flickers emerald green. White eyes, I'm shivering with fury. Muscles swell, clothes burst. The jokers are sent flying.

The them-and-me divide got worse and worse.

> The boy removes his hat to reveal a freshly shaven head. The golden circuit-like mesh glistens as it catches the sun, a spider's web woven into his scalp. As their hysterics continue, I see that they are in fact all the same. The gold is partially visible through even the thickest hair. Anyone with a trained eye can see it.

January 1985 marked Colin Baker's first full season of *Doctor Who*, and the programme was returned to its traditional Saturday tea-time slot. His companion, Peri, as played by actress Nicola Bryant, was captured at last on video. I fell madly in love with her that year. She was utterly gorgeous, and my heart ached to be with her.

Mum and Doreen would laugh as I peered, starry-eyed, into the sky. "Nicola, I love you," I would say in my heart. But, they *knew* what I was saying, all right. It didn't require genius to work it out. I was so besotted I couldn't eat!

January 1985 was also Mum and Stan's first wedding anniversary, and so they decided to hold off the New Year celebrations and mark the anniversary instead. As the party started, I began to sense the all-too-familiar signs of panic as the house got more and more full.

> Who do I talk to? What do I say? I'm feeling anxious.

I disconnected the video, carried it upstairs to my bedroom, and wired it up to a small portable TV. I now had a rather good way of avoiding the socializing without feeling too lonely. Or so I thought.

The early part of the evening was great. Doreen's son Karl came, and we caught up on old times. Karl had seen the latter episode of the latest *Doctor Who* adventure *Attack of the Cybermen*, but had missed the first one. We watched it in my bedroom and got stuck on a particularly funny line delivered by Northern actor Brian Glover. He, in character, challenges the Cyber Leader by impersonating the way he speaks. "Getting-a-bit-rough-is-it?"

Well, me and Karl just fell about, holding our sides and gasping for breath. We wound the tape back and watched the scene again. After another fit of hysteria, we wound it back a third time. Tears streamed down our faces, and the adults who had found their way into my room failed to see what was so funny about it.

Then three teenage girls arrived.

> PANIC!!! What are they doing here? No one told me girls were
> coming. Don't look at them. Don't look them in the eye. Oh, those
> mocking eyes, picking me to pieces. I hate it. Get away. Get what you
> need and get away.

In the dining room they leafed through some LP records, hoping to find
something "decent" to put on. Instead they found a Shakin' Stevens album,
which I still rather liked. The trio sniggered briefly and slipped it back in
the rack. Their snigger turned to bemusement as they plucked out another
title. "*ITV Themes*," one of them announced. "Performed by the London
Symphony Orchestra. *World of Sport? Coronation Street?*" The scorn in her
voice stabbed deep to my heart. It would only be a matter of time before
they would locate *Soundhouse* and *Doctor Who – The Music* by the BBC
Radiophonic Workshop.

I quickly trotted upstairs to my room, and shut the door hard,
returning to my Time Lord hero for comfort and escape. Eventually, it
dawned on the girls why I had fled, and they made their way to my room.

"Come on, William, don't be shy," said a female voice from outside my
door.

"I'm watching my video," I stammered. "Leave me alone."

They were right, of course, I was painfully shy…especially when
hounded by members of the opposite sex. But shyness was not my only
problem. I actually felt quite angry. I hated parties.

After a while, the trio just walked straight in. I was furious. I
understood that teenage girls went to parties in the hope of meeting boys.
They knew their parents were occupied downstairs, and so wouldn't really
notice if they went off with a boy. I was also aware of how far these games
could go.

I explained I was studying to be one of Jehovah's Witnesses, hoping
this would put them off. It didn't. There was a girl Karl fancied, and she
looked at my Witness books, slipped one off the shelf, flicked through it
casually, and said she was an atheist. She was also bored stiff, and I realized
that I had become her means of passing the time. "Prove to me that God
exists."

I showed her another book containing a cut-away illustration of a
microscopic cell, depicting in detail its inner workings: the supposed

earliest life form to emerge from Earth's primeval soup. "How could something so staggeringly complex come about of its own accord?" I asked.

She smiled, and I could see why Karl liked her. "It evolved," she replied.

I began to stutter. Talking to girls was terrifying enough, but engaging one in a religious discussion was something else again. "A complex living organism from dead matter? Without any intelligent guiding hand? No designer? All a freak accident?"

She shrugged. "I'm still not convinced."

By this time, my throat had completely dried up. I could barely speak. I looked to Karl for back-up. After all, he believed in God, and was far more confident and articulate than I was.

But he just sat on the edge of my bed and said nothing. He didn't want to lose favour with her, and deep down I could not blame him. She was very pretty and intelligent. If I hadn't been so intimidated I might have had a crush on her myself.

After a while, the group became restless and sloped off downstairs to play the few records that might have passed for remotely trendy. "God, he's *so* boring," one of them moaned, not quite to herself.

> Me, boring? You are the ones who only listen to chart music. You are the ones who follow the soap operas. You are the ones who let the media tell you what to think and feel. You are the ones who are so easily manipulated by the system. You are the ones who never think about where we come from and what it's all about. *You* are predictable. *You* are boring.

> I want to cry. I'm so alone.

I returned to my room, holding back the tears of exasperation, and switched on the video recorder. The Doctor was my friend, and Peri was my girl.

The party went on into the early hours. I lay on my bed, my eyes burning with fatigue. I was stone cold sober and desperate for sleep. Laughter, talking and music, laughter, talking and music. My mum's voice, the excitement of my brothers and Karl's brother John. Laughter and talking. No music. Creaking stairs and stifled giggling.

Oh no, they're coming back! Quick, put the chair over the door. I hope that will be enough. My heart is pumping hard. I'm panicked, I'm anxious. I'm Doctor David Banner. My eyes are bloodshot, but their colour is white. I'm shivering, my teeth gritted. Synthesizers, voices and strings.

I glared at the door as it started to budge. One of them whispered, "He's barricaded himself in." The ringleader raised her voice. "William, can we come in?"

"No!" I blazed, and the more I blazed, the more their hysteria grew. "Oh, *please.*"

"Go away!" I begged. "Just leave me alone."

There was a brief silence, and then suddenly the chair toppled over and the door crashed open. The three tormentors staggered in and began to laugh for real. I was so, so glad, when their parents called them down and all the guests went home. My own parents cleared away the party litter and I, so very grateful for the peace, fell into a heavy and desperate sleep.

Sometimes, I think Stan found it hard to understand what made me tick. He had formed a friendly relationship with my two brothers, but was still quite distanced from me. He and Mum would arrange family outings, incorporating a pub lunch along the way, and my brothers would get very excited. But I just saw it as an opportunity to indulge my fantasies, and so I always stayed home. It was the only way I could absorb myself in *Doctor Who* without being told to turn it off.

Mum and Stan were concerned about my shyness and self-imposed isolation. Stan believed that a few strategies to combat the bullies would help and so he enrolled my brothers and I in a martial arts club. To ease us into it, Mum joined the queue of white-gowned, bare-footed judo students and kicked the punch bag, or whatever it was, being held up by the instructor. She had convinced me that it was going to be great and that it would imbue me with self-confidence. I very much liked the idea of this, and imagined myself sorting out the trouble-makers at school, and making lots of good friends.

Yes I liked it – until we got there.

Jon and Matt followed Mum and kicked the bag. I just stood and watched. Mum turned and waved me over, smiling. "Come on, Bill, get in the queue. It's good." My brothers added their agreement to reassure me.

"I will in a minute," I replied, swallowing hard. "I'm just watching for a bit."

They accepted this until it became clear that I had little intention of joining them. I watched the tutor and the students, then my family, and the more I watched the more anxious I started to feel.

> They're all staring at me. They're all wondering who I am. "Look at him," they're saying. "Who's he? He's never been before." Odd ones keep looking at me. They're wondering why I'm still standing by the wall. Stan is watching me, smiling vaguely, frowning mostly. His eyes are saying, "Come on, Bill. What are you still standing over there for?" Mum is getting aggravated, I can tell. My throat is dry, my knees are going to give out. I can't breathe.

"Just try it once, William," said Mum, walking up to me. Jon and Matt nodded with great enthusiasm. "Go on, it's good. You'll like it."

I faltered.

"We'll come with you." My brothers, eleven and seven, were hoping I would take to it. They were so encouraging and so supportive. Even at their tender ages they understood how hard this was for me. The least I could do was have a go. And so I stood behind them in the queue.

Everyone smiled when they saw me get in line. Mum, Stan, Jon and Matt, even the instructor at the front. The nerves ran high as the minutes hand on the clock took on a speed like never before and it suddenly became my turn. I scrutinized the movements of the child in front to see how I would be expected to do it.

There I was, it was me, and *everyone* was watching.

> It's wrong to fight. It's wrong to fight. It's wrong to fight. It's wrong to fight. It's wrong to fight. It's wrong to fight. It's wrong to fight. It's wrong to fight. It's wrong to fight.

I walked up to the punch bag. The instructor smiled and held it. "Go on, son, give it a strong kick, the best you can do."

I kicked it, then blushed, so very, very embarrassed by the whole affair, and then turned to make my way to the back of the queue – or rather the wall. "Well done, son, that was great!" I heard the instructor call. Others chimed in, including my family, "That was good, that, Bill."

I stood at the wall, observing the others queuing up for another go. I felt so exhausted. All those people, all those eyes. I couldn't wait to get out. Mum came up to me and smiled. "There you are," she said. "It wasn't that bad, was it?" She pointed one of the boys out. "See him, he's a black belt. It didn't take him long. You could be a black belt if you kept it up."

I said nothing.

> I don't want to be a black belt. I don't want to fight anybody. I don't want to learn it. I don't want to be with these people. I don't want them watching me. I don't want to come here ever again. I want to be left alone. I hate it. I hate this world. I hate myself.

We emerged into the night air and headed for the car.

> Freedom!

Everyone was invigorated and on a high. Everyone except me. "So," said Mum, "shall we go again next Wednesday?" Jon and Matt were thrilled with the proposition and it showed on their faces and the way their steps took on a little skip. Mum turned to me, smiling. "It was good, wasn't it?"

I felt like bursting into tears. I could feel my bottom lip quivering, and my face burning red. I cast my eyes to the floor. "No," I said simply. "I hated every minute of it. And I won't be going next week."

In seconds, Mum's smile changed to a crestfallen look, then to a frown, and then finally to one of anger. She was so frustrated with me, and as a result I was with myself, because I *did* want to have friends, I *did* want to be able to defend myself, and I *did* want to feel normal.

> You're a failure. You're a failure. You're a failure.

I managed to hold off the tears.

For a time Mum entertained the idea of being a part-time foster parent. There was a couple who needed some respite from their son Anthony who had Down's Syndrome. He was a lovely little lad with all the expected characteristics, but he required constant supervision and drained his parents mentally and emotionally. Mum was given the OK to foster him for the odd week here and there and a single bed was set up in the back room for him to stay. His parents were quite surprised at how quickly he and I bonded.

No soon as he had stepped through the front door, he would be shouting, "Bin! Bin!" Bin was supposed to be "Bill", but he couldn't pronounce it. He would shuffle out of his anorak and charge upstairs to my bedroom. There were two single records he particularly liked, one was the Push Button Click song (he loved "Rule number two: We don't like school"!), and the other was the theme to the Muppet series *Fraggle Rock*. He would hum through the chorus of the latter until he could join in with a hearty "Down at Fraggle Rock" at the end. As soon as the record was over, he'd shout, "Again!", and I would have to play the record again.

"Doesn't William get tired of it?" his parents asked my mum. Little did they know that playing the same record over and over was something I tended to do whether Anthony visited or not. It didn't faze me in the slightest.

When Mum gave up the fostering I let Anthony keep *Fraggle Rock* and one of my copies of the song by Push Button Click. He was thrilled.

During the spring, the comedian Ken Dodd was doing panto at the Davenport theatre in Stockport. Stan and Mum decided to book me, my brothers and Karl's younger brother John in to see it. Transport to the venue was arranged by Stan's local pub, The Legion, and consisted of a double-decker bus packed with teenagers. Two adults presided over the affair.

I boarded the bus, already cursing my foolishness in thinking that this would be a good night out, and led my party to the back. Once the vehicle was in motion, the singing started. This would have been fine if the rowdy bunch hadn't started substituting different words and using vulgarities. One song was doctored so that it would be about the lady in charge of the trip. The "f" word featured prominently throughout the ditty, and she just threw her head back and belted out a coarse laugh. She wasn't bothered at all.

> Cock the gun. Release the safety catch. Squeeze the trigger. Fire blazing from the nozzle. Bullets dancing on the floor. Bodies wobbling and falling.

Jonathan, Matthew and John were visibly shocked by the language. They looked at me, slightly panicked by the aggression they were detecting in the voices of the youths and the casual dismissal of those in charge. I just looked back, helpless. We were not used to the adult world tolerating such behaviour. I was particularly angry because I'd been persuaded to miss *Doctor Who* for this, and I knew that no one would be at home to tape it for me.

The pantomime was a disappointment. Ken Dodd was not as funny in that genre as when doing his stand-up routine. *Doctor Who* was the highlight of my week, the only means of escape from the world I hated so much. And I'd missed it for this.

"Did you have a good time?" asked Mum when we got home.

"No," I replied abruptly. "It was rubbish." And with that went upstairs to play my records.

I vowed that day never to be persuaded to miss *Doctor Who* ever again.

Life at school trudged on, with the teachers putting great emphasis on our mock exams, and telling us time and again that after Christmas we would be sitting the real thing. They scared us half to death. It was as though life wouldn't be worth living if we left school with poor results.

Social Studies continued to be a bind. I was sure Stagg hated me. As part of the course, we had to do a project on an aspect of society. I chose Jehovah's Witnesses. "Why not do it on religion in general?" Mrs Stagg suggested. "Last year, the boy who did that came top."

She was only trying to help, but I was so neurotic by then. I stuck with the theme of Jehovah's Witnesses.

On one occasion Stagg took exception my quoting Matthew, Chapter 24, Verse 14, as part of my section about the preaching activity. "This good news of the kingdom will be preached in all the inhabited earth as a witness to all the nations; and then the end will come."

"William," announced the teacher. "Come here, please."

"Yes, Miss?"

"Why have you quoted a scripture under this chapter heading?"

"To show why the Witnesses preach from house to house, Miss. They are obeying that command."

"This is a Social Studies project," she retorted, "not a religious one. This would be fine in Mr Davenport's class, but not here. Take it off."

Writing the project was very easy for me, since the Bible and Jehovah's Witnesses were my core obsessions. *Doctor Who* and *The Tripods* withstanding, I thought about very little else, and knew great chunks of Witness literature by heart. This was to cause more problems for me, as Mrs Stagg, quite understandably, drew the conclusion that I'd copied everything out of the textbook. I protested, "I haven't, Miss."

"You HAVE," she insisted. "It's word for word."

> You hate me, you do. You hate me because I'm different. You hate me because my mum came in and argued with the headmaster. You hate me because I'm not a mindless sheep, because I won't row my boat with the others, because I'm going against the tide. You don't like me because I refuse to accept the norms. You don't like Jehovah's Witnesses. That's it, you don't like Jehovah's Witnesses. You're prejudiced. That's it – prejudiced.

"Don't try my patience, William Hadcroft. I don't want to see this book again. Understand?"

> Prejudiced.

"Now go and sit down."

> All the class are watching me. I'm beetroot red. I'm crimson. They're sniggering. They're pointing. They think I'm weird. Why am I weird? I don't know. I can't breathe, I'm choking, I'm going to pass out. I want to burst into tears. I wish I were dead.

One afternoon, Mr Davenport, beaming and enthusiastic, approached both Ian and myself with what he thought was really exciting news. "Boys, can I have a quick word? We've just been working out who to appoint as prefects for the fifth year, and we've been looking at the candidates in your year, and I'm pleased to tell you both that you've been selected."

Ian immediately broke into a broad grin, obviously very pleased with his appointment. "Thank you, Sir." I just smiled vaguely. The idea of being a prefect was repugnant to me, partly because I was still obsessed with the notion of being capped by the system, partly because I couldn't imagine the other kids following any instructions I might give, but mostly because

I simply wasn't interested in having a position of authority. Status, while it might have been the be-all and end-all, even for 15-year-olds, simply did not interest me. In fact, I believed it said a lot about the people who *were* interested in it.

"Sir," I piped, swallowing my nerves. "Is it all right if I don't be a prefect next year?"

Davenport frowned, unable to comprehend my request. "You don't *want* to be a prefect?"

"No Sir."

"But why?"

Nerves. Try not to look at him. Keep in control. Swallow.

"I just don't want to be, Sir."

And I wasn't.

As we approached Christmas, the school put lots of emphasis on exam revision. I wasn't as enthusiastic about it as I should have been. I just couldn't wait for it all to be finally over.

The months leading up to spring 1986 were spent retreading old lessons. Social Studies teacher Mrs Stagg took our finished projects to make one final analysis before submitting them to the examiner. I was so paranoid about her seeming dislike for my chosen subject, I pinned a little note to its cover. "Please don't let any personal opinions affect your judgement", or words to that effect. I feel absolutely awful about it now, but at the time I was utterly convinced that she couldn't stand me.

For some reason I was absent for the following session, but Ian filled me in on how Mrs Stagg had ranted and raved to the rest of the class about my insulting little memo. When I finally did go in, she went on at length about how she would never dream of doing such a thing, and how upset her husband was, and how I could think she would be so prejudiced. It was hard to take, although it wasn't a first. I was often faced with having to explain my strange opinions and unfounded suspicions to baffled teachers.

For example, Mr Davenport took a Careers lesson shortly before the exams, and arranged mock job interviews with various pupils. There was one boy who had a bit of attitude. He was all right, reasonably friendly, but I found his air of confidence intimidating. Davenport, pretending to be a potential employer, asked a few questions and the boy gave his response. Then facing the class, Davenport quizzed, "Now, what did you notice about his manner and the way he spoke to me?"

I put up my hand.

"Yes, William."

"He was arrogant," I offered.

The teacher's face screwed up into an almost pained expression, as though he was trying to fathom how I'd managed to see arrogance in the boy's demeanour. "Arrogant?" he said. "What do you mean?"

As usual, I clammed with embarrassment, looked down and said nothing. Davenport stared for what seemed like ages. Then he said, "I don't understand you, Hadcroft."

That's all right, Sir. Nobody does.

In the weeks covering the climax of the exam period, lessons became more relaxed, with teachers taking things very easy. There was a real sense that we were approaching the end of an era.

On one of the days Mr Davenport led a team of runners on a cross-country expedition. They ran from the school, across the old disused railway embankment, all round the surrounding streets, and then back into the school grounds, across the field, to the finishing point. It being the end of the year, Mr Davenport didn't care whether I ran in the race or not. Naturally I cared even less.

It'll be the last time I have to put up with this tiresome nonsense.

Markers were placed at various intervals across the field, showing the route the runners must go to get to the finishing point, and all those not running, me included, had to stand by the markers.

And so, with a definite buzz in the air, those participating set off on their cross-country run, with Mr Davenport timing the event on a stopwatch. The crowd set off at a pace, trotted down the main drive, turned right towards the railway embankment – and then silence. Nothing but the sound of distant road traffic and the tweeting of birds. Those of us stood on the field by our markers started to chat to one another.

I had trouble hearing what one of my classmates was saying and walked over to join him. We chatted at length and got really engrossed in whatever it was we were discussing. We laughed and talked, and it felt good. There was a really relaxed atmosphere. No more school, no more ridiculous concepts, no more sport games. I couldn't wait to leave.

The boy at the marker nearest the entrance to the field called over to me. "Bill, I can see them coming!"

I casually acknowledged this, "Right", and carried on talking to my classmate. The first of the runners emerged at the entrance, jogging rather than running, but still going, and quite away ahead of the others. His face looked pained, but he was still going strong.

> Rather you than me. What a waste of time and energy. Utterly pointless. Just so one person can claim he's better than the others. What's the point of that? It's childish. I've no patience with it.

He ran past the boy at the entrance, missed the marker where I should have been standing, and headed towards my friend. "No, no," waved the friend. "You've got to go past that one first." I confirmed it by nonchalantly strolling back to my marker. "He's right," I said. "It's this one first."

The runner backtracked to my marker and then proceeded with his original course. Davenport and the others followed and then we on the markers made for the finishing line. As I approached, the winning boy was bent over, holding his knees, and gasping for breath. Davenport stood by him clicking his stopwatch. "Ooohhh!" he moaned. He sounded genuinely disappointed. "You're just a couple of seconds off the school record. Never mind, you did very well. Well done, son."

The boy straightened up. I swallowed hard as he glared at me.

> What's up now? What have I said, or not said? What have I done, or done wrong?

"I went the wrong way," he spat, "because he wasn't stood at his marker."

Mr Davenport looked at me. "William?"

"I thought he knew where to go, Sir," I said nervously. "I thought he would just follow the markers. I thought it was obvious."

> And it's not that important anyway.

Davenport just stared at me. "You left your marker?"

"Yes, Sir."

"But why?"

I indicated my friend who had been on the next marker up from me. "To talk to him, Sir."

The winner poked an angry finger in my face. "I would've broken the school record!"

I started to laugh nervously. "Well, you *have* broken the school record, when you think about it, haven't you?"

Both Davenport and the boy frowned in unison. "What?"

"Well," I shrugged. "If, by going round the markers correctly you would have broken the school record, all you have to do is deduct the few seconds where you went back on yourself and then you *did* break the record."

Mr Davenport shook his head. "It doesn't work like that."

I was exasperated now, and a little panicked by their simmering fury. "If he'd have gone round my marker," I repeated, "he would have broken the record. Therefore he *did* break it."

"I didn't," said the boy. "And it's because of you."

He walked off to join some of his friends. "What's up?" one of them asked.

"Hadcroft's lost me the school record because he wasn't stood in the right place." The lad glanced round at me and I, shamed, kept my eyes to the ground. A slang word for masturbation reached my ears.

At the time I really didn't know what all the fuss was about. I understood that it was important to them, and that I had upset them. But that was all. Competitive sport meant nothing to me. On the scale of things, when one considered what other things were happening on the Earth, when one took on board where our puny world is in relation to the surrounding galaxy, and ultimately the vastness of the universe – whether or not some boy could run faster than another boy seemed insignificant, irrelevant even.

A few weeks before I was set free from school, an adjudicator came round to assess the teachers on how they assign marks. I was asked to do a reading. Thanks to my progress in the Theocratic Ministry School at the Kingdom Hall, my reading from John Christopher's *Tripods* trilogy went down very well indeed. You see, I had discovered that it was actually easier for me to deliver a talk in front of an audience than it was to socialize. The only person I had to consider was myself. No one was going to answer me back, I didn't have to worry about my raw honesty offending people, I didn't get anxious thinking about it all. I was in total control and, as a result, relaxed. My introduction was properly formulated, it aroused interest, it was calm, and my delivery of the reading was fluent, well paced, with variation in pitch. I put on little voices for the different characters.

Mr Simpson congratulated me on it, Mrs Morris seemed quite proud and Mrs Atkinson even said that the adjudicator had told her she hadn't given me a high enough mark. I was *good*, and I knew it. I had come top and impressed them all. This, a couple of weeks before leaving school…

When we finally did break up, I felt incredibly relieved. It was over at last. Now I would be working with mature adults. The excessive swearing, the aggression and vulgar jokes would be a thing of the past. People would treat me with respect.

I left school with a string of average CSE grades and two O levels, one of which was in English Language. My mother was very keen for me to go to college and pursue a career. Looking back I could have studied Creative Writing and followed my dream of becoming an author, or I could have done Media Studies and indulged in my passion for the television industry. But I refused point blank. My reason? Well the reason I gave was that I wanted to be a pioneer minister of Jehovah's Witnesses; that is, a house-to-house preacher devoting 90 hours a month to this work. Witnesses who did this normally worked part-time in a regular job to bring a modest wage which could supplement the pioneering.

While I did like the idea of this very much, I must confess that my real reason for refusing to go to college was much more fundamental than that: I was scared. I hadn't left the classroom environment of school just to enter another one at college. I was free, and I was determined to remain so.

Mum reluctantly gave in, reasoning that if pioneering was what I really wanted to do with my life, I should be allowed to do it. After a while she asked what I was going to do about getting a job. I kept putting this off, not because I was bone idle, but because I was terrified. I had absolutely no idea how to go about it. For those few weeks I wasn't earning anything and I wasn't receiving the dole. "When are you going to sort the dole out?" Mum kept asking. And I kept saying, "In a bit."

I thought that when you left school you automatically received the dole until you found a job. I was waiting for a cheque to turn up with my name on it!

When it became clear that I would have to visit a Job Centre, that I would have to fill in forms and account for my actions every fortnight, that I would have to talk to strangers and queue up alongside other unemployed people, the anxiety began to creep up again. How on earth was I going to cope?

I climbed further and further into my *Doctor Who* cocoon, watching my video recordings and listening to the BBC Radiophonic Workshop records. My obsession with it had reached a point where I could recite great chunks of script and would often be found doing so, staring out of the kitchen window or sitting on the edge of my bed – literally going over favourite episodes, playing them back in my imagination.

Then one afternoon, when I had put the theme music on for the umpteenth time, my mother marched upstairs, thrust open the bedroom door, and seethed. "I'm sick of it! No wonder you don't have any friends! You're driving us all bloody mad!" She marched over to the only pin-up I had in my room and stabbed a finger at the face of Colin Baker. "Don't talk to me about God!" she blazed. "HE'S your God! Doctor bloody Who!"

It's all I've got. It's all I've got. IT'S ALL I'VE GOT!!!

I held my breath through the onslaught, and then burst into relentless sobbing. "I know," I cried. "But I can't help it. I wish I could stop, but I can't." Mum softened as she watched my pathetic form sitting on the edge of the bed, tears streaming and body shivering. She left the room, as perplexed as ever. Once she had gone I shut the door, and in silence cradled the framed picture of Colin Baker in my hands. He stared back at me, all thoughtful and serious, his multicoloured coat marking him out as "different", the question marks on his shirt collar denoting his character. An enigma, an oddity.

He's like me.

Things started to look up a bit when a friend called Eddie came round to see me. He was relinquishing his early morning cleaning job at the local supermarket, and was wondering if I might want to take it over.

Somewhat apprehensive, I said "Yes."

The Real World, 1986–87

I T WAS FIVE O'CLOCK IN the morning when I arrived at the back gate of the superstore as instructed. Eddie took me in to meet Rose, my supervisor, and to show me the ropes.

I set to work pulling out all the rubbish from under the fixtures, a draining, exhausting, back-breaking task for someone not used to exercise. The idea was to get around every fixture in the store, preparing the way for a ginger-haired, middle-aged man called Arthur, who would then buff the floor with his machine. His job seemed a much better deal: just fill the machine with water and detergent, and then push it up and down every aisle until the whole shop floor is done.

> Can't I do that instead, Rose? I would be much happier doing that. A solitary job where I don't have to interact, where I wouldn't worry about people watching me and passing comment.

I was very conscious of the girls sniggering and pointing. They were in their late teens or perhaps their early twenties, plastered with make-up, hair bleached white, and poisoning the air with their foul language. I was a laughing stock again, and on that very first day the awful truth dawned on me: the working world was actually no different to that of school.

I had been looking forward to joining the outside world because I thought it was the world occupied by my grandparents, my aunts and uncles, and my mum and dad: a world where people are responsible and civil, where being "different" is readily accepted as part of the tapestry of life. But I had been duped. This was definitely not the world where people watched their Ps and Qs, and I began to realize, slowly but surely, that the illusion presented by the adults in my family was precisely that, an illusion.

It's exactly like school, but without the teachers. It's *worse*.

I started to notice that things were not what they seemed in other parts of life too. TV out-takes, for example, the bits of film that get cut because an actor or presenter has fluffed their lines. Respected, purer-than-pure children's role models swearing their heads off when they get something wrong. Politely spoken, well-respected celebrities effing and jeffing, no better than factory fodder and supermarket night-shift types.

They're false. They're all false. The world is one big lie. Two-faced. One thing in one set of circumstances, completely different in another. Everyone is acting. I hate it. I wish I were dead.

For the first few weeks I was a subject of idle mockery, with various staff members commenting on my crippling shyness, the fact I was still a virgin, the fact that I didn't share any of their interests. A lad not passionate about football? How strange. He still watches *Doctor Who* at his age? Even stranger. The girls would encircle me and ask me embarrassing questions. "Is it true you're still a virgin?"

Just look at the floor.

"Yes, that's true."
"Even though you're 17?"
"Yes."
"Why?"

Just look at the floor.

"Beck'll let you go with her, won't you Beck?"

Beck's shaking her head in mock denial. Just look at the floor.

"Haaa! He's blushing!"

I wish I were dead.

On my first day, Rose introduced me to the night workers whose job it was to stack the shelves and price up the goods. "This is William, our new cleaner." I put on my best smile and extended my hand to the lads: "Hi."

One of them sneered at my outstretched hand. "Oh, you're one of *them*, are you?"

One of what? I'm just trying to be nice, you cretin.

I was regarded as a harmless eccentric, I was a curiosity to them. After a while the packing lads warmed to me, and nicknamed me "Joe". One morning I asked one of the shelf stackers why they called me Joe. He said it was short for "Joe Egg". I quite liked that, and said, "Is that because I'm a good egg?"

"No," he replied. "It's because you've got an egg-shaped head." Oh, right... I earned £30 a week, 15 of which went to my mother, the remainder being spent on records, tapes and the ever-growing range of classic *Doctor Who* adventures released on BBC Video.

Of course, it wasn't long before I noticed one of the till girls, a certain Gemma, who bore a vague resemblance to Nicola "Peri" Bryant. Each morning I straightened my blue overalls and combed my long greasy hair (which at the very least obscured my egg-shaped head) and made, black liners at the ready, for the dustbins at the entrance. I never actually spoke to Gemma, I didn't have the courage; and even now I don't know the first thing about her. Once again I was in love with an image.

Buffer man Arthur found me exasperatingly slow when it came to clearing the floor. He'd bring his machine to the foot of the aisle in which I was sweeping and start tutting and looking at his watch. "I've got to have all this done by eight-thirty, Willy."

Don't call me Willy. I hate it.

He approached me and informed me of just how useless I was: "You know, Willy, every factory and every firm has a balloon working in it. You know, someone who trips up all the time, who gets everything wrong and holds everybody else up. And you're ours."

He pulled a couple of passing individuals to one side, with me in earshot, and talked very loudly, "Hey, I was just saying: every firm has a balloon working in it, and William's ours."

I was very hurt by this. I despised everything about the job: the time I had to start, the type of work I was doing, having to race against the clock, the teasing. I was lonely and depressed most of the time. Was it the job I hated or just myself?

It didn't go down too well when I was spotted by one of my colleagues looking in the Job Centre for a new source of employment, and one morning Rose approached me and gently advised, "Don't let Arthur get you down, love. He doesn't mean it."

If my shyness and awkwardness were not eccentric enough, then my attempts to win friends certainly were. I had realized that all I had to do was make them laugh and get them on to my wavelength, and life would be a lot nicer for me as a result. I tried to jolly things along by making a send-up audio tape of the supermarket crew. Called *But Yes But, But Nothing*, it was based loosely on the radio version of *The Hitch-Hiker's Guide to the Galaxy*. It featured my impersonations of various workmates and *Hitch-Hiker* style narration, set to sound effects and music. One morning I bit the bullet and played the recording as I did my job.

Some people kindly made comparisons with *Monty Python* and said it was a similar kind of humour, others said it reminded them of the local radio comedy *The Bradshaws* where one man did all the voices – but most just thought I was weird.

> A couple of tattooed lads stand frowning at the tape recorder. "What's this, Joe? Is it *you*? It is, innit? You're weird. Get it off and put the radio back on." They don't think it's funny. They just think I'm strange. I wish I were dead.

As with my first couple of years at secondary school, I became disillusioned and deeply unhappy. I became irregular, arriving late nearly every day, and taking odd days off. This in turn brought pressure from all sides; from the people I knew who also worked there, from Rose and, of course, from my mother.

I tried to defuse Rose's chastisement by saying I'd got stuck in a time warp, or that the TARDIS had landed me in the wrong time zone, thinking that this would perhaps amuse her. "I did actually arrive at five o'clock, but in the wrong year. So you see, I did get here on time, but three centuries ago."

At first it seemed to work, and she would go scurrying off to tell the others, and they would approach me to hear it for themselves. Everyone laughed; but after a while I came to appreciate that they were laughing *at* me, rather than *with* me. I also knew that my lack of punctuality was no comedy.

I felt like I'd fallen to Earth from another planet. They didn't understand me and I didn't understand them. My attempts to fit in were met with ridicule, bemusement and, at times, irritation. And their attempts to normalize me were repelled forcefully.

Meanwhile at home, John, brother of Karl, had spent most of the summer holidays with my family. He must have been as young as our Matthew, and yet we got on very well. He set up a camp bed in my room, and the nights would be spent lying there in total darkness listening to *Jeff Wayne's Musical Version of the War of the Worlds*. That was a brilliant album. Richard Burton's narration transported us to a time when Martians were invading the Earth. The superb score, which seemed to be a combination of electronic rock and orchestra, captured the mood of the story perfectly. I later learned that *Tripods* composer Ken Freeman actually invented and played the synthesizers on the record and that, actually, there aren't any conventional string instruments in it: the orchestra sounds are all keyboard generated, courtesy of Ken.

And so, David Essex sang about his dream of a new underground utopia, while Justin Hayward warbled that classic ballad "Forever Autumn", as well as the Professor's anthem about the chances of anything from Mars arriving on our world.

John, Matt and I never tired of this highly addictive album, which is more than can be said for Mum. I'll never forget the time when one of her friends came round and started enthusing about the LP. Mum gave a mock look of abject horror. "Oh no," she lamented. "Not another one."

> So what? Would it be different if I talked endlessly about Manchester United instead?

By the close of 1986 I was attending all the meetings of Jehovah's Witnesses: the Public Talk and *Watchtower* lesson on Sundays, the Book Study on Tuesdays, and the Theocratic School on Thursdays. My ability as a public speaker was coming on a treat, so much so that I felt more confident speaking in front of a hundred people than I did attending social gatherings.

The next step was to participate in the official house-to-house ministry. Needless to say I was terrified. I met with the Book Study group one Friday evening and was reassured by Ken that he would be doing all the talking. That *was* reassuring! After saying a prayer and then travelling to our assigned street, we split up into groups of two and began.

My knees felt as though they were going to give out as Ken and I approached the first door. Ken knocked hard, and my heart thumped faster and faster as the shadow of a man could be seen approaching the door through the glass. As soon as he opened the door, Ken went into his brief presentation about the latest issues of *The Watchtower* and *Awake!* magazines. The man listened, thought about it, and agreed to take the magazines.

Simple as that. Or at least that's how Ken made it look. My appreciation for the magazines grew at this point, as I came to realize just how much careful thought went into them. The principal magazine took its name from the Biblical metaphor of a watchman standing in his lookout post and announcing what he saw on the horizon. The magazine's full title was *The Watchtower Announcing Jehovah's Kingdom* and was the full-on religious one. Its companion, *Awake!*, was designed as a general knowledge journal but with a religious slant. The name was extrapolated from something Jesus said about staying awake to the real meaning behind current events. Some householders found the latter more palatable and just had that.

Magazine presentations were designed to be brief 30- to 60-second affairs, whereas the other form of witnessing, what they called Sermon Work, was more about having a conversation with the householder. It would involve asking questions and reasoning, and would normally climax with the placing of a book. All the publications were presented for the printing cost only, which meant that compared to shop prices they were extremely cheap. And no Witness ever received payment for his or her work, whether it be the preaching, being an elder or being a representative from the London headquarters. It was all voluntary, and it impressed me no end.

Ken was especially devoted. He was a pleasant, balanced young man, who had given up full-time work and now worked as a part-time joiner so that he could concentrate on the public preaching ministry. He was what they termed a pioneer, someone who devoted 90 hours per month to the ministry, calling on interested ones and conducting home Bible Study courses like the one he did with me.

I aspired to be like Ken and, on the 3 January 1987, I was formerly baptized as one of Jehovah's Witnesses.

My life at home continued to be fairly reclusive, and work was as challenging as ever. I clung to my Time Lord hero for relief. Sylvester McCoy debuted as the seventh incarnation of Doctor Who that autumn. The programme had been struggling to maintain its audience due to a number of factors, and my heart sank into my shoes when the BBC scheduled the new series against ITV's blockbuster soap *Coronation Street*.

September 1987 saw us holidaying at Butlin's once again, this time with Dad. We'd been to Pwllheli so many times we decided to try Skegness for a change. It was rubbish.

I had contacted the Push Button Click panto group by letter, and discovered to my horror that Jean Wren Productions had gone out of business. This year would see the last of the Push Button Click shows. I was devastated. Jean Wren had enjoyed my correspondence so much, she'd promised me a role in the Click when I was old enough to play a part. She had also promised to give me a guided back-stage tour of their new big London production of *Super Ted*. She had been so impressed with my dedication to the Push Button Click phenomenon. But now it was all over.

The whole week was tarnished by a series of events which, to this day, haunt me. It all started when, on the first day of the holiday, I befriended a 13-year-old girl. She sat with her stepfather, her brother and her half-brother at the dining table next to ours. It was when I heard them talking about the Push Button Click that I introduced myself.

I enjoyed her company, and she took to me as an older brother figure almost instantly. We spent the whole week knocking about together, a 17-year-old and a 13-year-old. It makes me boggle in this day and age, looking back to that unusual friendship. Now it would send shivers down people's spines and make adults worried that something else might be going on.

One evening, I decided to pay her a visit. As I approached the chalet, I found I could see in through the ill-fitting curtains. I gasped at what I saw.

She was lying on the floor, legs parted, and her ten-year-old brother was lying face down on top of her.

Shocked and greatly disturbed, I decided there and then to intervene.

Who else is there…?

I knocked on the door, my hands sweating with nervous apprehension. "Who is it?" said a voice. I frowned for a moment. The voice belonged to her stepfather. I couldn't believe it. He was actually in there with them.

"It's William," I said, shaking. "I thought I'd just pop round to see you."

"Oh…OK, hang on a minute."

After a lot of shuffling around, the door was opened. I looked disdainfully at the drunken slob of a stepfather. The girl was sat on the edge of her bed fully dressed, red faced and perspiring. "Hi," she said casually. She smiled.

The toddler was fast asleep in bed. The ten-year-old came marching out of the bathroom (or maybe a bedroom, I can't remember now) and greeted me just as airily. Their act was rehearsed to perfection. Poor kids. The rest of the night for me was spent thinking of how I could put a stop to that awful abuse.

Who else is there…?

It took most of the following day to pluck up courage and tell the girl that I'd seen them. She looked at the floor, red faced and shamed.

I touched her shoulder. "Hey," I said with as much warmth as I could muster. "Don't worry. I'll help you escape." She looked at me doubtfully. "Trust me," I said. "I've thought it through. I know how I'm going to do it."

"How?"

"Ever heard of Esther Rantzen and Childline?"

"No."

"I'll write to Esther Rantzen."

As soon as I returned home, I kept my word and wrote a lengthy letter to Esther Rantzen who, I knew, had established the Childline charity for abused minors. I think I wrote it care of the BBC programme *That's Life*, which she presented, and which was still in production at that time. A month or so later, Childline phoned me up, and before I knew it, I was being interviewed by the police.

Letters the girl had sent me were taken as evidence. One in particular interested them, where she had asked me to write to Esther Rantzen again, because her stepfather was "making her take her clothes off for five pounds".

A while after that, I received a letter from the girl herself, thanking me for my help, and telling me that all three children were now with foster parents.

It had been a depressing year, all told. The final blow came in December, as my mother and brothers awaited the imminent return of Stan from his latest Merchant Navy voyage. Mum was particularly excited, since she had succeeded in giving up smoking. Stan was a non-smoker and, although he never complained about Mum's habit, she had packed it in without telling him. We imagined his gleeful reaction.

Then, one afternoon, a white transit van pulled up outside our Roe Green house. Mum recognized the "Zapata" logo straight away. Had Stan come home earlier to surprise us all?

A dour-faced gentleman came to the door, and Mum reluctantly allowed him in. "I've got some very bad news, Mrs Warburton. Please sit down." Stanley had suffered tremendous headaches while at sea and had been taken to hospital. The man told of how my stepfather had lost consciousness, and had suffered a brain haemorrhage.

"But he's all right, isn't he?" my mother pressed.

"No," said the man slowly. He just stared for a second and then uttered those awful words that say so much without really saying anything. "Mrs Warburton, I'm sorry."

I felt my heart turn to rock as I watched the realization dawning on my mother's face.

"You mean…he's dead?"

"Yes. I *am* sorry."

She immediately broke into frenzied sobbing. "Noooo!!!" she screamed. "We've only been married for *four years!*"

It was horrible. One of the worst days of my life, maybe *the* worst. My brothers started crying. I just felt numb. It was as though I wasn't really part of the scene; it was like watching it on television and being moved silently. I was stunned and shaken, but I didn't give any outward signs of a reaction at all. I had been more demonstrative of my grief over the death of Adric in *Doctor Who* six years previously and had wept buckets for days. But for Stan, my stepdad, with whom I'd lived for four years, who had been a big and real part of my life… I just stared at my crippled family.

After the man had gone, Mum phoned Uncle Bob. "Robert? It's me." She started crying again. "Stan's died…"

Bob, along with my mother's youngest brother John Churchill, came round straight away.

Mum fell into a severe depression. She often had convulsive fits of vomiting, and people would remark on her sullen complexion. Grandma was especially grieved. "I saw your mother in Walkden last week," she said. "I was going to say something but thought better of it. She looked *terrible*."

I wasn't much help. I just retreated into my cocoon and ran for the TARDIS. I left them to it. I simply could not cope with the intensity of the emotion on display everywhere I looked.

Mrs Berry over the road collared me and said, "I bet you've been a tower of strength for your mum." I said nothing in reply and felt wretched inside.

When Mum and Doreen were discussing having Stan's body flown back to Britain, I failed to see why it was important. After all Stan was dead and all that was left was his shell. It didn't really matter to me whether the body decomposed in Britain or in Nigeria. To me it was an irrelevance. "I don't see the point. The real Stan can't be brought back. His body is just a husk of a shell."

I hate myself every time I remember that. It was, of course, nothing more than a quote from *Doctor Who*. I really was obsessed with it. The programme consumed almost my every thought. It sickens me now, to think I applied a quote from the programme to this awful situation. No wonder my mother hated it as much as she did. Flying Stan's body over to England so she could see him one last time and say an official farewell, to bring closure and start the healing process, was paramount to her, as it would be to anybody. But I had grown so detached from reality by this stage that it all seemed like a lot of fuss over nothing.

The Vomit of a Tormented Soul, 1988–90

JEHOVAH'S WITNESSES HAVE A REPUTATION for pestering people. You know the sort of thing, calling at your house while you're having lunch and resisting your pleas to call back later, standing on the doorstep for a good twenty minutes even though you'd made it very clear that you could only spare two. They ask for your opinion on certain issues and then argue with you until you want to swear at them and shut the door in their face. And if you fall into the trap of talking to one in the street, they don't take the hint, and follow you about until you turn nasty. They are, quite frankly, intellectually and emotionally challenged.

Or are they? Actually, most are just like you. They earn a living in a regular job, they pay their bills and mortgages, they send their children to school, they do their shopping at Asda, they take a holiday at least once a year, they watch television and go to see movies. Some are concerned about their health and join Weight Watchers or go down the gym, some play football, some form their own music bands, and some love science fiction. In fact, if they didn't visit your street in their suits and modest dresses, carrying their leather bags and being extremely polite, you wouldn't know they *were* Jehovah's Witnesses.

The governing body of the organization provide members with constant year-round training on how to present their message to the public. There are discussions at the Kingdom Hall about being reasonable and respectful, there are example presentations published every month to indicate how a doorstep conversation should be conducted. And the vast majority of members adhere strictly to the guidelines. They are balanced, reasonable people.

So why the reputation? Well it's all thanks to a minority, who perhaps struggle with a personality disorder, are lacking in tact and social skills, who fail to acknowledge that others see things differently, and who might be a tad obsessive about their own belief system. Add to that a command in the Bible to spread the word, and you have the stereotypical Witness. Of course, it's the confrontations with this brand of witness that one tends to remember.

And I'm ashamed to say that in my young adult life I was one of them. There are many aspects to being one of Jehovah's Witnesses, but it was the doctrine dealing with the last days and God's coming judgement which consumed me. All Witnesses believe that this will happen, and indeed yearn for it, but a minority who are open targets for bullies and struggle with their own feelings of worthlessness cling to it and obsess about it – the end of the hostile world. Again this was true of me.

I had become so depressed by January 1988 and so irregular at work that Rose had to "let me go". She was very good about it: the business with the girl on holiday, the death of two friends in a car crash and my stepfather's passing, all in the space of four months, had taken their toll on me quite considerably. It was mutually agreed that she would sack me so that I would qualify to receive unemployment benefit.

Before I left, though, there was one task that I felt impelled to fulfil, in fact as far as I was concerned it was a matter of life and death. Eternal life and death. The till girl on whom I'd developed quite a crush needed to hear the message. Of course, since I was dreadfully bashful around girls, and even more so with those for whom I had a fondness, I had never actually spoken to Gemma in the whole of the time I worked there. And so, just before I left the supermarket, I asked one of the women at Customer Services to give a package to Gemma when she had the time. The package contained the Jehovah's Witness textbook and a letter from me basically telling her that I really liked her and that I didn't want her to perish when "the end" came.

Whenever I contemplate these actions I start to feel a bit sick in the stomach, it's so embarrassing. The few times I've related the story to fellow Witnesses, they have grimaced at the thought and wondered what impact receiving the package might have had on the poor girl. Well, I can reveal exclusively here, folks, that a rather stern phone call from Gemma's brother ensued in which he charged me not to give her anything else and to stay well away. I was so shaken by the call that I had little trouble complying.

Many times over the last few years I have wanted to approach her and apologize, but I fear that any such attempt would be interpreted wrongly. So if you're reading this, Gem, I'm sorry I did that. I'm not a nutter, honest! I was just on the verge of a breakdown, that's all.

It was in 1988 that I became hooked on the music of Hue and Cry, a Scottish band headed by brothers Patrick and Gregory Kane. Their single "Labour of Love", a political protest song with a modern jazz line, had been a Top Ten hit the previous year. I bought the album from which it came, *Seduced and Abandoned*, some time after. The same year, 1988, brought the Top Twenty hits "Ordinary Angel" and "Looking For Linda", but it was the next single release that was to really touch me. Entitled "Violently (Your Words Hit Me)", I saw the promotional video for it on the children's magazine programme *Saturday Superstore* and decided there and then that I must buy it. Gregory's laidback keyboards and acoustic guitar complemented the crooning tones of Patrick's vocal, as he sang about being completely untouchable, brittle and hateful, and how the lady in his life had made him a different man. I viewed the song as a little prophecy; that one day there would be a woman in my life who would make me feel the same.

I played "Violently" more times than is good for a boy with severe melancholia, and went on to buy the album, *Remote*, from which the single came.

This was also the time when I realized that the Justin Hayward who sang the *Star Cops* theme "It Won't Be Easy" was the same Justin Hayward who had performed "Forever Autumn" on the *War of the Worlds* album. According to the sleeve notes Justin was lead singer of a band called The Moody Blues, so I set about writing to him to determine whether Moody Blues music was similar in style to the aforementioned tracks.

Justin replied to my letter promptly, telling me that the Moodies' music was indeed very similar to "It Won't Be Easy" and "Forever Autumn", and recommended that I try their very first album, *Days of Future Passed*, and their (then) latest, *The Other Side of Life*, which I did. The spring of 1988 brought their brand new album *Sur La Mer*, which I played daily, much to my mother's discomfort. She really hated the track "Want To Be With You", because, while it echoed my feelings perfectly, it also reminded her of Stan. I was quite happy to torment myself with mournful songs, but she wasn't! Sorry, Mum.

It was also around this time that I acquired a 15-year-old pen pal by the name of Dominic. He lived in Kent and I'd found his address in *Doctor Who Magazine*. To him, having a pen pal was a bit of fun, a way of making friends with like-minded people. But for me it was different. Dominic was a lifeline. His letters were the reason I got up in the morning and, being unemployed, I was able to write to him at the very least once a week. Each day I would hound the letterbox to see if anything had come.

I cherished the correspondence so much, I even bought him the very first black-and-white Dalek serial on video. A double-pack affair, and something I knew he wouldn't be able to afford with his pocket money. I also made what I called "tape letters", audio recordings where I would chatter on about different aspects of *Doctor Who*, *Blake's Seven* and *The Tripods*. It was a way of being myself without feeling like I should be apologizing all the time.

Please like me. Please like me. Please like me. Please like me.

I think Dominic's mum might have been a bit worried on the quiet, especially when I started phoning him.

I was desperately lonely.

I finally secured a part-time job at a hotel in Worsley. Overall-clad, and with a deep sadness in my eyes, I would slope onto the premises to do my little bit, mopping the corridor from the kitchens to the staffroom, cleaning the said room and the adjacent toilets. One member of staff, a waiter I think, was staggered to learn that I was only 19. "I thought you were married with children and everything!" he declared, somewhat shocked. "It's because you're so sensible."

If only someone would *want* to marry me.

In true William style, there were a couple of girls there I had crushes on. If they ever realized, they never made it known; and even if they had, I wouldn't have had a clue what to say or do.

One morning there was a bit of silly banter going on between one of the girls and a chef. He was pretending to maul her, grabbing hold of her and pushing her on to a table. She was laughing all the time he was doing this, even when he parted her legs and pretended to have sex with her.

Stop it. Stop it. You're dishonouring her. I hate it.

She caught sight of my crimson face, I being shocked at the enactment. The girl roared all the more, as did the others in the room. "Look! He's blushing!"

I would do my four hours every morning, come home, and collapse, exhausted on the sofa. Mum had no idea how to deal with me. "Huh!" she'd say. "Anyone would think you'd done a day's work, the way you come in like that."

The funny thing is, I *was* exhausted. Having to mix with people, having to think of conversation, having to pretend to be interested. It was so tiring. I was tired of it all, of the world, of life, of myself. Ever the alien.

In an effort to help me look and feel less "odd" Mum bought a bright paisley shirt. They were very much the in thing and my mother thought the youth of the day looked very nice in them. I enjoyed not sticking out like a sore thumb for a month or so. I say a month or so because the fashion suddenly changed, and paisley shirts were once again the province of the homosexual world. I'd acquired my new shirt right at the end of the phase. I was strolling casually through Bolton town centre one Saturday, when a gang of youths accosted me, chanting in camp effeminate voices, "Ooh, I like your shirt!"

Immediate rage. Shallow tiresome children. Teenage shaven heads, loud mouthed and smoking. Smoking to appear adult. Deliberately inhaling poison to look mature. Brainless youths. I'm shivering with anger. Cue white eyes and intense music, adrenalin rush and glowing DNA.

Fashion was, in my not so humble opinion at that time, like its adherents – pathetic.

One of the elders in my congregation, a man called Harry, who was very much a grandfather figure to me, invited me to a get-together at his house. This was an ideal way to meet new people – including girls. I weighed up the pros and cons, and decided that since Harry and his wife would be there, as well as one or two older folk from my own congregation, I would be able to manage it socially.

At first I was the usual fish out of water, saying and doing all the wrong things, trying desperately to be witty like the others. One of the older young people turned up wearing green cords, which I found a little bit in bad taste. I recalled a line from a *Blackadder* episode where Edmund's Scottish cousin MacAdder is described as the most dangerous man in Europe to wear a skirt, which I thought was side-splittingly funny. When I saw the young man's cords I announced to one and all, "The most dangerous man to wear green cords in Europe" – and everything went quiet.

> They don't think it's funny. Why aren't they laughing? Why is it funny on *Blackadder*, but not here? They're all just smiling politely at the floor. Now I'm blushing, I've done it again. I hate myself so much.

After the initial feelings of awkwardness subsided, I actually found myself settling in. There was a group of Jamaican girls there who had been invited from another hall. For some reason I found that I was able to relax completely in their presence, and I started to talk about the various characters in my hall and wheel out some of my dodgy impersonations. Despite not knowing who it was I was supposed to be "doing", they found my little party piece hilarious. One girl in particular let it be known to the host.

> I can't believe it! A girl who actually finds me attractive and amusing! And she's really pretty too.

Harry was thrilled for me. "I think you may have cracked it, William," he beamed.

A few months later there was a wedding at the other hall, and Harry, his wife and I were invited. This was the big opportunity to approach the girl, who no doubt had been primed, and get talking. But I found the atmosphere and the crowd unbearable.

It's absolutely packed. I–I can't do it. I can't go in. No, come on, this is your big chance. You *must* go in. You must.

All those people. They did the hokey-cokey, and I tried to join in.

This is utterly ridiculous. Why are we doing this? Because it's "fun", I suppose. After all, that's what it's all about, bum, bum. It's insane.

Then there was the barn dance.

First of all, we are not in a barn, we're in a community centre. Second, what is the point anyway?

Then the pop music started up, which of course meant dancing. I didn't do dancing. I hadn't the first clue how. Even closely watching the others I found I couldn't really copy it. Perhaps it was because I found it embarrassing, being over six feet tall and everything. Perhaps it was because my parents never danced at parties. They stood about talking and drinking wine and beer, but they never danced. Never ever. And so neither did I.

Harry approached, grinning all over his face. "Go and ask her to dance, William," he said. I immediately clammed up and stared at him in abject horror. He gestured to the picture of beauty sat nervously by the far wall. "Look, she's waiting. She's waiting for you to ask her to dance."

She is too. Primed and waiting, waiting for me to walk over and ask.

I managed a couple of words. "I can't."
   "Why?"
   "I can't dance. I'll feel like an idiot."
   "She's waiting, William. Just go over."
   "I can't." Panic was beginning to set in, and Harry was looking agitated. He was so hoping I could make it work with her. So was I. But I stayed put and just watched the dance from the wall. The tempo of the music changed as the DJ put on a different record.
   Plucking up courage, the girl got out of her chair, walked across the room, and smiling her beautiful, intelligent, innocent smile, extended her hand towards me. "Will you dance with me, William?"

My throat. I can't breathe. I'm choking. My eyes are burning, they're going to drop out of my head. I'm shaking.

I shook my head slowly. "I can't. I'm sorry."

Harry's wife: "Go on, William. Dance with the girl!"

"I can't."

The girl's smile faltered. She wasn't sure now, I could tell. "Why?"

"I can't dance. I don't what to do."

Her certainty renewed, she took my hand and yanked me away from the wall. "Oh, don't worry about that. It's easy. Come on, I'll show you."

> PANIC! I'm with a girl. She wants to dance with me. I don't know what to do. I'll look so ridiculous, towering above everyone else. They'll all be watching me. They'll all see how hopeless I am. I can't do it. I can't do it. I can't do it.

I snatched my hand back really hard and then staggered backwards. Everything suddenly seemed to go into slow motion. Her face. Just staring. So shocked, so hurt. I looked round and caught Harry's stunned expression. A voice. A woman's voice: "William!" The girl was still staring. She didn't speak, but her eyes said it all.

Like a wimp in a teenage soap opera I ran from the community centre, and once outside burst into tears. I was shaking with rage, but this time it was my own self-loathing that was the source. The only girl who had ever shown me the slightest attention, the only one who had ever seriously spoken to me, the only one who had ever found me amusing – and I'd humiliated her in front of all her friends.

> The creature. Faltered breathing, furrowed green forehead, tearful white eyes. Not comprehending, not seeing the reasons. Just the embodiment of raw emotion. The creature roars loud and long into the night air. Expressing itself the only way it can.

The desire to be a writer was simmering again. I submitted two pieces to *Doctor Who*. One was a script about an evil force buried deep within the TARDIS, which I submitted to script editor Andrew Cartmel; the other was a novel for juniors entitled *Doctor Who and the Mandroids*, which went off to Target Books editor Nigel Robinson. After a good while I received replies to both. Andrew Cartmel sent me an example of how a script should be formatted and I had to eat humble pie and accept I'd got it all wrong (which I did). And Nigel Robinson sent me some constructive criticism, part of which said, "I think you have some talent as a writer."

Thanks, Nigel. You've no idea how motivating that single sentence was to be. For someone with a very low opinion of himself it was the difference between giving up and carrying on.

Still desperate for a girlfriend, I turned my attention to the local congregation. There was only one young woman in the place who qualified for a serious relationship. She was bubbly and cheerful and seemed to be almost always laughing. She was delightful.

We got on quite well as platonic friends, and I clearly remember the meeting at the Kingdom Hall where she enquired about my age. When I said I was 18, her face screwed up in disbelief. "Is that all?" She was about 24, I think, and if there had been any romantic interest, it flew out of the window at that moment. Unfortunately, for me, I had fallen head over heels in love with her.

After a while I informed the person whom she looked upon as a father figure of my feelings for this woman. Apparently he and his wife had had a secret admiration for one another for months before they started courting. When I confided in him he got very excited, thinking that my situation might mirror theirs.

It didn't.

Things became very awkward after my confidant told the woman I had a crush on her. I had to see this girl twice a week for pretty much 52 weeks of the year, and it was a great source of anxiety for me. Unfortunately, I wouldn't take no for an answer: I embarrassed her quite a lot by staring and looking mournful whenever she was present. I also had a habit of filling up and walking out of meetings. The tears were real, mind. I used to cry myself to sleep at night.

My relationship with my mother was far from good. She accused me of being self-obsessed and arrogant. I didn't really have an answer to this. I was very confused. On occasion I would simply burst into tears while we, as a family, were watching television, and she would just stare at me, her face anguished at not knowing how to react or help. Sometimes I would attempt to explain my feelings.

In one breath I would say something like, "I'm different than other lads. I don't need friends and a girlfriend", and then later, in the same conversation, would put my problems down to not having any friends.

Mum would just stare, completely baffled. "You've just contradicted yourself," she would say.

I would shrug limply. "I know."

The truth is I contradicted myself because I had two opposing points of view battling away inside me. On the one hand I hated the shallowness of everything and the superficiality that I could see absolutely everywhere, and had no desire to win friends who were like that. But, at the same time, I did want friends. I wanted to meet others of my age who were like me.

There didn't seem to be any.

My mentor, Ken, had left the congregation at the Kingdom Hall to devote his life to working at the London headquarters. Now my closest friend was a divorcee named Tom. He was a friendly chap, very melancholy with a tremendous sadness in his eyes, but nice. He took me under his wing and we would go out for a drive in his car. He saw the world the way I saw it: completely fake. But while he was a pal in so many ways, the fact that I was 18 and he was approaching 50 meant he had little time for my childish obsessions. *Doctor Who et al.* were still solitary pursuits, as was my dream of being a writer.

When it became clear that I really wasn't going to pioneer in the house-to-house ministry and that I only ever did it at weekends (as full-time workers did), Mum decided that it was time I got off my lazy backside and took a full-time job. I didn't like this idea one bit. The part-time work was ideal for me because I could get away from the world and chill out. Now this was not going to be the case. I got quietly terrified of the whole notion, until Mum blazed at me so much I applied for a full-time warehouse job at a soft-drinks factory just to get some peace.

Mr Seagrave walked me round the warehouse and introduced me to some of the workers. I said "Hello" and extended my hand, and was greeted pretty much the same way I had been at the supermarket. My heart sank. If I got the job I would be trapped in this environment for eight hours solid. Eight hours of one dimensional conversation, eight hours' vulgar joking, eight hours of football chitchat, eight hours of being a laughing stock.

I wish I were dead.

Mr Seagrave took me back to his office and concluded the interview with a question. "So, then, what do we call you? William or Bill?"

"Oh, not Bill," I replied airily.

"Why not?"

"Well, it conjures up images of some smelly old dosser wearing a flat cap and duffle bag, living in a cardboard box under a bridge in Farnworth."

Mr Seagrave raised an eyebrow and smiled. "My name's Bill," he said.

Done it again. Wish I were dead.

I blushed straight away.

Bill gestured to the window overlooking his little empire. "Well, do you think you could do it?"

A small, T-shirt clad youth zipped passed on a fork-lift truck. The vehicle swung round at lightning speed, its cargo stacked quite high. The boy looked up through his fringe of fair hair, threw a couple of levers, and in seconds deposited his pallet of crates into position. "I don't know," I said, feeling what remained of my self-confidence draining from me. "I mean I doubt I'd have the nerve to drive a fork-lift like that young lad out there."

Bill grinned again. "You would with practice," he said. His tone changed slightly as he added, "And that young lad is actually a young *woman*. In fact, she's my fiancée."

DONE IT AGAIN! I DON'T BELIEVE IT! JUST GIVE UP SPEAKING, WILL YOU!

I walked from the premises knowing for sure that I'd blown it. Then, about a week later, I was asked to go in for a second interview, this time for a post in quality control. Apparently, Bill had recommended me to the production manager. Red-faced and intense, Mr Cordingley showed me the makeshift lab and the syrup-mixing room. It turned out I had been recommended for the role of quality controller. I accepted immediately.

Mum was very impressed. "Ooh, that's quite a responsible position, you know. You'll have to dress up for it." And so I did. I strolled in the following Monday in a navy blue suit, a white shirt and a bright yellow tie. An umbrella rested on my arm. A lot of the women working on the production line assumed I was a rep! I asked for the line supervisor, and a medium-sized, blond-haired man called Graham blithely approached, to whom I introduced myself as the new QC. His dreamy expression fell into a smirk as he looked me up and down and took in the ill-coordinated colour scheme. Then, both he and Mr Cordingley kitted me out with a white coat, disposable paper hat and a pair of wellington boots. I was to spend the first couple of weeks on the production line, then some time on the syrup-mixing procedure, finally moving on to the quality control.

John Greenhalgh, a young man in his twenties, was assigned to show me the ropes on the factory floor. I was so utterly overwhelmed by the sudden change in my working life that I barely spoke – and I *never* smiled. I had reverted back to the 11-year-old William who had just started secondary school.

All the same feelings. I want to cry. I hate it. I wish I were dead.

John concluded that I was a bit dozy, and tended to sing "We're wide awake!", the theme tune to the breakfast television programme *The Wide Awake Club*. The situation worsened when I let it be known that I was religious...

John's workmate, Mark, shook his head and waved his hands in mock determination. "Keep him away from me! I don't want no Joseph Witness over 'ere."

On my first break, everyone was curious about the new recruit. I sat in the canteen and suffered their scrutiny. They could tell all too easily what kind of boy I was. A shy boy, a bashful boy, a terrified boy. I was good sport.

"Who are you?" demanded one of the warehouse lads.

A woman in her early thirties sniggered like a giddy schoolgirl. "He's our new QC."

"What does QC stand for?" one of the others quizzed, genuinely bemused.

Before I could answer, someone said, "Queer c***!"

They all fell about in hysterics. I blushed a deep crimson, which made them laugh even more. All-too-familiar territory.

> Intense music. Eyes change to white. The creature turns tables over.
> The workers scramble for the exit, the women scream in terror.

September brought the twenty-sixth series of *Doctor Who*. Still screened against *Coronation Street*, which was now heavily promoting its new third weekly episode, it was a marvel anyone watched the Doctor at all.

The last episode of the season was transmitted on 6 December 1989, and there was no announcement following the programme as to when the series would return. I scoured the pages of *Doctor Who Magazine* for news over the ensuing months. Producer John Nathan-Turner announced his resignation. I wondered who would be replacing him and in what direction they would take the show next. The months rolled by with no announcement as to who would be succeeding John or, for that matter, when Series 27 would be screened. Then a dreadful realization began to dawn on me.

It *is* going to come back, isn't it?

Syrup-room operator Wayne returned from his holiday and began training me in the ways of the soft drink. I found the mixing of ingredients fascinating, but dreaded the day when I would be left on my own. I had to learn this before I could be trained in quality control.

While spending time with Wayne, I learned a great deal about his favourite rock star Gary Numan. Originally born as Gary Webb, Numan had suffered with fits of anger as a youngster and had been prescribed valium by a child psychiatrist. I found all this rather enthralling, especially as the unconventional singer had found it hard identifying with people and struggled to maintain friendships. Wayne told me that Gary started out as a punk in 1977 purely as a means of signing a record deal. As soon as he was established he switched to synthesizers. Nobody, including his record company, thought this would pay off. However, Gary's instincts were right.

The *Replicas* album of 1979 reached Number One, in the wake of Numan's Chart topping single "Are 'Friends' Electric?". His early music had very personalized lyrics set to a science-fiction backdrop. His themes of alienation and uncompromising individualism appealed very much. His debut album, *Tubeway Army*, though quite sparse by today's music standards, lyrically had much to offer a detached, lonely young soul like me. One of my big favourites was "My Shadow in Vain", where Gary sings about preferring to die rather than cry; wishing he was someone else; seeing things as black or white; not being able to discern lies; blotting out emotional pain with drugs; and standing at the crossroads of sanity and madness. Back then this was *very* potent stuff indeed.

Wayne told me that Gary Numan had enjoyed five years' success (1979–1984), before the major radio stations blanked him for not conforming to current music trends. I was staggered to learn that Numan was actually still going strong, thanks to a legion of loyal fans, of which Wayne was one.

My first experience of Gary Numan was a live album entitled *The Skin Mechanic*. I was blown away by the power of the synthesizers and the reaction of the crowd was awesome. The music seemed very similar to the BBC Radiophonic Workshop stuff I loved so much – but here it had lyrics too. Unfortunately, with the live album, I could barely make out what Gary was singing. It was only when Wayne brought in some studio albums with the lyrics printed that I started to appreciate just how much Gary and I had in common on an emotional level. Songs like "Are 'Friends' Electric?" appealed because of the sci-fi backdrop, but also the loneliness exhibited in the personalized parts. I loved all his early hits, which, with the release of his second Number One album *The Pleasure Principle*, marked a departure from the sci-fi fantasies and exposed the man at his most vulnerable.

"Cars", for example, is all about feeling safer driving down the high street than walking down it. "Complex" and "Remind Me To Smile" are about his deep-seated feelings of paranoia as he was suddenly thrust before an adoring public and a hostile press, while "We Are Glass" explores what it is to be both strong and delicate at the same time. Over subsequent albums, Gary progressed from vulnerability to depression and self-loathing, to pure unadulterated fury.

I later learned that the 'friends', in inverted commas, in "Are 'Friends' Electric?" are not just androids in a story, but rather a reference to his own struggle to maintain relationships. Listening to him speak on interview records brought further insight. He seemed so much like me in so many ways, his views about the world, his raw honesty, his knack of offending people without realizing it.

There were two areas where we were like chalk and cheese: I believed in God, he was a devout atheist; I was still a virgin, he'd enjoyed all that the rock and roll lifestyle had to offer. These issues aside, I found there was something about the man that drew me to him. His undiluted electronic music that touched my raw emotions, his obscure lyrics that were often just a garble of feelings, his war against convention, his determination to assert himself without compromise.

Life at Alpine Soft Drinks suddenly changed for the better during the run-up to Christmas. Once again I had made a comedy review on cassette where I impersonated some of the more idiosyncratic characters in the place, most of which were management. Unlike *But Yes But, But Nothing* at the supermarket, which tried to tell a story, this time I just went for little sketches, incorporating sound effects and music, and called the result *The Alpine Review 1989*. I took it in one afternoon when the production line had ground to a halt and played it to the team.

Well, the girls were in hysterics, and insisted that I play various sections back, including a song about them I'd written set to the theme music of *Neighbours*. They loved it, and as a result they loved me. I had, at long last, succeeded in persuading them that I had a fun side. Other end-of-year reviews included a horror-themed *Nightmare on Ravenscraig Road* and the sci-fi bonanza *Alpine Trek: The Search for Finney*.

Once I'd grasped the production line and the syrup room, the time came for me to learn the QC job for real. A man from Birmingham head office came up every fortnight in order to introduce me to the laboratory tests one by one. Named Ray, he was a gentle, quiet-spoken chap, who made me feel safe. I liked him a lot. He never rushed me, he never asked why it took so long for me to grasp certain principles, and he appreciated my honest streak. In fact, it made him laugh. "What I like about William," he would inform my managers with a big grin on his face, "is that if he tells you a lie to cover up a mistake he's made, he comes back half an hour later and confesses it!"

That was true. Sometimes I'd make a blunder and try to talk my way out of it. When Ray accepted the lie without hesitation, I would get a huge fit of guilt, and would go back: "Ray, that isn't what happened at all. I just made it up." He couldn't be angry with me because he found the confessions amusing. On another occasion he declared, "You could trust William with your life! And that's not something you can say about everybody."

Best not tell him I'm an out-and-out coward then.

I used to get anxious about the speed at which I could take information on board. Ray would look over his glasses and ask, "Now what do we do? Can you remember?" And I'd shake my head and feel pathetic.

"William," he'd say in exasperation. "You can quote me scripture chapter and verse."

"I know."

"So why can't you remember this?"

"I don't know."

They were hoping that I would be able to do all the tests by myself and, when I initially complained that it wasn't possible to conduct every test and check the fresh batches before they went to the production line every hour and on the hour, they dismissed it as me being a bit slow. But after a while they saw that I did indeed have a point, and trained one of the production line girls, Elaine, to be my partner. For the next five years she, John and I would enjoy a good working relationship.

Being in the company of the Alpine crew daily made me more and more aware of the vast differences between my religious stance and the views of the world in general. I would hear members of the team gossiping on a Monday morning about who had "copped off" with whom and, while at one time I would have found this kind of talk unseemly and revolting, part of me now was absolutely fascinated. The contradictory feelings had taken on a sexual dimension.

On one occasion a man in his early 20s started getting giddy and silly, winding up the staff. A girl identified the source of the man's playfulness. "It's because he hasn't had any for ages." She addressed the man. "You're desperate to get your leg over, aren't you?"

The man gave a mischievous grin and nodded. In reply the girl said rather casually, "Right, well go to a club tonight, pick up an easy tart, and give her a good going over, because you're doing our heads in."

The following morning the man breezed into work, confirmed that he had followed the advice given the previous day, and felt all the better for it.

I was astounded at how casual they were about sex. The moral framework within which I operated, and concern about unwanted pregnancy, sexually transmitted diseases and AIDS, simply were not there. I began to obsess about this kind of freedom, and secretly desired it. I was suddenly at odds with myself, wanting to respect the Bible standard, and at the same time being overwhelmed by the exploits of my workmates.

I was amazed when, one break-time, they discussed the subject of being unfaithful to their partners. After comparing examples, one of them blurted, "Let's face it, we all have except for William." I blushed and waited for someone in the room to protest, "Hang about, speak for yourself, *I've* not." I was both appalled and profoundly disturbed when no one did.

Sometimes the subject of religion would be introduced and people would fire questions at me. One man got agitated and announced, "I don't believe in all that crap. I mean, where is he, this God? Where is he when people need him? When disasters happen, and that."

My attempts at explaining were dismissed immediately. Then a younger man walked in. "What are we talking about?" he breezed. The first man scowled at me. "Religion," he said. The younger man, a Roman Catholic, retorted, "Well I believe that when your number's up, your number's up, and he takes you."

The first man nodded his agreement, God now suddenly looking cool and peer-friendly. "Yeah, I do."

FAKE! A completely pointless and sterile conversation.

My interest in *The Incredible Hulk* was rekindled when my local ITV station Granada showed the pilot film. Now 20 years old, I was appreciative of the writing, directing and production, and realized it was all down to one man, Kenneth Johnson. It was he who had taken the basic premise of the comic book and woven in all the stuff about tapping into one's hidden strengths and the manipulation of DNA to make the thing more palatable. It was also his idea to have a tabloid journalist relentlessly pursue the tragic David Banner across America. I watched the film repeatedly and Johnson became my new hero.

The desire to see episodes from the resulting TV series was strong and so I wrote to Granada and asked them to show some of the old series, which they did a few months later. I like to think they did it on my prompting. I identified with the David Banner character, arriving into a new town at the start of each episode and settling for dead-end jobs despite his great talents. One of the episodes shown was *The Psychic* by Karen Harris and Jill Sherman. In it, Banner attempts suicide, and laments that the curse is no longer the creature he turns into, but rather the man he has become. I *so* identified with that.

I was also completely obsessed with the opening title sequence to the series, which is made up of clips from the pilot film and is accompanied by narration, once again written by Kenneth Johnson. Whenever I felt threatened or anxious I would go over the narration to myself or mimic the metamorphosis sound effect. Sometimes I would just play the title sequence on video over and over.

The images, as in my childhood, were potent: Dr Banner strapped into the gamma radiation unit, his DNA mutating with the overdose, Banner wrenching himself while undoing a wheel nut on his car, the transformation, the relentless pursuit by reporter Jack McGee, the exploding laboratory and the creature being blamed for the apparent murder of David Banner.

The final scene is of David standing over his gravestone. He sighs deeply and looks directly at the viewer. At that moment the picture freezes and the right hand side of his face becomes that of the raging creature, with the legend "The Incredible Hulk" superimposed.

Around the same time, a superb London Weekend Television adaptation of *Jekyll and Hyde* was screened. It starred Michael Caine, and he gave a brilliant performance as both the ethically troubled Dr Jekyll *and* his evil, corrupt darker side. I recorded the film and watched it many times over, Caine being so mesmerizing in the two roles. This Robert Louis Stephenson classic was written and directed by David Wickes. The revelation that Jekyll and Hyde are one and the same person is not really a shocker these days (what with the expression "like a Jekyll and Hyde" being in common usage!), and so Wickes produced a great character piece exploring the motives of the protagonist, as well as weaving in some contemporary fears about genetic manipulation. In this regard it bore more than a little resemblance to *The Incredible Hulk*.

All my life I had been drawn to stories where an individual undergoes a metamorphosis or suffers from a split personality. I had an obsession with characters who could possess in themselves strong opposing points of view and yet still be the same person. The Doctor in *Doctor Who* was the ultimate example: seven very different interpretations of the same man. The aforementioned David Banner and his rage unbound in *The Incredible Hulk* was another.

The conflict between my religious instincts and fleshly desires was growing all the time. It was as though I was dividing into two people who hated one another, the one operating on principle and despising godless conduct, the other resisting the restraints placed by spirituality and resenting the chains of the moral code. I was becoming a walking paradox, and the *Jekyll and Hyde* TV movie reflected it like a mirror.

Some Witness youths had organized a night out in Manchester. They were going for a Chinese meal and, for once, they had invited me. My first instinct was to say no, but I knew that this was an ideal way to make friends and perhaps project myself in a fresh light. So, rather nervously and reluctantly, I said yes.

I got dressed up and made myself look as presentable as I could. Mum was really excited in my behalf. "You never know," she said. "This might be where everything changes for you. You'll probably get on with everybody like a house on fire and make new friends. You might even meet a girl you like."

Don't think I haven't thought of it!

Everything Mum said seemed very plausible and realistic. I had eased up somewhat since starting at the factory, I'd become more assertive, and so it didn't appear fanciful that I might come home with lots of phone numbers and make the right impression with the girls. I couldn't wait for the evening to begin.

The group consisted of a few local young people and an assortment of youths from a different congregation. There were no older people present, which was contrary to the advice given in Witness literature, and something I did not feel comfortable about. I tended to feel safer around older people. We arrived in town a little early, and so paid a visit to a nearby pub.

> I hate it. Too many people. I'm sure they're staring at me. I must stand out like a sore thumb. They will surely know I've never been out before. Women are looking me up and down, women with low-cut dresses, their eyes burning right through me. Younger girls in tight black leather, smoking, smoking and watching. Too much noise, the music's loud. Too much pushing and shoving. I'm feeling nervous, I'm feeling ill. I wish I were dead.

Sensing that I was having trouble, one of the lads I had respect for tried to break the ice. "I've got that video in the car for you, mate."

Someone else said, "Oh? What video's that?"

"Gary Numan," he replied. "I borrowed it."

Straight away there were groans amongst the company. "He's queer, isn't he?" someone piped.

I cleared my throat. "Er, no. I don't think he is."

A young woman put in her contribution. "Oh, he *is*. It's obvious."

"What is?" Someone else quizzed as they brought their pint across.

"Gary Numan's a queer."

"Oh, definitely."

I said nothing.

> HE ISN'T!!! Seething fury: shivering in the night rain, adrenalin rush, glowing DNA, white eyes, dramatic music.

During the actual meal itself, everybody talked about friends in other congregations and exchanged gossip. They all knew one another and were catching up on old times. Occasionally, someone would turn round and say, "All right, mate?" I would nod and smile, and then they would turn back to the conversation. I so wanted to be a part of it, but nothing they talked about interested me. It was all clean and wholesome and a world away from the soft drinks factory, but it still tended to revolve around who was going out with who, what someone in another congregation had said about someone else, the latest developments in the football world, someone's new car and how fast it goes, and what they all thought of the current pop music scene.

What do I say? They might as well be speaking another language.

For two hours solid I sat at the end of the table and said nothing. All I could think of was how I so desperately wanted to go home and listen to some Moody Blues. "Melancholy Man" – very apt.

Eventually I was dropped off at home, and as I slid in my front door key, I anticipated telling my mother what a complete disaster the night had been. She had been so enthusiastic and I, in my mind's eye, had seen just how great it was going to be.

"Well?" she said excitedly as I walked into the living room. "How did you go on?"

I burst into tears. "It was awful. I just couldn't find a way to get in with them, even though they tried to involve me. I'm never going to have any friends. I'm just not like them." Then a thought occurred to me. "I can't see how I'm ever going to fit in. Even when the New World comes I'll be on my own."

Mum looked very pained and tried to subdue her frustration. "Don't be ridiculous," she said. "Everything will be perfect in the New World. It will be different for you then." Although she had not returned to Jehovah's Witnesses herself, she didn't like any indication of me giving it up. She worried that I might withdraw from society completely and she wanted me to mix with people. She was also probably very well aware of my gullibility and believed that I would be safe among Christian people.

I'm always going to be on my own. I wish I were dead.

It really did seem to be me *versus* the rest of the world. I confided in my pen pal Dominic, and in response he sent me a video to watch. It was of the 1968 television series *The Prisoner*, starring Patrick McGoohan. He thought I might identify with it, and boy was he right!

The Prisoner tells the story of a government agent who turns his back on the world system and becomes resigned to maintaining his individuality. While at home, packing for a much-needed holiday, he is rendered unconscious and then imprisoned in a strange island community called the Village: a bizarre parody of the world he thinks he's left behind. There are a lot of colourful people in the Village, but no one is identified by name, only by number. He is Number Six, and his various interrogators take the station of Number Two. But who, wonders the prisoner, is Number One? Who is the unseen ruler of the world?

My mother told me she had always found the programme irritating because there were no clear answers. She thought its creator and star, Patrick McGoohan, had pulled a massive con trick on the TV viewing public, and she wasn't alone in that opinion. But while I acknowledged that the series was deeply allegorical and complex, its basic theme seemed pretty obvious to me: *we are all prisoners of the system and, ultimately, prisoners of ourselves.* This is borne out by the fact that Number Six never really escapes, and in the end he and Number One turn out to be aspects of the same person.

After a while I concluded that those who couldn't see what it was really about couldn't see it because they, in real life, simply went along with the flow. People who watched *The Prisoner* and *The Tripods* and dismissed them by saying things like "Oh, I'd just tell them what they want to know and live in the Village", or "I'd just get capped and be happy", were revealing to me more about themselves than they realized. I abhorred such thinking.

One of my favourite episodes is *The General* by Joshua Adam. Is education a means of indoctrination? In this instalment a professor has developed something called Speed Learn whereby citizens can acquire a university degree in 15 seconds. This is done through a super computer nicknamed the General. It's claimed there is no question it cannot answer. The Prisoner rises to the challenge and feeds it a single word which results in the machine's destruction. The word? The only question the General cannot answer: "Why?"

Another episode I closely identify with is *A Change of Mind* by Roger Parkes. Are psychiatrists and psychologists merely reinforcing the system's brainwashing? Still refusing to conform, the Prisoner is branded "unmutual" and is shunned by the Village community. When that doesn't work Number Two threatens "instant social conversion", a process involving the removal of the aggressive frontal lobe of the brain. After a while the Prisoner realizes that nothing has actually happened, he's just been conditioned to believe it.

Certainly I was feeling trapped, as though I was the poor subject of some sick joke and that the whole world was in on it. The more they laughed at me, the more I resisted them. The more they tried to make me conform, the more I was determined not to crack.

> "I will not be pushed, filed, stamped, indexed, briefed, debriefed or numbered."

I had found a new lifeline.

Simple Babylon, 1991–92

EVERY NOW AND THEN WE in quality control would get a visit from site manager Alf Hunt, whose serious no-nonsense approach and commanding voice scared everybody half to death. I was especially nervous of him, until one day, when I was checking some Britvic grapefruit compound and had to declare that it was well and truly off, Alf commended me for saving the company thousands of pounds. After this I felt more at ease with him.

Alf became rather fascinated by my religious beliefs and whenever he visited the factory he would approach me out of the blue and ask a question. "All right, William, where in the Bible does it say you mustn't swear?" And I'd reply without hesitation: "Ephesians Chapter five." In response he would roar with laughter.

One of the managers, a man called Ian, also enjoyed a good religious discussion, and sometimes we would get carried away and forget about our work.

Production manager Graham took a slightly different approach. He would slap me on the back or give me an exaggerated hug, and adopt an overtly cheerful smile. "So then, Willie. When are Ji-nova and his lads coming to do us all in?"

A young girl once approached me and said, "God, I bet you're dead brainy with loads of O levels and A levels and all that." Very reluctantly I owned up to having O levels in English Language and in Art and a string of CSEs (which are a step down from the GCE qualification), and no A levels at all.

She frowned, really perplexed. "So how come you talk dead posh and know loads of stuff?"

> Well, first of all, I'm not dead posh.

I shrugged. "I suppose it's because I read obscure material. *Doctor Who Magazine* and *TV Zone* are full of stuff about television production. And I learn a lot about religion, science and history through *Awake!* magazine and the Kingdom Hall." Her eyes had glazed before I'd finished my sentence.

In a different context, John Cordingley, the production manager, observed that I had a slightly aloof tone of voice. "I'm afraid, son, you've got a bit of a chip on your shoulder." I objected to his saying this at the time, but in retrospect I know he was absolutely right.

Christmas parties were a great highlight for the staff, and I would ache inside as they recounted their extravaganza. Their photos said it all. Eyes dilated, sagging faces, slouched profiles. My mind boggled when I heard of various individuals pairing up for a bit of one-off sexual excitement. I would grieve at the sight of the pictures. Pretty young girls looking haggard and spaced out. What a waste.

> They seem so happy. They really don't care. They don't worry about the consequences, they just enjoy themselves. Ideas of God and morality never come into it. I wish *I* didn't care. I wish I could be free.

One woman was having an affair and openly talked about it. "I told him," the gossipy tale would begin. "I said, 'What are you doing with a woman like me?' And he said, 'But I love you, kid,' and I said, 'You're mad. You should be out there, going with as many girls as you can.'" And she meant it too.

One of the most popular characters in the place was the fitter Dave. He was so utterly relaxed about life and very cynical. He reminded me of Rowan Atkinson's Blackadder character, rolling his eyes in mock boredom when people said things not to his liking and making sarcastic quips about royalty being parasites, hating the corruption amongst politicians, and referring to a certain BBC soap opera as *Deadenders*. He never spoke about life at home and no one dared to ask. I thought he was great. He really made me laugh with his wry observations.

He once walked into the canteen, his face a right picture as he had had quite a day of it, looked out of the window and addressed the heavy grey clouds above. "You can keep your everlasting life!" By rights I should have been appalled at his addressing God in that way, but I'm afraid I just started laughing.

The inner conflict was growing all the time. If I wasn't going to abandon my religion, the wisest thing would have been to put the "other" side of life out of my mind and just get on with it. But I couldn't. The other side of life fascinated me, it occupied my thoughts quite a lot, especially if my workmates were indulging in some juicy story – the details would stay with me for the remainder of the day. I was both loathing it and revelling in it. I was obsessed with it.

My workmate John heard a new REM song on the radio, and was so put in mind of me, he bought me a copy. It turned out to be "Losing My Religion", in which singer Michael Stipe talks of being in a corner and choosing his confessions. I couldn't be offended because I appreciated John's motive. He was simply saying, "This is like you."

By this time I had become absorbed in *Dead Poets Society*, a movie starring Robin Williams as inspirational teacher John Keating, who has been assigned to his old prep school. In the film he encourages his students to seize the day, to be free thinkers and embrace their passions and ambitions. Each of the boys has a dream or an aspiration, one to be an actor, another to overcome his crippling shyness.

One of my favourite scenes is where Keating has the boys walking about a courtyard in a way that reflects their personality. When one of the boys doesn't join in and Keating inquires why, the boy shrugs and says he's exercising the right not to walk. The teacher loves this because it demonstrates that the boy has understood the point.

However, the other teachers at the school voice their concerns over Keating's methods. The system demands conformity, the purpose of the school is to prepare students for university – not to encourage free thinking. The boy Neil, who wants to be an actor and who admirably proves his talent in an amateur production, has to battle not only the system but his own dictatorial father, who demands that he abandon his acting and concentrate on studying Law. He is so forceful and rigid that Neil commits suicide – and Keating gets the blame. To the horror of his loyal students Keating is reprimanded and dismissed from his job.

I was so moved by the story and had personalized it so much that I talked at length about it to anyone who would listen.

It's so true. It's so true.

A presenter on a young people's TV talk show declared, "I saw that Dead Po-its So-sigh-e-i last night. It was crap!!"

Enough said.

The situation with the girl whom I loved at the Kingdom Hall had reached breaking point. I wouldn't take no for an answer, clinging on to the slightest hint of her possibly changing her mind (signals that were *not there*, I have to say in retrospect), and she getting all the more impatient as a result. A chat with my now favourite elder Phil set the wheels of reconciliation in motion, and we made an appointment to visit the girl in her flat. Even then I was hoping that once she had spoken to me properly in relaxed surroundings there might be a change of heart.

I took in my surroundings quickly and imagined myself living there as her husband. Phil acted as mediator and we aired our grievances. Once the tension had abated, I made some attempts at humour, which fell completely flat. Both she and Phil responded with awkward silences and just smiled at the floor or into their cups of tea. I'd got it wrong again.

The visit concluded and Phil took me home. On the way, lost in thought as I mulled over different parts of the conversation, I absent-mindedly ran my fingers across my chin. Something appeared to be stuck on it, rough and hard. Was it a spot? It didn't feel like one. I dug in a fingernail and prized off the artefact. My face flushed and I could feel my cheeks burning with a mixture of emotions: deep-seated failure, embarrassment, *anger*. My eyes filled as I rolled the blood-stained toilet paper between my finger and thumb. Then I cleared my throat. "Phil?" I asked.

"Mmm?"

"Did I have this paper stuck to my chin all the time I was in there?"

It was Phil's turn to clear his throat. "Yes, William," he said gently. "You did."

I wish I were dead.

Mum and Stan had bought a caravan on an attractive site in Cheshire. I attended the local Kingdom Hall there, and found to my delight that one or two couples actually lived on the site as permanent residents. A couple named John and Val became firm friends. I got on very well with John because he didn't suffer fools gladly and I found him amusing. Val was more like a second mum, and she doted on me a little because I reminded her of her son who had, like me, suffered in times past because of his sensitive disposition.

There was one woman in the congregation to whom I warmed pretty much immediately. She was 18 years my senior, but looked considerably younger, and in many ways seemed quite my mirror image. We got on very well and she laughed at my jokes – and genuinely laughed at them too. I felt so secure and at peace that I could have married her there and then. She seemed to realize this (perhaps learning that I'd written a poem about her!) and gently let me down. That night I wept buckets at John and Val's. In retrospect I think a lot of my other emotional anxieties probably contributed to the breakdown, my latest crush simply being the trigger.

Sometime after this, I took another break from work and visited the caravan. I went to the local Kingdom Hall meeting and was offered a lift back to the site by a pleasant man in his forties and his teenage daughter Melanie. I was quite struck by her because she bore a little resemblance to the girl whom I'd helped while on holiday. Anyway, they parked up at the site and began telling their life history, that the wife had gone and they were a single-parent family. Mel was in the pioneer ministry and was quite impressed that I was going it alone in the Witnesses. The foundations of a nice friendship had been laid.

The following morning I met with the local group for the ministry – and there was Mel, as beautiful as I'd remembered, with her fine brown hair and sparkling blue eyes. Her smile greeted me as I entered and my heart performed a rather impressive backward somersault. "I was hoping you'd be coming out," she enthused. "I had a dream about you last night. It was weird. I dreamt I was working with you on the ministry."

I was rather staggered by this, and hoped I was reading the signs correctly, for by this time I appreciated I had a problem interpreting facial expressions and body language. I didn't always get it right.

And so Mel and I paired up and knocked on our first door. Her presentation was so eloquent and skilled I felt like a complete idiot. What I did on the doors was quite bumbling and shambolic, my nerves getting the better of me. I also had a problem thinking of something to say *in between* doors. I was so overwhelmed by her beauty, and by the simple fact that a *girl* had chosen to work with me, with the express intent of getting to know me better, that I couldn't think of anything remotely interesting to say. I started to talk about ridiculous things, trying to be funny. Later, as we met up with the rest of her group, I saw Melanie's friends looking all excited and raising their eyebrows, as if to say, "Have you hit it off?" She gave a slight shake of the head. That I *had* read right.

> I've blown it AGAIN. I want to burst into tears. Give me another chance, Mel. Have me round for dinner with your dad, like it was when you gave me a lift. Sit with me in the Book Study and listen to my answers. Chat with me at the end. Come to my congregation and see me give a talk. The person you were interested in is still here. I'm here, Mel, locked up inside. If you find the right key, you'll find me. Just one more chance, Mel. Just one more chance. Please.

At times I would hear her crack a joke with her friends and they would all laugh at her observations on life. She had my sense of humour. I once heard her impersonating comedian Ben Elton and retreading a routine she'd seen on his BBC programme *The Man From Auntie*. The other young people had tears streaming down their faces.

> I love that, Mel. I watch that show. I appreciate his take on life. Just one more chance, Mel. Just one more chance.

Dominic had proved to be a good pen friend, and so I scoured the pages of *Doctor Who Magazine* and *TV Zone* to try and find a female equivalent. One particular entry caught my eye. A *Star Trek* fan called Julie, who was about my age, seemed like fun, and so I mailed her a letter and tape and hoped for the best. The tape contained the usual sickening self-obsessed babble from me, detailing my tastes in sci-fi and my rather traumatic childhood. I also put on a few Moody Blues tracks including "Nights in White Satin", as well as one or two Gary Numan songs.

Please like me. Please like me. Please like me. Please like me.

It was at this stage that I started to call myself Will as opposed to William. I had always liked my name because it is associated with having such qualities as resolve and determination, but it tended to sound too regal. My family had called me Bill from a very early age, and while in the family this felt perfect, it didn't quite gel when outsiders said it. I decided it was time for a bit of re-invention. There was Will Parker in *The Tripods*, Will Riker in *Star Trek: The Next Generation*, the actor Wil Wheaton and Will Smith in *The Fresh Prince of Bel Air*. For the first time in my life I was going to do something trendy, and on the tape I addressed to Julie, I introduced myself as Will.

What I got in return was a huge packet containing a multi-paged letter (which made references to my "gorgeous voice"!), a tape containing childhood history, examples of musical tastes and a photograph. But it wasn't from Julie. She had passed my letter onto her younger sister Karen because she thought that we had more in common.

And indeed we did. Karen adored *Star Trek: The Next Generation* as much as I loved *Doctor Who*. She had also been bullied a lot at school due to being "quite a bit overweight" and felt rejected by her parents, in particular by her father. Suicide attempts and self-mutilation had followed as a result. She hated herself.

Through the correspondence we enjoyed over those autumn months, we got to know one another very well. I plied her with compliments to try to counteract her feelings of self-loathing and she did likewise for me. Tapes, videos and books were exchanged. We got on famously.

> One problem: I'm one of Jehovah's Witnesses. She is not. I have deep-seated religious views, she does not. I attend three meetings a week, she does not. My view of the future is moulded by my beliefs, her beliefs are completely different. I don't celebrate Christmas or birthdays, she does. I don't have any time at all for practices rooted in ancient pagan religions, she loves astrology. We're incompatible. No we're not. Yes we are. No we're not. Yes we are. I have a choice: give up the Witnesses or give up Karen.

The inner conflict was there again.

I told Karen about my religious beliefs and discovered that she knew a bit about them. Her uncle had become a Witness and had been ostracized by her family as a result. One of her workmates was an ex-Witness too.

Don't tell anyone about her at the Kingdom Hall.

After several long chats on the phone, we decided to meet.

Would Granada Studio Tours be open on New Year's Eve? Karen told me it was, and so that became our meeting place. The weather was atrocious, the wind raged and the rain heaved.

I couldn't believe what I was doing. The approaching car park would contain a Ford Escort and my very first date. I laughed to myself and contemplated how most lads would have had several dates and lost their virginity well before the age of 21. I peered over the wall of the car park, scanned the sea of vehicles, and there she was. Long gypsy-like garments draped around her form. Her dyed-black hair was tied up in a bun and long earrings dangled over her shoulders. She stood with the car door open, looking cold and terrified. I waved and she smiled vaguely. Synchronized throat-clearing followed as we both realized what we were doing.

I felt extremely awkward and paranoid. I'd heard that the gentleman was supposed to walk on the outside of the pavement to protect his lady, and since I had only remembered to do it half way through the date, I got quite anxious. As I started to explain myself, she told me I was doing OK. In fact she was amazed that I didn't mind walking with her in public. Apparently she had a friendship with a young man who would ring her up and tell her all his problems, and they would meet and talk in his car. She was a sort of agony aunt to him, but only ever in his car – he didn't want to be seen with her in the street because she was overweight. By comparison I was quite reassuring.

I couldn't understand the weight thing myself. All right, so she was a bit overweight. So what? She was also very pretty, quite a looker, in fact. As the date neared its end I told her that I didn't know what all the fuss was about and that I thought she was very attractive. She responded with a smile and said, "Well I think the same about you. You're not that bad-looking actually."

You're only saying that because I said you are pretty. You're just being nice.

Once we got back to the car, I decided to try something. Not the sort of thing most lads try when they go in a car with a girl they've fallen for. I reached into a carrier bag and produced a Bible. She froze as I started telling her all about the last days, Armageddon, the New World, and what she had to do to get there.

Now come on, girls, isn't that just the best way to reach a woman's heart?

Amazingly, the friendship did not come to an abrupt end there. We continued to chat on the phone and met up a couple more times after that. My mother took to her instantly, and in her own mind decided that this girl would probably be my future wife. I was in a dream, and I was in love.

"I love you, Karen."

"I love you too, Will," came the silky reply. I adored that voice. But I knew each time she said those words, they would be followed by "as a friend".

I knew that Karen loved me deeply and affectionately. There was abundant evidence in the way she looked at me, the way she spoke to me. We went for walks in Worsley Woods, and for the first time I felt complete. Now *we* were one of those couples laughing and walking hand in hand.

She showed me the songs she had been writing on her guitar and synthesizer. They were really good. One, called "Friends", reflected her love of wildlife and her anger towards those who endangered it; another one, "Standing in a Field", told of her great loneliness and how she wished someone would just come and sweep her off her feet. It was little wonder that she reacted to my tape the way she did.

The one thing she had that I didn't was the maturity to see that our friendship couldn't really be anything more than that. I refused to accept it, but she very bravely embraced the awful truth. She couldn't entertain the sorts of things I believed, and I couldn't abandon them. No one was making me adhere to a religion I didn't want: my parents weren't in it, it had been my choice all along. I could have walked away at any time, but I wouldn't – and she *knew* I wouldn't.

I had always wanted to attend a *Doctor Who* convention and, for the first time, one of the main events was to be held in Manchester. I was terribly excited about it and looked forward to seeing the actors who had starred in the show and meeting other fans.

Karen accompanied me, but was preoccupied with her grandma who was seriously ill. In the end, she decided to go home, and I felt awful afterwards because I did not abandon the show to comfort her. The one thing her attending *did* do was give her the convention bug. She and Julie attended numerous *Star Trek* events after that!

And so my younger brother Matthew and I continued to mix with the *Who* faithful. I was quite overwhelmed by all these people from across the UK who had gathered together to celebrate the good Doctor. I was even more astounded to hear tales of individuals tape-recording episodes from the television before the advent of home video. How on earth could we have all thought of doing the same thing without having ever met? Then my eyes fixed on a sweatshirt someone was wearing. The legend read "Gary Numan Outland Tour 1991". How absolutely bizarre.

I was desperate to make friends with at least one person there. Oh, we would have *so* much in common. I approached one of the stewards. "Hi," I said. "I'm Will. I've never been to one of these before. Have you?"

The steward was very friendly. "Oh yes, lots of times. I helped organize it."

Imagine that. He helped organize it. Now – what to talk about.

"What do think about John Nathan-Turner?" I quizzed. "I think he ruined *Doctor Who*. I think he killed it off doing stupid stories. When you think of *Delta and the Bannermen* and *The Happiness Patrol.*"

The steward just looked at me. "He also produced *The Keeper of Traken* and *Logopolis.*"

I had to admit they were two of my all-time favourites. "Well, yeah."

"And *Kinda, The Visitation, Earthshock, The Five Doctors, Revelation of the Daleks, The Curse of Fenric.*"

And they were classics too. I decided to change tack, still pulling a face. "And then he kept altering the theme music."

The steward made a show of glancing over my shoulder and being busy. "I've just seen someone I need to talk to. Excuse me." I smiled and nodded – and completely failed to see what I had done. It was only afterwards, when I went back over the conversation, that it dawned on me.

It was little wonder I had no close male friends of my own age. I didn't make any new ones that day.

At home after my first *Doctor Who* Convention, 1992.
My eyes and non-smile say it all.

My friendship with Karen peaked when we attended the Warner Bros cinema in Bury to watch *Star Trek VI: The Undiscovered Country*. This was a great milestone in *Trek* history as it marked the very last adventure to feature the original cast, Captain Kirk, Mr Spock, *et al*. As such it was quite an emotional climax.

Karen and I sat near the front, cuddled up and held hands. It was a warmth I had never experienced before, and I craved for more of it. Every so often, she would glance down at our clasped hands, and I knew the occasion was just as special to her as it was to me. On arriving home, I plucked up the courage to kiss her on the cheek. It took me ages to summon the courage, but she knew me well and understood. She gave me a bag of goodies, including a brooch and a poem about friendship. I was really moved by this.

She came down a few weeks later and we played records and chatted. I had opened the budgie cage to allow the bird room to exercise its wings. As it flitted from the cage, it sounded off an unexpected squawk. Both Karen and I jumped out of our wits. In shock she swore under her breath.

And this was the point where I woke from the fantasy. I wasn't offended or disgusted, I just realized that we were both playing off to the other's expectations. I had learned not to talk religion, she had learned to watch her Ps and Qs. Both of us were playing parts in a story; we weren't ourselves, not truly.

A while after, I raised this issue on a tape, and I breathed a sigh of relief when the reply came back. She felt exactly the same way.

Winding the relationship down was an awkward business. If I didn't know how to go about courtship, I certainly didn't know how to stop one. The problem was partly confounded by the fact that I really loved her – the Karen that I knew, at least. And I'd always had a weakness for pretty faces. She was very pretty.

The dynamics at the Kingdom Hall were starting to change. There had been a couple of marriages among the younger folk; some had moved to different congregations; Ken, as I mentioned earlier, had gone off to the London complex. This left one of the old "cool" set and me out on a limb (well, him anyway. I was used to it). His name was Michael, and whenever he got bored and lonely, he would invite me to go out for a drive. I really liked the idea of this, but had to lay down strict rules as to the types of places I could go.

"I'm not a pub person," I would say. "I can't stand crowded places and rowdy youths." And Mike would smile and accommodate my demands. One Friday night he drove me round Bolton moors and we stopped off at a very dark and forbidding tower to look at the lights in the valley below. Then he suddenly announced, as though he'd just had a brainstorm, "I know the place. It'll be right up your street." And it was.

He took me to a quiet country pub in the middle of nowhere. Called Old Rosins Inn, it was set back on a moor just by the old Roman Road in Darwen. I loved it. There were no yobs, no stupid tarty girls – just married couples and middle-aged loners. I told myself that whenever I met the perfect someone and got married, Old Rosins would be where our reception would be held. I was always making myself little promises like that.

On the way back home I expounded to Mike the reasons for the Doctor's many faces, why the TARDIS was in the shape of a police box, how the Daleks were a parody of the Nazis, how *The Tripods* could have been done better and why *The Prisoner* could not be taken too literally.

And he still came back for more. Boy, he must have been lonely.

By this time my mother's father had become very ill. He had been suffering from senile dementia for some time and had been confined to a special home near where Grandma lived. I found visiting him a bit of an ordeal, not because Grandad often didn't know who I was, but because of all the people in that place *watching* me. On the few occasions I did go, it felt like absolutely everyone was looking at me, which, of course, is ridiculous. If another family member walked in, perhaps an aunt or an uncle, I would struggle to think of things to say, and I wouldn't know where to look if someone else's relative came in to see their family.

> They're looking. What do I do? What do I say? I'm feeling very uncomfortable.

It was even more of a trauma if a female nurse paid me any attention, or even if she was just in the room seeing to someone who needed her help.

There was one time, it must have been Christmas 1991, when a doctor came to see a few people, and he brought his teenage daughter with him. Man, she was beautiful. And intelligent. And polite. And talkative. She was talking to me.

> What do I do? What do I say? Just keep watching *Star Wars* on the TV.

She was really nice, and even started talking about *Star Wars* in an attempt to get eye contact. She never got it. I couldn't look a beautiful girl in the eye without feeling judged, sentenced and executed.

> Don't look at her.

I rarely visited Grandad. He died in that hospital.

The 12 September marked that year's circuit assembly and yet another trip to Northenden Assembly Hall. I loved it there, and preferred it to the summer conventions held at the football grounds.

Having been advised by my friend Lee that I'll only find a girlfriend when I stop trying to impress, I made a conscious decision not to have anything to do with members of the opposite sex and just enjoy the talks and panels presented. I also took a volunteer job changing all the bin liners to keep myself occupied in the dinner hour.

It was while I was engaged in this activity that a lady from Farnworth congregation approached. I didn't recognize her, but she clearly knew who I was. "Oh, it's William, isn't it?" she enthused. "Ee, you used to come to the Kingdom Hall with your mum, and then you started coming on your own, didn't you love?" I nodded, somewhat perplexed.

It was then that I noticed a slender woman with lovely auburn hair gazing at me in fascination. She was very pretty and girlish, and I estimated that she'd probably be in her early to mid-thirties. A tall, thin teenager with sad droopy eyes languished by her side. I could read the pain in his eyes.

> So much pain. Awkward, nervous, not sure what to say. A fish out of water. I know where you're at. Believe me.

"When was that, now, love?" the older lady continued.

"Well," I began, not used to such full-on attention. "I started coming back when I was about 12, when the *Live Forever* book was first released. I came to the Sunday meeting on and off, and had a study with Joan. Then Ken took it over and I was baptized in '87."

The lady, who I'd managed to discern was called Pat, grinned broadly. "Oh, he'd be brilliant as a friend for our Paul."

I looked at the teenager and he looked at the floor. Pat introduced me to mother and son. "This is my sister Carol." I looked at Pat and then at the slender, auburn-haired beauty in the navy blue jacket and skirt. My expression must have betrayed my thoughts, as she continued, "I know you wouldn't think so to look at us. This is Paul."

The mithered lad stepped forward and forced a smile. But his eyes gave the game away. Big, blue and so desperately sad. I shook his hand and he gulped nervously. Instinctively Carol took over the conversation and started enthusing about the morning's session of talks and demonstrations.

I couldn't believe it. Someone who felt as passionately about these prophecies as I did. It transpired that she had been associated with the Witnesses for years, left when she was 15, got married, had two children, returned briefly in the early 1970s and got baptized, left again, and had now returned to the fold for good. She was very attractive, both physically and as a person. I concluded there and then that I had no chance.

The young lad was obviously struggling to accept the break-up of his parents' marriage and the sudden move from North Wales to Greater Manchester. And Carol – well – old enough to be mother to a 15-year-old? I asked for their name and address so that I could write to Paul and encourage him. Carol gladly obliged. They went on their way and I returned to my bin liners, and thought no more about it for the rest of the assembly.

About a week later, I mailed a tape message complete with musical tracks from Hue and Cry, Gary Numan and the Moody Blues.

> Please like me. Please like me. Please like me. Please like me.

I waited a couple of weeks but received no reply. So I took it upon myself to pay him a visit.

It was nerve-racking. I stalked down Peel Lane in my red-and-black tracksuit, carrying a multicoloured umbrella in one hand and a bag of chips in the other. I stood at the mouth of their address for a few seconds, held my breath, and then went for it.

> Knock, knock, knock. This is even more nerve-racking than the ministry.

Carol opened the door and frowned at me for a moment. Dressed in my multicoloured affair and not my brown suit, I looked completely different and she didn't know who I was at first. Then I wasn't sure about her. She was wearing a greyish tracksuit and had her hair tied back in two "Indian" ponytails. But the hair was auburn, so I said, "It's William. From the assembly."

Then recognition. She smiled a lovely, excited smile and opened the door wide. "Come in, come in."

As soon as I stepped over the threshold, I was greeted by a black-and-grey Blue Merle/Labrador mongrel. He wagged his tail and looked longingly at my bag of chips.

"This is Ben, he won't bite," Carol assured. A door to the left opened onto a barely decorated living room. I quickly surveyed the whitewashed walls, the ancient coffee table sitting on the patchwork carpet and the bulky 1970s sofa dominating the far side. A four-row wall of bricks ran beneath the gas fire up to the portable colour television in the corner.

"Paul's upstairs playing on his computer," she said. "Would you like a drink?"

"Tea, please."

Carol leaned over the banister of the stairs and called up, "Paul! William's come to see you."

I heard the bedroom door fly open. "Who?"

"William. You know, that lad from the assembly who wrote to you."

"Oh, right." Paul trotted down the stairs and shook my hand. That pained look again. Every muscle in his face was trying to smile, but his eyes betrayed him. "All right, mate," he said. I shook his hand.

I proposed that I come on Friday evening to prepare the *Watchtower* lesson for the following Sunday. It was a way of gaining common ground, a way of getting to know Paul and his mum and, more important, a way of making me feel calm. His mum leaped on the idea and so it was arranged. The only person who wasn't really consulted was Paul himself.

It became a fixture. That Friday I introduced them to Matthew, who at that time was having a personal one-to-one Bible Study with me, and thereafter the four of us would meet every Friday and get down to our prep. Carol would make tea, we would go through each paragraph, underline the answers, check the scripture references and make notes in the margins. Usually about half way through the session, Paul would get fed up and trot off upstairs to play "Sonic the Hedgehog". If Carol protested I'd raise a finger. "Leave him," I would advise. "He's had enough. If he wants to go, let him go." At the end of the prep session, Matt would shoot off upstairs and join him.

Then Carol and I would be left to talk in the living room. We exchanged histories and I learned that she had a daughter named Marie who was actually only a few months younger than me.

Just how old *are* you, Carol?

The 15 October was a day of great excitement, as I passed my driving test. A week or so later, my mother bought from Uncle John a Vauxhall Chevette. Jonathan came with me for a few trips round Roe Green and surrounding districts and helped me gain a bit of confidence.

I was now free and liberated from those awful feelings of paranoia that dogged me socially, at bus queues and when walking down a busy high street. I could now see with great clarity what Gary Numan had been singing about. Here in my car I felt safest of all. Cars certainly were the only way to live. And thanks to my new freedom I could visit Carol and Paul more often.

Each visit finished up the same way. Me and Matt going round to their house, Matt joining Paul on the computer, me talking with Carol. The inevitable feelings of romance were starting to develop. They got stronger and stronger until they became a full-blown crush.

And we all know how this usually ends up.

For about a fortnight I stayed away. It seemed easier just to carry on with life and cool the situation with Carol. She was older than me, had two grown-up children, and had just come out of a marriage that, near the end, was quite turbulent. She was enjoying her freedom. Telling her how I felt would probably terminate the friendship, and I didn't want that.

Eventually I couldn't resist paying her another visit. There was no doubt about it, I had fallen head over heels with the woman. When Paul let it slip that his mother had just turned 40 I thought he was joking. But it was true. I was 22, she was 40. Only 18 years' difference then.

Carol's daughter Marie paid a visit and, unbeknown to me, Carol was hoping that we would hit it off as an item. Now there are a few things you must know about Marie. She is in fact partially sighted, not that this has been an obstacle, quite the contrary. Marie went to a boarding school and then to university where she gained all manner of qualifications. She is very intelligent, very sharp and in possession of a quirky sense of humour. We got on well and it's easy to see why Carol thought we were compatible. But Marie already had her man, fellow university graduate Daniel Hill. I got to meet him later, and we got on famously too, I being more than a little impressed by his songwriting.

As I say, I had no idea that Carol was hoping to fix me up with Marie. Apparently, once I'd gone home, Carol said excitedly, "Well, what do you think?" To which Marie replied, "Yes, he's very nice. But I'm afraid he's only got eyes for you."

Carol was completely taken aback by this. "But he's my friend," she said.

The Christmas break loomed on the horizon. We, that is Matt, Paul, Carol and myself, went out to places like Blackpool and Old Rosins Inn and had a whale of a time. It felt like a family unit. It felt right. My emotions were boiling up now, I found it hard containing myself. I wrote Carol a poem called "First in the Queue", hoping she would realize what I was getting at. She just stared at it. "Yes, yes, it's very nice." Didn't she understand what it meant? I decided to come clean.

It'll ruin everything. Tell her. It'll ruin everything. Tell her. It'll ruin everything. It'll ruin everything. It'll ruin everything. Tell her. Tell her. TELL HER.

"I've got something to tell you, but I'm not sure how you're going to take it."

She smiled that lovely warm smile. "OK, go on."

It took me ages, I kept stalling. In the end I confessed. "I'm afraid I've got a crush on you."

Carol laughed. "Is that your big awful secret?"

"No, I mean a *really bad* crush on you."

"So, what's the problem?"

Wasn't it obvious? I turned into sarky Sixth Doctor. "Well the feeling does have to be mutual before it can go any further."

She laughed again. Her eyes sparkled, her hair bounced, so feminine, so utterly beautiful. "Who says it *isn't* mutual?"

Oh, I wasn't expecting that.

"I beg your pardon?"

Carol Catherine – The Making of Me, 1993–95

THAT WINTER WAS THE MOST romantic time I had ever experienced, as we walked the dog through the gentle drifting snow of a February evening. Hand in hand, laughing and giggling like there was no tomorrow. We would stand in the lamp light in the nearby hospital grounds and embrace. This was completely new for me. I was wanted and loved, not for any other reason than for simply being me.

Carol had a sense of being whole too. She loved my candid honesty, a quality that some had interpreted as bombastic and arrogant, but that she viewed as pure. There was no hidden agenda, no secrets, no other life going on behind her back. I said what I meant and I meant what I said.

When it started to become clear that we were an item, voices of discomfort and concern sounded off in certain quarters. The age gap seemed to be a problem for some; others thought Carol was rushing into something she would later regret, it being only a year or so since splitting with her ex-husband. My mother's main concern was my fanaticism; she couldn't accept that Carol would know about it and accept it. But Mum hadn't really seen us together, hadn't seen how compatible we were, nor how the relationship was reshaping my priorities. My girlfriend had filled a massive chasm of loneliness and despair. While I still loved those interests, I no longer *needed* them to survive.

Among the people who supported us unconditionally were Carol's mother Lily, whose one response (after wondering if I had a touch of Down's Syndrome!) was, "You have the same temperament, love." Others included my brother Matthew, and Carol's daughter Marie.

My mum, once she had met Carol, said, "Well I can certainly see why you like her." But again she was doubtful about the relationship.

We weren't doubtful one iota. We discussed the implications of the age gap: when she's 50 I'll be 32, when she's 60 I'll be 42, when she's 70 I'll be 52, etc., etc. I told her that I didn't really care about any of that. The stark loneliness which I had experienced since puberty had been unbearable, to the point where I had been trying to think of ways to commit suicide. Companionship was what I needed more than anything else – to be loved for who I was, warts and all, and to give love.

On the subject of children, I knew there weren't going to be any more. This was fine by me, in fact it was more than fine. I'd observed the stress experienced by new parents at the Kingdom Hall and did not fancy it one bit. Because of my personality, I knew I would find fathering a child emotionally challenging. I would expect my child to have the same values as me, which would either bring a life of persecution and bullying or would make him or her want to live a double life, compromising at school. Either way, I would be severely troubled. Then there was the issue of my anxiety attacks and my depressions – and my *anger* – I still battled deep-seated negative feelings. While they were always internalized, I believed no child should grow up in that environment.

So Carol was perfect for me, and I was perfect for Carol.

After a while the families and the congregations accepted us as an item. We were invited to the wedding of one of Carol's nieces. It was a big church do and many of Carol's family were looking forward to meeting her new toy boy. I arrived at her house all suited up and ready to go and then, as we were about to depart, I began thinking about the church and just how many people were there.

> It'll be a big grand church. There'll be a clergyman, and hymns and prayers. It'll be different to the Kingdom Hall, the routines will be different. All her family will be there. Crowds and crowds. Masses of people, watching me, pointing at me, scrutinizing me, picking me to pieces. I can't breathe, I can't breathe.

"Are you all right, Will?" said Carol. "You've gone red."

I burst into tears and sat down. "I can't do it, I can't do it."

She frowned. I had told her about these episodes many times, but this was the first time she had actually seen one. "You're shaking."

Paul stared at me. "It's only a wedding, Will. You'll be all right." I appreciated him trying to help but I knew it was no use. Carol accepted that I was now out of action and went to the wedding without me.

> They'll all be asking where I am, and Carol will have to try to explain. I've embarrassed her, I've embarrassed me. I've ruined it.

Except I hadn't ruined it. Carol accepted my limits and I loved her all the more for it.

By April, we were invited to another wedding. This time I agreed to go. The reception was held at Smithill's Coaching House in Bolton, and I was so shy about meeting the family I refused to go in! Carol's brother Geoff, with whom it had been said I shared some traits, came out to get away from it all. He became another supporter after we had chatted.

I was preoccupied throughout the whole thing, feeling with the tips of my fingers the felt-covered box in my pocket. I'd simply not had the opportunity all day. So after returning to her house, I asked Carol if she fancied a drive out to get some fresh air. Thankfully she said yes. Dan and Marie, who had come up for the wedding, were happy to stay in alone, and so at 11 p.m. we drove down to Worsley village and stood on the old humped bridge astride the famous orange canal. After a few minutes' hesitation, I produced the box. "Carol?"

She looked round to find me on bended knee. "Yes?" It took a second for her to realize what I was doing.

"Will you marry me?"

She didn't have to think about it. "Yes," she said, overwhelmed as she handled the ring. "I would love to marry you."

Dan and Marie were the first to know, and rejoiced in our behalf. Again, others were less enthusiastic and thought we should give it more time. Young Paul was not ready for it at all. He hadn't even discerned that we were courting. When we told him of our plans to get married he broke down in tears, our approaching wedding putting paid to his dreams of his mother and father possibly getting back together. This proved to be our only regret, that we didn't give Paul more time to adapt.

On the same day we got engaged, the girl on whom I'd had that terrible crush at the Hall got married. It was assumed by some that I'd missed their wedding because I couldn't face it. Everyone soon found out, though!

The next thing to do was set a date. The Kingdom Hall was not available to us and I didn't fancy a Hall wedding anyway because the two congregations would have turned up and this possibly might have caused me problems. I wanted it to be simple and low key. So we went into Swinton Registry Office and set the date: Wednesday 4 August 1993. We were so excited when we came out, it felt as though we had got married there and then.

The Alpine crew were thrilled to hear my good news, but some of them were not so thrilled to learn that no one from work was actually invited. I had a particular vision of how I wanted the wedding to be, and jokes about sex were not part of it. I was so clear and direct about my reasons when asked, I suspect I offended quite a lot of people. If you were one of them, I *am* sorry. Graham made light of it. "On a Wednesday, eh, Willie? You never know, we might stop production and come down and surprise you!" On the quiet one or two said they didn't blame me for restricting it to just family and close friends.

By now I was completely overwhelmed. I thought and spoke about little else, my bride-to-be had turned my life right round in just a matter of months. One evening at the Kingdom Hall I was approached by a very concerned Harry. "William, I've just found out about your Matthew. Why didn't you tell us? We could have had it announced."

"About Matthew?" I said in a daze.

Harry tried to contain himself. "We didn't know he had a cancerous growth on his head. Your mum told us when we visited her."

I was instantly shamed. I'd completely forgotten about it. "Oh yeah," I said. "They've cut it out and given him a bit of plastic surgery. We hope he'll be all right now."

"He's only fifteen, William," Harry reproved. "It could have been very serious."

"Yes, I know."

And so the big day arrived. No best man, no bridesmaids, no pomp and ceremony. No having to wait for the bride to turn up a bit late, as was the custom.

What a RIDICULOUS custom.

I was so nervous about Carol changing her mind, I arranged to pick her up and take her to the registry office myself. The wedding ceremony itself was well supported. Everyone seemed to be in a really good mood. They took their photographs and their handshakes were firm. "Take care of her, son," said my new brother-in-law Bob. "She's had a rough deal." I took his admonition to heart.

Afterwards we drove up to Old Rosins for the reception. Very mindful that the vast majority did not practise a religious belief, we had our friend and local elder Arthur say a prayer to which everyone present could say "Amen" before we tucked into our meal. More customs were dispensed with as Carol and I gave speeches explaining why we had invited the guests – rather than guests making speeches about us.

On the right, my rather lovely wife Carol
on our wedding day, 4 August 1993.

Our pitiful earnings, and the fact that I still couldn't stand currants and raisins, meant that we didn't have a traditional wedding cake. But Marie came to the rescue on the day and paid for the staff to wheel in a full chocolate fudge cake. We were highly appreciative and lived on it for the rest of the week.

Mum ended the day by saying, "I know I wasn't sure, but now I've seen you together properly I can see how happy you are." Carol's brother Bob phoned Lily and declared, "Ee, it's the first time in years I've said a prayer over a meal!" And Grandma told one and all that ours was the best wedding she had ever been to.

The day had been a grand success. We had done it our way – the best way. We watched our guests depart, and then it was off to Lily's caravan in Garstang for the honeymoon. We spent the week taking trips to the village of Scorton, and we had a couple of days in Blackpool. We even managed to afford a show at Winter Gardens, where Brian Conley was performing. A further trip to Morecambe paid off when I found a Justin Hayward tape called *Moving Mountains* going for a couple of quid in a second-hand shop. It was really good as well. The ballad "Lost and Found" summed up our feelings for one another and joined Hue and Cry's "Violently (Your Words Hit Me)" as one of "our" songs.

The year 1993 marked the 30th anniversary of *Doctor Who* and, while there was still no sign of a new series, I did enjoy the BBC's documentary *Thirty Years in the TARDIS*, which carried numerous interviews with writers and producers, a mine of information for any would-be author. By this time Virgin Publishing were into their third year of full-length adult novels *Doctor Who: The New Adventures*, which continued with the Seventh Doctor and Ace, and a new companion created exclusively for the book range, Professor Bernice Summerfield, "Benny" for short. I'd enjoyed Terrance Dicks's 1991 novel *Timewyrm: Exodus* very much, but because it tended to take me weeks to manage a full novel I had shied away from trying any of the others. However, in 1993 I decided to have another crack, this time with *The Dimension Riders* by Daniel Blythe. I absolutely loved it, and I wrote to the author to say thanks for getting me back into reading.

Of course, what I really wanted was to write a *Doctor Who* novel myself. But there were certain obstacles to my succeeding, and most of them were down to my attitude. For a start, I didn't really plot a novel out before I started writing. In addition, there were a number of grammatical errors which were creeping in, like mixing modes and making the author's voice heard rather than telling the story through the development of the characters. My greatest obstacle, though, was my refusal to let others look at my work and offer constructive criticism. My mother would often say "Let me look at it, love" and I would say no because I couldn't bear to hear any negative comment.

There were a couple of interested people attending Kingdom Hall at this time and I determined to take them under my wing. One had been studying on and off for quite a while and in the end didn't commit, while the other made steady progress. He had heard about the doctrine from his work colleagues who were studying it in Stockport. He had been brought up Roman Catholic, had abandoned the religion in his teens and now, in his twenties, was quite taken with the idea of God's Kingdom restoring the Earth and bringing mankind back to perfection. He studied with Arthur, a man who had once served as a Witness missionary in Sri Lanka and who was now a pioneer. He himself was named Anthony.

One Thursday evening I plucked up courage to introduce myself to Anthony and invited him back to our house for a cup of tea and a chat. I was thrilled when he said yes. Carol and I befriended him and before long he was a regular visitor to our house. I quickly discerned that, while he liked football on a general level and drove a fashionable car, he wasn't inclined to talk endlessly about them – which for me meant a possible friendship in the offing.

By this time *Star Trek: The Next Generation* had secured itself as a big favourite and I knew that if Anthony liked science fiction generally he would take to some of the better episodes. And he did. Patrick Stewart as Captain Jean Luc Picard and Brent Spiner as the android Commander Data quickly became as worthy in his eyes as the legendary Captain Kirk and Mr Spock. I introduced him to the new villain Q (a sort of mischievous/vindictive spirit being) and the force-to-be-reckoned-with known as the Borg.

Once Anthony was hooked on the series, I back tracked through some of the original series episodes, which he lapped up, having appreciated them as a youngster. Then I went in for the kill, and introduced him to what I *really* wanted him to approve.

My strategy was simple: show him the sort of *Doctor Who* he was likely to remember, then some of the better older stuff, then progress forward with the best ones from the more recent series.

I was, of course, unashamedly attempting to brainwash Anthony into liking *Doctor Who* so I could have someone with whom I could discuss it on an intellectual level. And because he appreciated the stories and the background information supplied by me, he did indeed take to it like a duck to water. In fact, only recently he was telling me that the subject of *Doctor Who* came up at work and someone was reminiscing, and Anthony found himself putting story titles to the memories and explaining perceived anomalies. Apparently it's all my fault that he is able to do this. I have to say that I don't feel remotely repentant.

The January sales of 1994 gave me the opportunity to buy a new synthesizer, one that was a stage up from the one Mum had bought me a year or so earlier. While I couldn't play a keyboard or follow written music, I had theorized that I would be able to find the notes that I wanted and, with a pre-programmed backing track, would be in a position to write and record my own songs. The earlier model didn't have a good enough backing track, and so my songwriting had ended rather abruptly. But now, with my Realistic Concertmate 1000 and a karaoke machine, I was able to put together a little album. I resurrected four songs from my earlier sessions, "Simple Babylon", "Belief", "The Wrong Girl" and "The Love Repellent", reworked them and then added some new titles. "A Changed Man" was adapted from a poem I'd written on behalf of a lad at work who wanted to apologize to his girlfriend.

"Simple Babylon" was supposed to be charting the change in me that had occurred since asserting myself at Alpine and it became the album title for the set.

A really melancholy piece, entitled "My Dear Brother", described a situation Jonathan had got himself into and the effect it was having on me. I actually wrote that lyric straight off in one evening. Then came an up-tempo piece about Carol being "the one". I'd had an idea a couple of years before about writing a poem about the girl of my dreams where each verse would end with a question and each time the answer would be "she is". And so "She Is" became the penultimate track, while the ballad "Fear" – that is, Carol's fear that our marriage was too good to be true – rounded off the set.

Jonathan's best friend Che was quite taken by my ingenuity, that I was able to produce an album with no knowledge of music – so much so that he went off and wrote a poem called "Just Sometimes". He brought it to me, I split the piece into a chorus and verses, found a tune and rhythm on the keyboard, and recorded the song in an afternoon. It was quite a collaboration.

The album received a mixed response. Most people would just snigger at the poor production values, and so I learned not to let people listen to it. You see, when I heard it, I could imagine what it was supposed to sound like. I knew that with a decent keyboard, some nifty computer sampling and mixing, and one or two proper musicians involved, the songs would actually sound rather good. A handful of people did enjoy my melodies and lyrics. Carol's nephews, some of whom are into music, loved it for its organic quality. One of them even produced it as a CD and wanted to distribute it to some friends, but I was too embarrassed by the pathetic production values to grant his wish.

It didn't stop me writing some more, though. In 1995 and 1996 I produced two more sets. *Winter Days* carried Che's song "Just Sometimes", which some people rather liked; a track about false people called "Superficial", which our Paul liked; and another dreamy ballad for Carol, to mark our first anniversary, that also served as the album title.

The *New World* album was better written in my opinion because it was written around my limitations. I didn't try to sing notes I knew were impossible for me and I didn't attempt instrumental breaks. As a result I had songs where the synthesizer music was strong, the singing was fair and the lyrics had depth. I also tended to wait for the lyrics to come after I'd devised a tune and style, whereas before I was largely converting poems into verses – not a satisfactory way to write.

My two big favourites from *New World* are "Paranoia Zone" and "Stay Away (From Me)". Musically the former was a heavy synthesizer-rock affair and I really enjoyed creating the big string section for it. I left it on tape and waited for the appropriate emotions to surface so that I could write a fitting lyric. The emotions came one Thursday evening. Paul had been attending some Kingdom Hall meetings, and on this particular occasion he had stayed behind to socialize after his mother and I had come home. When he finally caught up with us he was fuming. Apparently he had been chatting with a couple of young men and they had started to reminisce about the sort of person I'd been prior to getting married. And they revelled in it. "You know that [someone at the Hall who was a bit of a misfit]?" they jeered. "Well your William used to be just like them!" They roared with laughter.

I was quite touched by Paul's loyalty to me. He was furious. And I was furious too. It angered me deeply that these individuals were dragging stuff up and perpetuating my old persona. I thought about how easily social skills came to them and how they'd strolled through life at ease, being popular, having plenty of friends. They had absolutely no idea what they were laughing at, or how much pain they and their sort had caused me. I didn't want to write about just those two young men, but rather absolutely everyone who had ever treated me as they had. I went up to the spare room, played back my new music, and wrote the lyric for "Paranoia Zone" almost straight off.

You don't understand
And I bet you don't even try to
You don't even care
And I doubt you'd ever want to

A voice in my head
Saying they hate me
This voice says I'm dead
If they get to see –
That I fear them

Tense – I can't move
My throat – I can't breathe
Nerves – No control
Help – I can't stand this scene

Fear grips my soul
They are laughing at me
Fear has taken hold
They torment me – And there's
No way out

I'm trapped in paranoia zone!

Do you know the feeling of constant dread and fear?
Erosion of confidence making men shed their tears?
Can you comprehend being seized by a force
A power so real you'd die to stop its course?

Do you feel a laughing stock walking down the street?
Do you feel embarrassment every time you speak?
Does everyone think you strange because you're a little different?
Do they point and snigger, your observation resent?

Then you cannot understand me.

I'm trapped in paranoia zone!

I'm so overwhelmed
I just want to hide away
There is no escape
Can't take their eyes off me

The voice in my head
The disease of my soul
Please hide me away
So I can be all alone
And at last feel safe.

With "Stay Away (From Me)" I wanted something sinister. The music had to sound threatening and the lyrics needed to reflect the darker side of me, the side which surfaced when I descended into the depths of depression. Even though life had got much better since meeting and marrying Carol, I still struggled with society and hated the falseness of it all. I got heavily depressed at least twice a year and withdrew into a cocoon.

I was delighted to find that I wasn't the only one who had these episodes. Marie's husband Dan commented, "There is one track on this new set which really touches a nerve with me." When he spoke the title his empathy was very apparent. "'Stay Away (From Me)'. You know, that is exactly how I feel a lot of the time. If you don't like my views, if you don't want to hear how it really is, just stay away."

It's here again inside my soul
So stay away from me
It feeds on hate and rotten thoughts
Stay away from me
A heart of stone swelling with rage
Stay away from me
It's evil born from memories
So stay away from me

It's taken years to grow
Stay away from me
Dark thoughts come
Stay away from me

It's invaded my mind, got control
So stay away from me
The "Hyde" of man, all that is bad
Stay away from me
If my countenance frightens you
Stay away from me
If you don't want to hear some home truths
Then stay away from me

The disease you can't see
Stay away from me
It's pain without relief
Stay away from me

Just stay away.

But overall I had grown weary of the limited production values of my equipment, and so vowed not to record any more songs until I had the finances to buy some decent gear.

For our first wedding anniversary, we holidayed at the caravan site in Cheshire. There was a pub in the town that had an old-fashioned railway carriage positioned on a bit of track outside, and this served as a restaurant. Carol and I had often wondered what it might be like to eat in it and so, after much agonizing, I managed to go there alone and book a table.

I must stress here that this sort of thing was usually unheard of. Approaching waitresses and barmen was quite an ordeal for me. Even at Old Rosins, it was Carol or Anthony who ordered the drinks and carried them over, I was so paranoid. But I managed to do it, I booked a table for two, paid for it and then surprised Carol that night.

She got dressed up and put on her make-up, and as we drove up the main stretch she kept asking, "Where are we going?", and I would smile and reply, "It's a secret." Her face was a picture when she realized. "How have you done this? You're terrified of talking to bar staff."

But I was getting braver.

Me and Ant at Old Rosins Inn, 1994.
At one time this would have been impossible for me.

Meanwhile, back at the factory, depression had really set in. When I first started there, there had been a sense of urgency and a determination to get things right. My and Elaine's role as quality controllers was a valued one. However, the atmosphere had changed since then. Among the workers there was this all-pervading feeling of doom, that the company was on its way out. This wasn't helped when the Birmingham branch closed down. Oh yeah, the workload increased for us, but we knew it was only because we were the only complex left.

I could also see that their door-to-door delivery system was really a thing of the past. Numerous persons had said to me, "Alpine? Oh yeah, we used to get that. They used to come round with these big glass bottles with a little rubber washer in the cap." Everyone knew the name and remembered it fondly. It was a household name, but it was dying. Soft drinks were now sold in two-litre plastic bottles in supermarkets. The days of buying one-litre glass bottles on the doorstep were long gone.

I became extremely lax in my approach, turning up at least two minutes late every day. I was so depressed with the place. On odd occasions, individuals would observe, "You know, you should be in an office not a factory. You belong somewhere like that." I used to smile and nod, "I know", and then contemplate my poor academic qualifications and lack of experience. I knew I probably would be good at filing and photocopying, writing letters, taking incoming calls – but I also knew I didn't stand a chance. I was also afraid. Afraid of change, afraid of having to settle in somewhere new all over again, afraid of failure.

Because we were now the only factory left, a new evening shift was inaugurated to cope with the Britvic contract. During this period, Wayne and Elaine would go home at the normal time, and I would take over as QC with a lad called Jim as syrup mixer. We had quite a rapport going between us. He had been brought up Roman Catholic and had rejected it, I was one of Jehovah's Witnesses. He liked reading the big science-fiction authors Arthur C. Clarke and Isaac Asimov, I loved classic TV science fiction.

"You know, Will, I love these chats that we have," he'd say, and he meant it too. Then, at break-time, he would go and join the others in the canteen and completely change personality. I was always disappointed when that happened, but he explained to me that he thrived on the factory atmosphere. He told me he once saw a comedy sketch by Mel Smith and Griff Rhys-Jones where they and a few others played a typical factory mob. He said he loved the superficial banter, and while I couldn't comprehend how anyone *could* love it, I accepted that he did.

The falseness of people really bugged me. It was something I was never able to come to terms with. People swearing a lot, yes; people having different beliefs, yes; people having no beliefs whatsoever, yes. But not people being fake, either individually or *en masse*, like the tabloid media for example.

The depressions were getting worse. I had grown to hate absolutely everything about the place. As a result I threw myself more and more into my religion. I would sit in the canteen and stare out of the window, wishing that God would bring his day of judgement and an end to my misery, either in a wrathful execution for my sins, or salvation into the New World as he wiped out the existing system.

Sometimes I would actually say it aloud. "Oh, roll on Armageddon. I'll be glad when it's all over." Then I would clam up, realizing what I had said. The others would suddenly go silent and exchange glances. I knew that they knew what Armageddon meant: the destruction of the world system, a system some of them embraced.

"You think you're better than us, don't you?" odd ones would say, barely able to conceal their contempt. "No," I would reply. (Frequently I believed I was worthless. Only Carol was keeping me afloat.) "But I do think I'm *different* to you." My pompous Colin Baker-esque delivery didn't do me any favours.

In the run-up to Christmas 1994 Elaine and I were told that one of the QCs would have to be demoted back to the production line, since the company needed to save money. I didn't have the heart to demand that Elaine go back, even though I was the original quality controller. In addition, management didn't want someone who had become lax and who never turned up on time to be the only one in the role. And so, as of January 1995, I was back in production – then in the warehouse – then back in production – then back on the QC job when Elaine was ill – then back in the warehouse… I had been reduced to an odd job man.

The last straw came when I was put in the syrup room. Wayne had a particular system to which he worked. He knew where all the flavours and colours were, and not all of them were labelled. Anyone new to the job would struggle. Anyone half used to it would struggle if the mixes were low ones: mixes that would be finished in under 20 minutes.

They didn't like the production line stopping. As soon as one flavour was off, the next one would be sent down.

> I can't keep up. The vats are running out quicker than I can make them.

I went into the canteen and spoke to one of the bosses. "I need someone to give me a hand. I can't cope in there."

"Look, son," he breezed, waving his hand dismissively. "Don't worry about it. If it runs out, it runs out. It's not the end of the world." And so I went back in and soldiered on. I was down to just two vats. I made one while the other was in production.

> It's going down too quick. It'll be out before the next one's ready.

"I'm sorry, I really do need some help here. I can't keep up."

"What did I tell you? If it runs out, it runs out."

> I can't cope, I can't do it. Adrenalin rush. Dramatic music. "Aaarrrggghhh!" White eyes, green skin, coat ripping down the back. Faltered breathing, salt in my saliva. I can't do it, I can't keep up. Red faced, tearful eyes.

> Suddenly calm. All right, I will take this as seriously as you do.

When the vat emptied, I washed it out with the hose and left it. As the last flavour worked its way down to the production hall I visited the canteen and bought myself a coffee. I was calm. I did not care one jot. When the final flavour came to its finish, I rang the bell to let production know, and then rinsed out the empty vat.

John called up from the floor. "Can I have the pineapple now?"

"No."

"Why not?"

"Because I haven't made it."

John rushed up the stairs and into the syrup room. "What do you mean you haven't made it?"

"I haven't made it," I replied simply. One of the managers walked in, wondering what the hold up was about. Then came Elaine to test the next flavour. "What's going on?"

John opened each of the three vats and then closed them again. "William," he said slowly. His face showed both confusion and mock horror as he realized mutiny was in the air. "There's nothing in any of these."

"I know," I said. "I couldn't keep up. I kept saying I couldn't keep up but they wouldn't send someone in to help me."

The manager who had been so blasé made a show of examining the recipe book and then began assembling the ingredients quickly. Or at least he tried to, as he soon found that a lot of them were not labelled. "Why have you done this, William?" he asked as he mixed some sodium benzoate with hot water. "We need to get this out tonight before the lorry leaves."

I shrugged, holding off a Tom Baker grin, and declared, "Well, if it runs out, it runs out." It was now five o'clock. I had no intentions of doing any overtime whatsoever. I simply went to my locker, got my coat and went home.

Amazingly I wasn't sacked. The following morning I was given a strong pep talk and told never to do it again. I accepted the discipline, but after another couple of days in the warehouse, decided that it was time for a trip to my local GP.

"I can't believe I did it," I said. "It's so unlike me."

Dr Tauk put his hands behind his back and thought long and hard. "Mm," he said finally. "It sounds like an anxiety attack. Do you suffer from depression and panic?"

I was surprised at his astuteness. "I do. I get very angry as well. I don't mean angry in that I'm throwing things about or hurting people."

"But angry inside," he concluded for me. "The gentle giant who bottles up his rage." I nodded in agreement. Dr Tauk sat at his desk. "Do you think you need tablets, like antidepressants?"

"No, I wouldn't say so. I just need to talk it out."

"Mm," thought Dr Tauk aloud. "I will put you on sick leave for six months and refer you to a clinical psychologist."

A psychologist? Someone to recondition me, someone to reinforce the brainwashing. I am going to have my "cap" examined to see why the process failed. I am going to have electrodes attached to the aggressive frontal lobes. They are the hammer and I am the anvil. They are going to hammer me into the shape they want. They'll want information, information, information, but they won't get it. By hook or by crook, I will never be a number.

Thus began the next chapter of my life.

Introducing Will Hadcroft, 1995–97

"RIGHT," SAID STEPHANIE, MY PSYCHOLOGIST, as I arrived for my second appointment. "I've thought about the things you said last week, and I think it's important we get two points out of the way before we go on."

What could they be?

"First of all, you're not mentally ill."

Phew, that's a relief.

"Second, your attachment to *Doctor Who.*"

Oh no, here we go.

"If you hadn't have used *Doctor Who* and the other sci-fi stuff as a means of escape, you almost certainly *would* have been mentally ill."

This was quite a revelation for me, as I'd been struggling with guilt feelings over the way my obsessiveness had intruded on the lives of my brothers, and in particular my mother. I told that one to Mum, and she accepted it.

"You say I'm not mentally ill," I began. "But there must be something mental going on, otherwise I wouldn't keep running into these people problems."

"It's more emotional than it is mental," she countered. "You have suffered a series of traumas that have affected you very deeply. The bullies at school, the death of your stepfather, the part you played in helping the girl who was abused."

I could accept these points because they were true: I had been deeply affected by these traumas. But I remained privately convinced that there was more to my problems than this. All the individual problem traits were identified over the ensuing 18 months. But I wanted a *name* for what was wrong, an umbrella to define those traits collectively. If I could put a name to it, to discover that there is in fact a recognized condition, I would be half way to handling it. The number of times people had asked what was wrong or had exhibited a look of surprise when I suddenly couldn't do something or had a panic attack. If I could have said "Well you see, I've got this thing called Blah", I'm sure individuals would have accepted it. Unfortunately, whenever I did try to suggest that something was fundamentally wrong they would dismiss it. "And has this been diagnosed?"

Stephanie was not forthcoming with an official name for my complaint. This was either due to a line of thinking common amongst psychologists and psychiatrists back then, namely that if they told the patient what it was, the patient would start to live up to it; or it was because I hadn't in fact been diagnosed with a recognized disorder.

Trying to explain my feeling "different" while at the same time being quite normal was very difficult for me. Stephanie only began to notice it for herself when I contradicted myself, as I had often done in conversations with my mother. I would begin a session by saying something like, "I don't need other people. I am self-contained. I enjoy my own company. I get sick of them trying to make me conform. I'm an individual." But by the end of the tirade I would be saying things like, "It's because I have no friends. I'm so lonely." To which Stephanie would smile and reply, "You've just contradicted yourself."

I would frown and say, "I know."

It was embarrassing having to explain myself, and I would either lose my train of thought or I would not say what I truly believed. I was also convinced that if I said too much I would be sent to a mental hospital and given electric shock treatment, as depicted in the film *One Flew Over the Cuckoo's Nest*, and so I deliberately held back.

With the self-contradictory stuff I so desperately wanted to say, "I actually feel both, you see. I want to be left alone *and* have lots of friends. I want to have a religious code *and* ditch God. I hate the sexual promiscuity of my workmates *and* I wish I were like them." The same was true of various debates and arguments. I could often see the validity in both sides and then struggle to marry the stark opposites together. These heavy thinking periods often triggered the dark depressions.

"You used a very disturbing phrase to describe yourself last week," said Stephanie in an early session. "You said you were 'schizo'. What did you mean by that?"

I shrugged. "That I sometimes feel like two people in the same body. I don't hear voices or anything like that, but I do get very strong thoughts that are contrary to my normal beliefs and feelings. Fighting them wears me out."

Of course, some of this self-war was due to my being one of Jehovah's Witnesses. All practising religious people have it, the war between one's spiritual principles and the carnal fleshly desires and impulses. Not just resisting practising things such as having sex with someone to whom you're not married, but trying to resist even thinking about it. Telling lies is bad, but to the religious person even little white lies are bad, because they are still lies. Determining what was due to my religious beliefs and what was natural to me proved difficult. I had a hunch that some of the aspects, such as not wanting to swear, not smoking and not getting drunk, would be present in me even if I weren't a Witness. Rowdy pubs and nightclubs made me feel ill because of the assault on my senses by the lights and the loudness of the music (to this day I have never been in a nightclub). And I seemed to have an inbuilt abhorrence to lies.

Gary Numan was a good example of this sort of thing. He had absolutely no religious beliefs whatsoever. Not only did he not believe in God, but he had grown to despise the concept of religion generally. In an interview, however, he said that he wasn't much of a drinker, didn't smoke and never told lies. When quizzed about the latter, he said that he had tried it, but his complexion and his eyes always gave him away. I had similar feelings, and felt an affinity with Gary despite our radical views about the origins of Man and the existence of a Creator.

My exasperation with superficial people and bodies of people, such as the tabloid press, were not easy to deal with. "Take, for example, that business when Stephen Fry ran away to France because he couldn't cope with the reviews he was getting for his play." The comedy actor turned thespian suffered with gross feelings of failure and self-loathing. I identified with him very much at that time, and a number of people had likened me to him, in the way I spoke and the way I moved. "They milked that for everything they could get out of it. One minute they are all over someone and paying them huge compliments, and the next they're ripping them to pieces."

Stephanie used a phrase that, at first, I didn't much care for. "Social skills." I thought it was ridiculous that the process by which people engaged in conversation actually had it's own label. It reminded me of my Social Studies lessons at school. Everything has to have its pigeon hole, even the way people communicate. I also resented the way the label implied there was something wrong with me.

What about the way everyone else lacks "individualism skills"?

After a while, though, I began to see what she was getting at, that there were unwritten rules in conversation: when to speak and when not to speak; maintaining eye contact; talking about appropriate things; showing interest in what others say. Apparently most people picked up these rules automatically as part of their development as an infant but and for some reason, for me, the penny hadn't dropped.

"We're going to do an experiment," she said. "Between now and our next appointment, I want you to listen to the sports news and make notes of points that might be used in a conversation, and then when the situation arises, try to employ them."

I look at her sceptically.

It won't work. I'm not remotely interested in sport.

I decided I should at least give it a try, and did exactly as instructed. Throughout the week I sat with a note pad and pen, and waited for the football news to come on at the end of the main news bulletin.

Football shouldn't be included in the BBC news because it isn't news. It's just a game. And teachers and employers shouldn't be lenient when pupils and employees pretend to be ill so they can stay home and watch the World Cup. "There won't be many in today, it's the World Cup." So what?

There was some new development about Bolton Wanderers. I wrote it down, and within a few days I was able to put it to use. It was while I was travelling by taxi. At first I didn't speak – because I had nothing to say that would be of interest to the driver. That was my policy: there's no point in talking if you've got nothing to say. I believed that small talk was ridiculous because no one involved in the conversation really cared about the subject under discussion.

> "Cloudy today, isn't it?"/ "Yeah. They reckon it's going to pour down later." / "Do they?"/ "Yeah. Could last all week." / "Oh dear."
> / "Still, it should brighten up next week." / "Yeah."…UTTERLY POINTLESS, and no one is really interested anyway. They do it because they can't stand the silence. I prefer the silence. It is therefore *they* who have a problem.

"Shame about Bolton, isn't it?" piped the taxi driver suddenly. This was it, my big chance. Normally I would say that I didn't follow football and the conversation would be terminated, followed by an awkward silence. This time, however, I actually knew what he was talking about. I responded by acknowledging the particular problem, and I have to admit I did feel better than usual. Less alien, I suppose. Everything went fine until he brought up another detail about Bolton Wanderers that I knew nothing about. "I don't know," I said honestly. "I don't really follow it."

"Oh," replied the driver. Then after a pause he asked, "Which team do you support then?" And I had to concede that I actually didn't follow any of them and that football was not my cup of tea.

When I reported back to Stephanie, she seemed quite excited. "How did you go on?"

I told her the truth, that it worked a little, and that I could see the value in learning about other people's interests, but as far as football was concerned, I had absolutely no desire to go any further. It was obvious to true fans, from my awkwardness and my lack of eye contact, that I was merely repeating what I'd heard or read. They knew I wasn't really interested.

I had always approached these sessions with an open mind. I wanted to be adaptable without betraying my principles, and to a point it was working. I had become more reasonable, I listened more, and when people talked about their favourite subjects I let them go on for a bit, appreciating how it feels when someone says abruptly that they're not bothered. On the other hand I learned to assert myself. Should, for example, someone walk into the living room while I was watching *Doctor Who* and start laughing at it, or worse just start talking through it, I would now say "Excuse me, I'm watching this", instead of going off in a huff.

Another little assignment involved keeping a diary. We had recently moved to a private rented house in Farnworth. The road it was on looked really nice and the house itself was a considerable step up from where we had come. But there were two problems. On the one hand the house backed onto a fairly rough council estate and a passage leading to it ran up the side. Youths and children would throw stones at the door or at the side of the house as they passed. On the other hand we had problems with the children who lived directly opposite, especially on Friday nights.

I had major problems with my internalized anger. The stones hitting the door made me jump, as did the football which frequently crashed against the living room window. Marie had the fright of her life one evening when a brick hit the bathroom window while she was in the shower. The thugs who lived at the back were utterly brainless. Those who lived over the road were worse in some respects because they were teenagers and appeared to come from respectable families. Their trouble usually started when their parents went out on the town, often until as late as two in the morning. No sooner were their backs turned than their little darlings broke open the wine and the beer. By midnight they were plastered. Then the fun would start.

My hatred for them ran deep, and I struggled to maintain the Christian personality described in the Bible. Instead of turning the other cheek I imagined a squad of Daleks trundling round the corner and performing a group extermination, or I would dream that they had been reduced to doll-sized corpses. On one occasion they played knock-a-door-run, in our case shouting "Bible bashers!" through the letterbox, and this at half past midnight. On another they smashed one of the smaller living room windows with an apple core. When they were confronted they simply laughed. Threats of telling their parents had no effect because they knew it was pointless.

And so my diary was filled with thoughts of anger and fantasies about them meeting a timely end. The final straw came one afternoon when a football hit the window for the umpteenth time. I threw open the door and took the ball inside. When they asked for it back, I stuck a knife in it.

"I've been reading your diary," Stephanie began. I braced myself for what was coming next. "I find all this stuff about the children in your street a bit worrying."

"I hate them," I said, seething on my chair. "Why won't they leave me alone? I've had this sort of thing all my life, at school, at the supermarket, then at the factory when I first started, and now here."

Stephanie smiled. "You seem to see these incidents as one long continuing problem."

"They are," I said.

"Well, hang on a minute." She pulled out a marker pen and began writing on the white board. "School. The supermarket. The pop factory. The kids in your street. Are they all the same thing or are they separate?"

"Well," I said slowly. "Each incident is separate, obviously."

"Right."

"But they involve the same sorts of things: name calling, winding me up, etcetera."

"And how do you react?"

"I get angry."

"So the thing that is continuing down through the years is not just the way people treat you – but the way you react to them."

Bullseye. I could see what she was getting at. She began drawing a circle on the board. "You have as a starting point *The Past*. It's always there in the back of your mind. Then you have *A Trigger*, something happens and the emotions come into play. You get *Angry*. These feelings remind you of similar incidents that have happened before. You *Dwell On Them*. And then you are brought full circle back to *The Past*. And then it feeds on itself, round and round."

It was an accurate appraisal of my thought processes. She rubbed out the line of the circle linking *The Past* and *A Trigger*. "You need to break the cycle here," she said. "When the trigger is activated, stop and ask yourself how the incident started. Ask yourself if you did anything to exasperate the situation. Then ask yourself how you might repair it. Tell yourself each time that it is a new situation and that you can influence the outcome."

This was the sort of stuff that proved beneficial in the end. After a while I was also able to apply the principles to other areas of life, and other emotions. It wasn't only anger that went round in circles. Sometime in 1996 I ventured with a handful of friends to the cinema to watch *Star Trek: First Contact*. While there I bumped into my onetime almost-girlfriend Karen. I was overwhelmed as soon as I caught sight of her. She was so pretty and so feminine, I was conquered by her smile. All my old feelings came tumbling back and I was severely troubled by them for several days. The fact that we had both admitted to one another that we had been living a fantasy didn't figure in it. All I could feel was what I used to feel before we both came clean.

Just as I had found it hard to divorce the anger of the past from the present, so it was with these affections. Once I had recovered I decided it best to avoid that particular cinema. Not because of her, but because of me. And then came the crushing guilt: Carol was the best thing that had ever happened to me, she loved me and I adored her. What was I playing at?

The self-confidence problems were also remedied. Rather than feeling guilty about my bouts of internalized anger, I was encouraged to consider whether it was "righteous anger", because even in the Bible there were accounts where righteous people became indignant about injustices and the like.

I also had to dwell on my achievements. Author Daniel Blythe had advised that I contribute to science-fiction fanzines, which I promptly did. One, a new release edited by Gavin Wilson entitled *RQC* (that's *Really Quite Cosmic*), published a number of pieces by me, including my appraisal of *The Tripods*. The article "Has It All Been for Nothing?" was later deemed fit to go on the Internet. I had got as far as the top 200 in the Channel Four Film Challenge, out of 2500 entries. And I had been published in the glossier fanzines connected to *Doctor Who* (*Skaro* and *Matrix*) and *In The Village* (*The Prisoner*), as well as publishing letters in the professional monthlies *Doctor Who Magazine* and *TV Zone*.

My letter about Tom Baker, which I sent to *Active Life* magazine in response to an interview they had conducted with the actor, won me a kettle. Every time I brewed up, I was reminded of how I'd come by the kettle. In addition, someone at the *Doctor Who* Exhibition in Llangollen, North Wales, read the piece, and was so impressed they forwarded a free family ticket to my address.

I had to keep these truths to the fore of my mind when the depression threatened.

Stephanie said that she sometimes had to deal with alcoholics, and if an alcoholic turned up for counselling under the influence, she would just send them away: "Sober up and then we'll talk. But I'm not taking you on like this." She advised that I view my darker, angry self in the same way. When the unwanted thoughts come, just tell myself, "I'm not talking to you while you're like this." It was an attractive metaphor, and it sometimes helped, but the other me was so overwhelming it proved difficult not to get sucked in to the darkness.

She also gave me a paper demonstrating the differences between aggression, assertion and non-assertion. I found this fascinating. I could recognize the bullies of the world as demonstrating the first behaviour, believing themselves to be assertive, but actually being aggressive; getting what they want, yes, but at the expense of others, and making enemies as a result. The last behaviour, non-assertion, fitted my personality like a glove. I tended not to assert myself at all, always backing down in fear of being ridiculed or of over-compensating and coming across too strong. And so, out of a desire to avoid confrontation, I let others have their own way. The solution might have been peaceful but it did nothing for my self-respect. What I really wanted was to be assertive, to make my voice heard without intimidating people, to have the courage to stand up for my views. To have self-respect. The paper warned that first attempts might not always work but that, after a while, I would start to see the benefits.

And I did. True to my nature, I became obsessed with the concept of assertion and photocopied the sheet for anyone whom I felt needed it.

Finally, Stephanie gave me a series of questions that I had to ask myself whenever I sensed the old feelings mounting up. The first one was *Am I Personalizing This?* I tried not to interpret criticism of the things I was interested in as criticism of me. Second, *Am I Catastrophizing?* I tried not to make a mountain out of a molehill, I tried to stem my tendency to imagine every possible outcome and worry about them all as though they had actually happened. Other questions included *Am I Expecting Myself to be Perfect?*, *Am I Focusing On the Negative and Excluding the Positive?*, *Am I Assuming Things?* and *Have I Ever Behaved Like That Myself?*

When I sensed that I was beginning to succeed in mastering these qualities I started to notice that my dealings with other people were more balanced and, as a result, I was happier and content. My self-respect grew, as did my respect for other people.

The major plus for 1996 was a co-production between BBC Worldwide and Universal Television – a TV movie of *Doctor Who*. It was screened during the May Bank Holiday and saw Sylvester McCoy reprise the role of the Doctor. In the film he lands in a San Francisco back street and is gunned down by youths. Attempts at a local hospital to save him trigger his next regeneration.

Popular British actor Paul McGann became the Doctor's rather dashing eighth incarnation, while Hollywood star Eric Roberts featured as the Master. It was hoped that the film would spark a new TV series or series of films.

The movie was to be the only new TV episode of *Doctor Who* in the 1990s.

The great irony came a few months later when the BBC held an awards ceremony. I was utterly staggered when *Doctor Who* won the "Best Loved Drama" category. At that moment I wished I was an active part of fandom. I wanted to phone everybody up and celebrate. But the only people I could have phoned definitely wouldn't have appreciated it.

So I celebrated to myself.

Carol's mother Lily wanted all her family to have a spring holiday with her at the Hotel Sheraton in Blackpool. My being out of work on sick leave meant that Carol and I were certainly available, and thanks to Lily's generosity we were able to join Carol's sisters and her mum. I took to the Sheraton immediately because most of the guests were either middle-aged or elderly. I felt safe in that environment and got on with Carol's family famously.

It was while in Blackpool that I decided to try my hand at script writing. I wanted to do something fresh and interesting, and while walking down the sea front, hit on the idea of a boy who becomes imprisoned in a nightmare parody of his school life. In that situation he would be the only one in colour, while the school building and the other occupants would be in black and white. The whole thing would be a dream where he worked out the meaning of his life. At the time I was drawing heavily on *The Prisoner*, but in retrospect I can see it owes just as much to *The Wizard of Oz*. For the school coat of arms I had the idea of having a single fingerprint, as this would denote individualism. Later on, my brother Matthew suggested putting a red "No Entry" sign over the top of it to show that individualism is condemned by the system.

Damn! I wish I'd thought of that.

Finally I needed a quest of some sort. Something symbolic that would turn out to have a profound effect on the protagonist when he woke up back in the real world. Ever since leaving school I had regarded the education system (that's the *system*, not education itself) as a means of social conditioning. One didn't just learn the rules of Mathematics, the grammar of English Language or where certain countries are in the world – one was also bombarded with etiquette, social conformity, political notions, religious beliefs, speculative science, and all sorts of other propaganda, some of which were in the curriculum, some of which came from the teachers themselves. I only realized this when I left school and started my first job. The school system was the blueprint for adult society.

A lightbulb moment: *The Blueprint*. "Find the blueprint and change it," advises a mentor. "Only then will you find the way out."

It was while I was at Blackpool that I caught a bit of playwright Dennis Potter's final interview with Melvyn Bragg. Potter had written such classics as *The Singing Detective*. He often wove in aspects of his real life and, more often than not, childhood experiences. His abuse at the hands of a relative influenced repeated themes of sexual misconduct and the theft of innocence. Potter believed that sex scenes should make a point and further the plot rather than simply serve as a means of boosting ratings. He lamented the demise of the single play and hated what he called pappy soaps and mini-series where one could punch the buttons of predictability.

He also said that he hadn't quite thrown off the idea of God, which intrigued me, since it implied he'd had a good go at getting rid of him. But the religion of his childhood was rooted deep into his psyche, the stories of the New Testament and of Jesus, and the hymns he used to sing, were all etched into his brain. Images and themes from Christianity feature prominently in Potter's work.

At the time of the interview, the writer only had weeks to live. He spoke of having come to terms with being a coward. This also struck a chord with me, as did his comments about being perceived as arrogant and opinionated. He claimed to be actually very shy, and that his attempts at compensating for the shyness made him appear outspoken and pompous.

I was extremely moved and fired up by the interview, so much so that I ordered a video copy of it. One particular comment had a profound effect. Potter said that if a writer were to try to establish himself in television today with original, thought-provoking ideas, he would be shown the door.

Taking all this to heart, I had to ask myself whether anyone would welcome a story where a child questions the way we are educated and concludes that he would be better served by personal tuition at home. I decided to shelve *The Blueprint* and devise something more formulaic, something a publisher would feel comfortable with.

I spent an hour or two every afternoon walking the dog around an old mill pond near where I lived. Century Mill had now been converted into workshops and businesses, and the stretch of water that was once the lodge was now a haunt for local fishermen. The grassed wastelands sandwiched between it and the new housing estate provided the peace I needed to think.

The first idea which sprang to mind was doing a children's adventure series akin to *The Famous Five* where the children were the heroes. Two boys and two girls, it was the obvious split. I decided one would be sensible and compassionate, another would be very trendy and socially aware, the third would be the geek, a kind of clumsy scruffy boffin who would provide the comedy, and the fourth would be superhuman in some way. I drifted back to my childhood days and recalled the things I was interested in. A child that could run fast, leap high walls, bend metal bars with his bare hands and see long distance – a sort of bionic child. At first the bionic child was going to be one of the boys. Arnie or Andy – short for android. Then one day I thought how cool and original it would be to have one of the girls as the robot for a change.

The basic concept of three children being guardians to an android 11-year-old fell into place, and I started to get really excited about it. But I needed a name, a catchy name, a name that on the one hand seemed quite normal but on the other told everybody what she is. I pondered on the word android: "Android. An-droid…" My eureka moment. "That's it: Anne Droid!" Then I contemplated how I should spell the surname. Droid sounded a bit like Boyd, or the German surname Freud. I decided to spell the name Anne Dreud, and then thought better of it because children would probably pronounce it "Drood". In the end I just changed the 'i' to a 'y' and called her Anne Droyd.

Anthony accompanied me with the dog on Thursday evenings after the meeting. "I've got her name," I enthused.

"Go on."

"How about Anne Droyd?"

His reaction was immediate. He grimaced, "Ugh, corny."

I wasn't dissuaded. "I know it's corny, but kids will love being in on the joke," I said. "It's like K9 in *Doctor Who*. A robot dog, a canine whose name is K9. All the adults groan but the children love it."

I wrote one 20-minute television episode of *Anne Droyd* in pen and ink, and then shelved it.

My writing continued to appear in fanzines, and when Mum saw that I was serious, she paid for me to enrol on The Writers Bureau correspondence course. She also bought me a word processor so that I could present my assignments in a professional way. The course served me well and I gradually began to appreciate what I had been doing wrong time after time. I started to ask other people to read my work before I submitted it, and pondered thoughtfully on any advice given. I also took into consideration the wishes of editors and stopped sending in material they had made clear they didn't want.

I was also always on the look-out for magazines that were in their infancy, reasoning that I stood a better chance getting work accepted by them. And I was right, because the one thing new magazines didn't do so well was pay. Writers tended to get their rewards in kind: review a book or video and get to keep the item afterwards, that sort of thing. But any starter aware of where he is on the ladder would be pleased just to see their name and work in print. I certainly was.

The first magazine I was published in was *Eclipse*, a new science-fiction journal that had managed to get stocked by WH Smith. Sadly after a few issues it folded because it wasn't cost effective. A man called Simon Clarke edited it, and I thank him for giving me my first little break. A few months later I discovered issue two of *Classic Television* magazine. They had high hopes and took me under their wing as a regular contributor. I in turn did my bit to publicize it locally. There was a real feeling of working and making progress.

In 1997 my psychologist Stephanie let it be known that she had been given a promotion, and that she felt my being passed over to someone new to, in effect, start all over again would be a step backwards. I wasn't too thrilled about this because I'd come to regard her as a highly valued confidante. I also felt that we hadn't quite hit the nail on the head in one or two areas. But she discharged me back into the world at large, I came off sick leave and began claiming the dole. I now had to get a job again, and to be honest I was quietly terrified by the prospect of having to meet new people and learn new tasks.

Then, one afternoon, there was a knock at the door. It was John from Alpine asking if I wanted my old job back on a part-time basis. I very gratefully said yes. With my new-found social skills and assertion, life at Alpine would be a lot easier than had been before.

Or so I thought.

Pursuing the Dream, 1997–2002

T HE ATMOSPHERE AT THE FACTORY was even more doom laden than before. Elaine was leaving to start a new job as a carer. "I should have done this years ago," she said. She walked me through all the QC procedures and voiced her astonishment at how little I had remembered. Thankfully it didn't take too long for me to pick it up again.

The management's attempts to keep the business afloat were pitiable. They had reworked the recipes so that they didn't need to include sugar. The reason? They hadn't paid the sugar company for the last delivery. Having lost the Britvic contract, they decided to create two new lines: (wait for it) *Pep Cid* and *Tan-goers*. We all roared with laughter when we heard about them. Why, even the labels had the same colours as the original big name products! There was a real sense that Alpine's days were well and truly numbered. Depression set in again and I returned to my old custom of staggering out of bed and arriving at work exactly two minutes late. I despised the place.

Sure enough, by September 1998 the situation was grim. Production had been reduced to half days with some of the crew being given the option of going home early without pay. Then one morning Bill Seagrave paid me a visit. "We've had a meeting down at the front," he said. He was staring at some papers on what passed for a workbench. "We're making some cutbacks." He half smiled, half laughed, as though in defeat, and then turned to look at me. "And I'm afraid you're one of them." I didn't know whether to burst into tears or jump for joy.

My depressions were getting deeper. A number of issues were conspiring against me. I got so anguished my head hurt. I hated the kids in my neighbourhood, hated my own sense of worthlessness and hated the fact that my writing wasn't really taking off. It felt as though I was going nowhere. It was time to re-evaluate a few things. I'd come to regard the world as capped and other people as prisoners of the Village, but how could I be sure it wasn't the other way around? How could I be sure that *I* hadn't been capped, that *I* wasn't a prisoner of my beliefs? I questioned everything. I really wanted out. Being all too aware of how innocent people were suffering all over the world, and not always because of humanity's greed, but because of old age and natural disasters, also contributed. Where was the all-loving Creator when we needed him?

And so, for the first time in my life, I embarked on an unbiased, open-minded attempt at discerning the truth. It had to be something that made sense, something that held water, that could withstand scrutiny. It had to be right, not just emotionally, but logically and intellectually. If it meant abandoning God, then I would do it. If it led to rejecting cherished beliefs and a change of course, I would do it. But it had to be right.

I had to address the issue of where the universe, the planet Earth and the life on Earth had come from. Scientists agree generally that the universe had a beginning. But what caused the beginning? What was there before it was created? They say a minute particle of densely compressed matter, a singularity, exploded, and what it released gradually settled into the pattern of the universe we have today. So perfectly ordered, so mathematically precise. But of its own accord? Without any intelligent guiding hand? Order from chaos? And what was the singularity doing before it exploded? Where had it come from? What existed *before* the singularity?

For all its claims to explain the origins of the universe, I concluded that speculative science did nothing of the sort. Most of its answers merely provoked more questions.

Then there was the issue of how life came to be on the planet Earth. Two theories prevailed, the first being that all the chemicals required for life were lying dormant, millions of years ago, in a primeval soup. The atmosphere at that time was radioactive. There was a flash of lightning, and in an instant all the right amino acids fused together to form a protein molecule. (Have you ever seen an artist's impression of the inner workings of a cell? Simple it ain't.) Somehow, the molecule survived the poisonous primeval soup and the radioactive atmosphere and began to reproduce. Again there was no intelligence at work, it was just a molecule. How the molecule knew it needed to survive, given that it had no conscious mind, self-awareness or desire, is not an issue easily resolved.

According to the theory, as the millions of years passed by, the molecule's descendants evolved from single-celled organisms into the two sexes, male and female. How or why they did this, and how they existed in the period between states, is again a complete mystery. Some developed into fish, others found their way onto land. Some became plants and trees. Of course, simultaneously, and quite by chance, the atmosphere was changing to accommodate these new creatures. Over millions of years every form of life on Earth developed, fish into reptiles, reptiles into birds and back again, then mammals, and finally ape into man.

Scientists taught the theory of spontaneous generation of life as fact for decades, until they were forced to accept by laboratory experiments that the chances of life coming about of its own accord, living matter from non-living matter, were so remote they were impossible. And so the second theory was born, namely that life arrived on earth from outer space, perhaps on the back of a meteorite. But this doesn't explain *how*, it simply relocates the origins to somewhere else.

As you can imagine, by obsessing about all of this I made myself quite ill. The more I questioned it the more it fell apart. It angered me greatly that this stuff was being taught as fact in schools and on television. Wildlife presenters would use phrases such as "Through the miracle of evolution", and the public accepted it.

I so desperately wanted to jilt God and change course, but logic was staring me in the face. What is designed has a designer. What is constructed has a builder. Laws, even natural ones, logically have a law maker. If computer programs require a programmer (and even self-programming computers need someone to create the original instructions), so does the program that drives and develops life – the DNA.

I longed to believe that it all just came about by chance and developed of its own accord.

I can't quite throw off the idea of God.

My stepdaughter Marie, who had been through a similar crisis of faith, became my confidante. She had concluded that there was insufficient proof on both sides of the debate and had become an agnostic, someone who doesn't know what to believe. I wished I could become an agnostic too, but it seemed a pretty tormented sort of existence, not knowing whether God is there or not. To leave the Witnesses, to upset the apple cart with my wife and Witness friends, as I would surely do, I needed something stronger than "I'm not sure it's true."

To be genuinely open minded I had to consider the case for a Creator. Interestingly, at the very start of the question, I ran into the same problem as I had with the exploding singularity. Before God created the universe, what was he doing? Before he created the spirit beings in his heavenly realm, he was alone. Being eternal, like the singularity, he existed endlessly into the past, without beginning. Logically, there had to be a time when he hadn't created anything.

What had he been doing all that time, alone? But if God wasn't eternal, if he was actually created, who created *him*? And who created the person who created *him*? And who created *that* person? I had to accept that, if God exists, he/she/it must be eternal. But then, using the same logic, the singularity in the Big Bang scenario could also have been eternal.

Either time stretches endlessly into the past, which contradicts the notion of a beginning, or it did have a beginning, which begs the question of what was going on before it began (which is impossible to answer because one can't go back to before the beginning of time. *Aarrgghh!!*).

I was compelled to reason that this creative force must possess immense energy, and it must have applied a high form of mathematics to the relationship between matter and energy to arrange the various systems (superclusters, clusters, galaxies, solar systems, etc.) and maintain them.

Another question. Is God just an impersonal force or is there a distinct personality? The care and attention in designing such things as the weather cycle, the seasons, the different kinds of animal and plant life, miracles in our own bodies such as the five senses, would denote someone who *cares*. And if he/she/it cares so much, there must be a purpose, and there must be a reason for permitting innocent people to suffer as they do.

I entertained several theories about the person of God. One which appealed very much was the concept of God being mad, that he was both loving, kind and forgiving, *and* cruel, vindictive and merciless. Another was the theory of the uninterested God, but that fizzled out because I couldn't see why a bored creator would bother to maintain the universe.

In the end I drew the conclusion that both systems of belief, natural evolution and God, were riddled with mind-mangling contradictions and required faith to fill in where the facts were absent. For me, the theory of a deliberate act of creation had the upper hand.

I haven't quite thrown off the idea of God.

I was back where I started – almost. I say almost because, having put myself through that gruelling form of self cross-examination, and having come very close to not believing in anything, I now had greater respect for other people's beliefs, no matter how flimsy they seemed. The glazed look that I might have had in my eye from "knowing" the truth had gone. Instead of telling people "It's the truth", I would now say, "I believe it's the nearest to religious truth that I have found." And if anyone suggested that one day I might leave Jehovah's Witnesses, rather than react with abject horror at such an idea, I would say, "You never know. Maybe I will. But it would only be because I had become convinced of something else."

People seemed to like this sort of answer because it wasn't dogmatic, it wasn't "I'm so definitely right, and you're so definitely wrong". I guess what I'm trying to say is that the agony of questioning everything made me more balanced. After a while I noticed that a lot of my Witness colleagues were also very balanced. Without realizing it, I had been the stereotypical dogmatic Jehovah's Witness so often depicted in newspapers and television dramas.

The other good thing that had come out of the trauma was *Cerebral Vice*, a fourth album of songs. This time I refrained from recording them and just carried the basic melodies in my head. The lyrics came to me fairly swiftly. Lyrics like "Is It Me?". Have you ever stopped and thought about your perception of the world, and wondered "Someone's got it all wrong here. Is it me or is it them?"

Is it me? Is it you? Is it them? Is it us?

The swarming crowd of frantic shoppers
Pushing and shoving for life's no-hopers
Number One, he takes over
A simple truth of our kind

No one cares that I can see
No one sees that I can care
No one knows what I see in caring
A simple truth of our kind

Is it me? Is it you? Is it them? Is it us? (Is it me? Tell me if it's me)
Is it me? Is it you? Is it them? Is it us? (Is it you? Tell me if it's you)
Is it me? Is it you? Is it them? Is it us? (Is it them? Tell me if it's them)
Is it me? Is it you? Is it them? Is it us? (Is it us? Tell me if it's us)

Paper notes in exchange
For popularity, to make a name
Number One, he's insane
A simple truth of our kind
Men in suits, they decide
Telling us to believe the lie
They lie and say that we decide
A simple truth of our kind

Is it me? Is it you…?

An angry crowd in derision
Loathe the man of truthful vision
Number One, his selfish mission
A simple truth of our kind

Shout the truth from the roof tops
Tell the world it's got to stop
Number One's behind the plot
A simple truth of our times

Is it me? Is it you…?

Is it me?

The title track got its name from how I was feeling, that my head was trapped in a vice and that it was getting tighter and tighter. It also has a secondary meaning, a moral one, as I was entertaining vices condemned by my religion. "Tired" is all about depression and despair.

I'm so tired
Of being beaten black and blue
Of a greedy material world
Denial of truth

I'm so tired
Of empty philosophy
Of meaningless belief
Refusing to see

It's hard to breathe in and out these days
Hard to get out of bed
It's hard to hide the depth of despair
Hard to get it out of my head

It's hard just going on with life
Hard on the old routine
It's hard to smile at the passer-by
Hard to really feel

I'm so tired
Of waiting for better days
Of dreaming up Utopia
And answers to prayers

I'm so tired
Of loving people full of hate
Of their seducing eyes
Of their tempting bait

It's hard to breathe in and out these days...

I'm so tired
Of affliction on the innocent
Of suffering lies
Modern pestilence

I'm so tired
Of this world we're living in
Of false promises
And what they call sin

It's hard to breathe in and out these days...

"What If?" questions the things we all take for granted. How do we know our perception of the world is the right one?

What if I've got it all wrong?
What if you're not there?
What if there's no plan?
What if nobody cares?

What if the world's not round?
Just suppose it's flat?
What if Einstein's theory
Turns out to be total pap?

What if goodness is weaker than bad?
What if sanity is just me being mad?
What if morality is reason to be sad?
What if I've got it all wrong?

Is the majority always right?
And am I following a pointless plight?
Am I all wrong and they're all right?
What if I've got it all wrong?

What if two times two is five?
What if things fall up?
What if freedom is within my reach?
But then again, what if it's not?

What if this life is all there is?
What if I'm wasting my time?
What if I could be all that I dream of?
What if it could all be mine?

What if goodness is weaker than bad...?

"Excuse Me" explores my paranoia.

Excuse me
Are you laughing at me
Because I'm not such a pretty picture?

Excuse me
Are you speechless because
I've said something not quite your cup of tea?

Excuse me for saying sorry again
I get the feeling that no one can take to me
Excuse me for paranoid delusions
I know for sure that the world is against me

Excuse me
Are you shocked because
I don't get on with the elevated thinkers?

Excuse me
Are your eyebrows raised because
I sound like I don't belong here?

Excuse me for saying sorry again...

The album represented who I was at that time so purely, I longed to record it. But I wasn't prepared to knock out another set of poor-quality recordings. I held on until I would be in a position to make them properly on decent equipment.

My progress as a writer was steady. My tutor at The Writers Bureau, Margot Raneri, marked my assignments and sent them back always with plenty of praise. I took my time with the assignments and became convinced that this was the only way I could ever reach my goal. Even if I had gone to college or university I might not have been able to keep up. This way I could go at my own speed. It took a while for the penny to drop about certain bad writing habits, but when they did the lesson was learned well. Margot loved my idea for *The Blueprint*, and it came back with ticks right through, and the comment "An excellent plot for a novel." I was getting there.

The magazine *Classic Television* was making a few waves. Publicity director John Ellis and editor Martyn Jackson were attracting the attention of mainstream distributors who could see potential in it. The various teams would say things like "It's good but we think you need to put more science fiction in it", or "It needs a few more soap opera articles. If you do that we'll consider taking it on." However, Ellis and Jackson prided themselves on having a magazine that was different to the others. They focused on comedy programmes and kitchen sink dramas.

The Writers Bureau had taught me that it's no use having a grand plan if there's no market for it. People buy magazines about science fiction and soap operas. There are no mainstream magazines devoted to *Only Fools and Horses* or *Casualty*, even though these series continue to be huge hits. For *Classic Television* to get picked up it would have to compromise.

Around October our landlord went bankrupt. The upshot of this was we had to vacate our house as soon as possible. Carol succeeded in finding two one-bedroom flats in Little Hulton, one for her and me and one for Paul, and we moved that month.

Amazingly, on the day that we were in the process of moving I received a phone call from Channel Four Television. I had written to the programme *Right to Reply* about the BBC's treatment of *Doctor Who*. The year 1998 was the 35th anniversary and, while it was being marked on satellite TV, nothing was being done by the corporation that invented it. I was greatly irritated by the BBC putting out lots of anniversary merchandise without giving us a series of repeats on terrestrial television. I believed they were exploiting the fans and giving nothing back.

Both Carol and I were invited on an all expenses paid trip to London to record a feature. After the phone call, I went upstairs to pack a few more things, and Carol continued her vacuuming downstairs. I smiled as I heard above the noise of the cleaner my wife excitedly singing the *Doctor Who* theme.

The director of my particular bit was called Claire. She was joined by a researcher named Donna, a camera man called Mark, and a sound man by the name of Ben. I tried to jolly things along by enthusing about Spike Milligan's famous Pakistani Dalek sketch. "Put-it-in-the-cur-ry!" I chanted. Donna just looked at me, and then I realized why. She was of Pakistani descent.

Sorry Donna.

First on the agenda was some filming in front of the blue screen at Channel Four. Then a trip to the Museum of the Moving Image to interview *Doctor Who Magazine* editor Gary Gillatt. I caught sight of him as we pulled up, and my stomach churned.

It's Gary Gillatt!

I shook his hand and smiled. Claire seemed a bit surprised by my approach. "Oh, have you two met before?" I had to concede that we hadn't, but I felt I knew him because of his editorials in the magazine and his appearances on spin-off documentary videos. I found the whole thing overwhelming and struggled to remember my assigned questions.

Next stop BBC Worldwide, 80 Wood Lane, to interview the editor of the book range, Stephen Cole. The BBC had assigned him to represent them.

It's BBC Worldwide!

Once inside the building, Carol and I sat in a lounge area and waited. After a few minutes it dawned on me that the person sitting on the other sofa was none other than Gary Russell, co-producer of the famous Audio Visuals (fan-made radio-style plays), ex-*Doctor Who Magazine* editor and author of numerous books. I plucked up the courage to go over and introduce myself.

It's Gary Russell!

I complimented Gary on his novelization of the Paul McGann TV movie: I considered his book to be superior to the actual film. Gary seemed rather pleased about that, and introduced me to Mike Tucker, onetime special effects man during the show's latter years who had now turned author.

It's Mike Tucker!

I shook his hand and told him how I'd enjoyed his novel (with co-author Robert Perry) *Illegal Alien*. I thought it was fantastic.

At last Stephen Cole was ready for us.

It's Stephen Cole!

We recorded the interview, but again I kept clamming up. After a while Claire asked if I was all right. She was concerned that I wasn't enjoying my day. I had to explain that making an appearance on television was a dream come true and that, although the likes of Gary Gillatt, Gary Russell, Mike Tucker and Steve Cole were just media people to her, they were in fact heroes to me. In the end I told her, Mark and Ben about my little break-down and my sessions with the psychologist. I thought it might explain a few things.

"Well, you've done very well," said Claire. "That Gary Gillatt knew who you were."

"Did he?"

"Yes. Did I not tell you? When I first rang him up he asked, 'Who's doing it?' and I said, 'He's called William and he's from Manchester,' and he said, 'Is it William Hadcroft?'"

I smiled and nodded. "He must have seen my name in the fanzines." So my plan was working. Get the experience, get my name bandied about.

Finally we stopped off at the legendary Who Shop in East Ham to interview Alexandra Looseley-Saul. A genuine TARDIS prop stood in the corner. Another childhood dream was fulfilled when I stepped inside it.

"Oh, are you coming next weekend?" Alexandra asked, almost as an afterthought.

"Next weekend?"

"To meet Tom Baker. He's signing his autobiography here."

Reluctantly I explained that I was unemployed and that there was no way I could afford to come back to London to meet Tom Baker.

My segment was broadcast in November and all the family were thrilled. A number believed that it would lead to my being picked up by some editor, publisher or producer type and given regular work. Alas, it was not to be. Following the broadcast, Claire phoned to see what I thought of it. I was privately obsessing about her using a catchy version of the *Doctor Who* theme and the way it jarred against my slow "moody" delivery. She detected the reservation in my tone and worried that I hadn't enjoyed myself.

The *Right to Reply* office very kindly stumped up the train fare so I could go back to London and meet Tom Baker.

I had regarded Tom Baker as a father figure over the years. I was quite taken with his emotional response to seeing clips from his stories in the video *The Tom Baker Years*, and he'd spoken to camera about his dream of sharing a glass of wine and a slice of cheese with the viewer (the fans) in the independent video *Doctor... Who On Earth is Tom Baker?*. He seemed to feel about me the way I felt about him. And so all the way to London I thought of something short and concise that would make him understand just how important he had been to me.

I recalled that he loved the writings of Charles Dickens to such a degree that he read a portion every day.

I love you and your work the way you love Dickens.

Upon arriving at East Ham I met up with *Classic Television* publicity director John Ellis. It was nice putting a face to the voice after all this time. Nervous, I turned down his offer to go for a pint and we went to a café instead. I then regaled him with a brief history of my life and told him just how much I loathed football. I'd forgotten that he loved it. Thankfully, he wasn't put off.

And then it was time to meet Mr Baker. I heard his oh-so-familiar voice as I entered the Who Shop. Alexandra introduced me to him and told him of my exploits the previous week. "Yes, yes," he said. "I don't watch it regularly but I know the programme you mean." I bought my copy of his autobiography and he signed it: "Happy days. Tom Baker."

"Tom," I said sheepishly.

"Yes?"

"You know how you feel about Charles Dickens?"

"Yes."

I swallowed hard. "Well that's how I feel about meeting you."

He smiled at me. Not the big toothy Doctor Who grin that he used to do, but a sort of modest embarrassed half smile. After clearing his throat he boomed, "Well it would be a bit difficult for me to meet Charles Dickens!" And everybody laughed.

Everybody except me. The years I'd spent dreaming of what I would say to my hero if I had the chance to meet him. When I met Colin Baker I had said nothing. Now, when I met Tom, I made a fool of myself. "You understand what I'm trying to say?" I said. Then he nodded, as if realizing that I should be handled sensitively. "Yes," he said, "I understand," and handed me my book.

Not content to embarrass him by my expressions of undying loyalty, I lingered by his desk for the whole of the signing while other fans had their two minutes and moved on. I was the stereotypical fan, the obsessed groupie who couldn't see the difference between a character and an actor.

John Ellis accompanied me on the Underground as I headed back to Euston station. Inside I was crushed by the realization of how I'd conducted myself, and at the same time mithered by the silences on the Tube. "Hey John," I began excitedly, "I've been thinking about *The Incredible Hulk*. Don't you think it's clever how Kenneth Johnson wove all that stuff in about DNA and tapping into hidden strengths?"

"Er, yes," replied John, rather taken aback. Two girls sitting opposite simultaneously broke into a fit of giggles.

I'd done it again.

In early 1999 I applied for a part-time job at a old folks' nursing home, thinking that it would be the perfect environment for me. Gentle elderly people, staff who had to maintain a level of kindness and sensitivity at all times. And I was right, it was exactly like that. But it wasn't the perfect environment for me. Why? Because it had people in it.

The staff were the most pleasant staff one could wish for. A young man in his late teens showed me the ropes, and my early tasks took the form of cleaning and setting dinner tables, changing and making beds, that sort of thing.

One day I was asked to wash some pots in the kitchens. They had to be done within a certain time, and I started to panic. The tins were covered in brown stains that were very difficult to remove, despite my attempts. I was half way through the task when someone walked in. "Have you still not finished that, William? What have you been doing? You've got all the coffees to do yet, you know."

I feel like crying.

"I can't get this brown stuff off."

She walked over, frowning, and took a look. "You don't have to get that off, you daft thing. You just have to get the bits of food off. I thought you used to be a hotel porter."

"I did."

Not a very good one, though.

"I was told to wash these tins," I offered lamely. "No one said anything about leaving the brown stains."

She tutted. "You shouldn't have to be told, it's obvious. Where's your common sense?"

Oh, that old thing. I don't always have it.

She very kindly took my place while I went off to make the coffees and teas. This was very easy, until it came to dispensing them. Not only did each resident have his or her particular preferences about milk and sugar, but quite a few had tablets that they washed down with their drink. Others had diabetes, and sugar in their drink could put them into a coma. As I looked down my list of names and wheeled my trolley from room to room, those oh-so-familiar feelings drifted over me. My breathing became increasingly measured, my complexion changed, my eyes watered.

I looked at my watch. The drinks had to be done by a particular time and I was only half way through. The coffee had also started to go cold. One of the residents was talking to themselves, others were just smiling and waiting. I could hear staff members busying themselves outside.

I can't breathe. I'm going dizzy. I'm going to cry, I can feel it. My bottom lip is starting to quiver.

The manager stared at me as I appeared in the corridor. "Are you all right, William?"

"No," I said, undoing my tie. "I need to sit down."

"What's the matter?"

"I'm having an anxiety attack."

"OK, you sit down, I'll get someone else to take over."

The usual big confession followed: childhood history, not fitting in, a tendency to obsess, poor social skills, unpredictable bouts of paranoia, appointments with a clinical psychologist.

I had lasted one month in the job, and now I was back on sick leave and down to see another psychologist for booster sessions.

My feverish interest in Gary Numan tailed off when his music went heavily into the realms of anti-religion, with his album *Exile* depicting a Judgement Day and Armageddon where God and the Devil turn out to be one and the same person, two sides of the same coin. While on an intellectual level I found the concept tantalizing, especially given my recent bout of inner torment, I could not stomach the idea of Jesus being anything other than the righteous man the Bible depicts him to be. I also felt that someone endlessly banging on about how he hates God is no less an irritant than a person who forever sings the Almighty's praises.

And so my zeal for Gary Numan's music simmered down. That said, I was still very keen on the earlier material and Gary the man.

My first appointment with clinical psychologist Suzanne covered a lot of old ground, and focused on my anger and depressions. This series of sessions was nowhere near as extensive as the ones with Stephanie had been, and I interpreted this as my not being as ill. I hadn't gone right back to square one. Suzanne believed that my anger was a leftover trait from the days when we were ape men.

> There's virtually no evidence that we were ape men. There are millions of apes and moneys, and millions of humans. There are only a handful of skulls to represent ape men, and most of them are incomplete. Conclusion: ape men are a figment of scientists' imaginations.

I found it hard controlling my obsession with evolution and it showed, especially when I gave Suzanne a Jehovah's Witness book on the subject. "Thank you," she said kindly. "I'm not actually allowed to accept gifts from patients, but I'll put it in the hospital library when I get back. It might come in useful for my colleagues to consult."

As far as I was concerned, my anger stemmed from my deep-seated feelings of failure and my disdain for our fake world. My emotions could be regulated, my appointments with Stephanie had proved that. I was taught how to cope again.

After a while, I was deemed fit enough to go back into the system, and back on Job Seekers Allowance. This time I would be stuck on it for a period of three years. I had no intention of going back to a factory, and no intention of putting myself in environments that would likely trigger off more anxiety. I wanted an office job doing things that I knew I was good at, and working with people who were on my wavelength. I attended the interviews but got no further. No experience equals no job.

Carol and I lived on very basic money, with little more than fifty pounds in the bank at any given time. Walking the streets and using public transport was a nightmare for me, especially when school children and yobs were present.

> I might commit suicide or I might be completely all right.

But I soldiered on.

It was circa September 2000, while I was in Carol's nephew's rare records shop "Acoustic Soup" in Bolton, that a significant turn of events began. Carol's brother-in-law Ken was manning the place, and I was browsing through some records, really killing time until the bus came, when I overheard an interview on the radio. It was BBC Greater Manchester Radio and someone by the name of Nigel Bent was talking about a new publishing company in the North West. "Turn it up, Ken," I said excitedly.

Nigel represented a small press outfit called CK Publishing, who were going to have a launch party in Stockport the following month. They published a quarterly magazine of poems and short stories called *Writer's Muse* and were about to move into the realm of paperback books. They were on the look-out for possible submissions. I couldn't write down their details fast enough.

A friend of mine, William Murray, who was also interested in becoming a writer, joined me and we booked ourselves places for the launch. In advance I sent manager Calum Kerr some sample issues of *Classic Television* as a way of introducing myself and having something to talk about. When I got there I seemed to be the only person, other than Messrs Kerr and Bent, wearing a suit. Still, my Writers Bureau training was coming in handy, I was being as professional and serious as I could.

William and I listened to the readings of poetry from the saddle-bound pamphlet books that were being released that night, and then I plucked up the courage to speak to Nigel Bent. He reiterated that they were hoping to publish *bona fide* paperback novels in the coming year. I informed him that I had a couple of ideas for children's novels, and he looked quite keen. I told him I was aiming at the 9 to 12 age bracket, but I was unsure whether the modern generation would appreciate my ideas. He said, "Well you send us three sample chapters and a synopsis, and I'll give them to my 10-year-old daughter, and we'll see what she makes of them."

Afterwards I introduced myself to Calum Kerr. He was delighted to meet me, being a bit of a sci-fi buff himself, and a fan of *The Hitch-Hiker's Guide*. I told him of my plans to submit a novel and he said he would look forward to receiving it.

Getting back home, I said to Anthony, "Right, I have two things I can develop. One is the deep controversial thing, *The Blueprint*, the other is *Anne Droyd*." Ant recalled our discussions four years previously and replied, "It's gotta be *Anne Droyd*, mate. It's got the right formula, it's got the gimmicky marketable name, and there's nothing controversial about it." The reasoning made perfect sense.

I worked out a plot and set it on the actual housing estate surrounding Century Lodge. Nazi scientists and underground bases were thrown into the equation, and Anne's bizarre surname was explained by calling her father Professor Wolfgang Droyd, which I believed I would just about get away with.

As for the characters, I wanted to do a bit of a Dennis Potter and weave elements of my life and personality into the story to give it a human interest angle. I decided that it would have an undercurrent exploring what it is to be different in a world which demands conformity. I wrote three long chapters, the last of which ended with the introduction of Anne and the Professor.

The first two chapters were "tested" on Carol and Jonathan one rainy Saturday afternoon. I wasn't sure whether they were just patiently listening or really engrossed. When I finished reading, they were ecstatic. Carol was convinced it was a winner and Jonathan compared it favourably to children's TV dramas of yesteryear. I also gave a copy to a friend of the family, 12-year-old Karina, who told me she couldn't concentrate on the novel she was currently reading because she was thinking about my characters. Her current novel? *Jane Eyre* by Charlotte Brontë. A further copy was given to Carol's niece Lily-Anne and more favourable comments came back.

With all this in the figurative bank I went to my mother and asked her to proof read it. Most pages, I'm pleased to say, were left untouched, while a handful had extensive comments in the margins.

I posted off the sample to Calum and waited. After what seemed like forever he e-mailed to ask if I had the rest. It took me roughly three months to write the remaining nine chapters, all the while consulting my young friends, my mother, my wife and my best mate. Anthony would laugh whenever I explained a plot device or a bit of characterization. "You started out with something gimmicky and marketable, but it's ended up all deep and philosophical anyway! You don't seem to be able to help yourself."

And it was true. I contrasted the families of my characters Gezz and Luke by making one religious and the other entirely materialistic. This was not done to promote religious values, but rather to explore the different ways a concept could be interpreted. The third character Malcolm would be a thinker, a philosopher. These developments came about because I began to realize that Anne Droyd would question absolutely everything and if I as the author gave simple pat answers I would be accused of preaching a doctrine through the story. As it turned out, Anne would be fed alternate and often conflicting information.

I was also able to explore the concept of difference.

Gezz is different because she conforms to a strict religion. She attends chapel and her parents have got rid of their television set. Malcolm is different because he has his own views on matters. He is also a bit of a loner when divorced from the group. He is shy and lacks social skills. Anne is different because she is a robot and has no emotional capacity. She merely processes information. This causes her to question all that is illogical or poorly explained. She takes things literally, which can be a source of amusement, but more often than not gets her into trouble. The only character to fit in with his school peers is Luke, but among his close friends he's the odd one out because he's the only character to concern himself with fashions and trends.

I discussed with my family and with Anthony the likelihood of adults reading between the lines and accusing me of preaching old-fashioned religious values because, if anything, the concepts projected had come out of my own inner theological debating rather than a desire to lead the way. They reassured me that if any such comments did come back, they would reveal more about the commentators than they would about the work.

Calum Kerr received the full 87,000-word manuscript by the end of January 2001. It was April that year when he telephoned to confirm that he was indeed going to publish it. Many more discussions were had over the ensuing months, and I worked on a couple of rewrites to tighten things up. Artist Jim Whittaker was assigned to produce a colour painting for the cover.

In the meantime I needed to keep myself on the ball. Now that I had a novel under my belt I wanted to try my hand at script writing. I had read that the likes of Gary Russell and Nicholas Briggs, who were now making BBC-licensed *Doctor Who* plays starring the original actors and releasing them straight to CD, started their audio careers making their own unofficial adventures on cassette way back in the 1980s. At the present time, other amateur dramatic groups had sprung up and were doing similar things. I decided to track them down and pitch ideas.

The first person I approached, just prior to the publication of *Anne Droyd*, was Bolton-based writer/producer Gareth Preston. I acquired some of the stories already on CD and was impressed by the acting and the production values. My favourites were *Present Infinite* by Lawrence Ahlemeyer, *Second Chance* by Adrian Hudson, and Gareth's own double-CD escapade *Trick of the Light*.

This was my first real attempt at scripting a *Doctor Who*. Before starting, I meditated on what I considered worked best in the TV series. Period pieces were often the finest productions because they were alien to our time but still set on Earth, and nineteenth-century stuff was very potent because of the Industrial Revolution, Charles Dickens and the mystery of Jack the Ripper. In fact, the TV series had already given us *The Talons of Weng-Chiang* from that period. So I fused those elements with themes from David Wickes' adaptation of *Jekyll and Hyde*, and then sprinkled in the Dennis Potter factor; that is, something personal from my own life.

The human aspect to this story is my own inner battle, spirituality *versus* base desire, and it manifests itself in my character Dr Charles Winston, a scientist not unlike Dr Jekyll. He wants to give Man unlimited access to his animal instincts and be free of moral constraint. Opposing his experiments is Pastor Jacobs, who objects to Winston's experiments on moral grounds. What Winston refers to as animal instincts, Jacobs calls sin. I looked up the Hebrew and Greek words for sin, Hamartia and Chattath (the Ch is usually pronounced "K", and the second vowel is probably round: "Kattaith"). I plumped for the latter and titled my synopsis and episode one script *The Chattath Factor*.

Admittedly I was surprised when Gareth replied and, acting as script editor, wanted changes making. Rather arrogantly, I had assumed that an "amateur" producer would be so pleased to receive a script from outside his circle of friends he would just snap it up. But there was nothing amateur about this man. He made me work and get the script to standard, and then commissioned the remaining two episodes. The discipline did me good. In the end Gareth paid me a great compliment by describing the piece as "an intelligent script".

From there I approached an Australian team led by Matthew Kopelke and Witold Tietze, who not only did their own *Doctor Who* stories, but also had unofficial not-for-profit versions of *Blake's Seven* and *The Prisoner* in the pipeline, along with an ongoing semi-pro series entitled *Beyond Traditional Recognition*. I asked them if they fancied doing an audio adaptation of John

Christopher's *Tripods* trilogy which would be very loyal to the books and, in effect, put right what the BBC had got wrong. They jumped at the chance and I set to work on adapting the first novel *The White Mountains*.

Anne Droyd and Century Lodge was released in paperback on 13 June 2002. Needless to say I was ecstatic.

Anne Droyd and Century Lodge:
The Dream Come True

B<small>Y 2002 I HAD BEEN UNEMPLOYED</small> so long that I qualified to make use of the facilities at Action For Employment (A4e) – in fact I *had to* as a condition for receiving Job Seekers Allowance. I attended regular meetings in Walkden hosted by Cath Barton and was assigned to a special self-employment course in Salford run by Steve Sumner. It's thanks to these advisors and fellow job seekers that I was able to drum up the courage to organize my own publicity.

If money was lacking, ingenuity was the answer. First off, I advised anybody who enquired about my book to order it from the Bolton bookshop Sweetens. They were all that was left of a chain of bookshops and were now independent. I hoped to make an impression with them. Sure enough, family and friends flocked to Sweetens and the manager Stella Morris began ordering copies for the shelves.

In the meantime I was contributing to any and every fanzine and website that would agree to publish my work. I had also begun a correspondence with audio producer Robert Dunlop. He became quite a fan and went to considerable lengths to promote the book. He was also very keen to know about the sequel *Anne Droyd and the House of Shadows*. I actually had ten sequels in mind which would form a complete series. Rob was so taken by it that he began to speculate about what the other stories might be about and how the series would end. He advised killing off a principal character and had definite ideas as to who it should be!

The A4e team kept talking about approaching the local newspapers. In time I worked up the courage to phone the *Salford Advertiser*. I was amazed by the response. Journalist Ben Murch lapped it up and presented it as a human interest story: working-class lad publishes book against the odds. A photographer came round and took some snaps with me holding the book near my face. I was so astounded at how easy it was to talk to the local press. I got on to the *Bolton Evening News* the same day and dropped heavy hints about Sweetens bookshop.

Both articles came out in close proximity, and before long I was shown by my sister-in-law Lillian the Saturday edition of the *Bolton Evening News* which carried the Top Ten bestseller list. The list was compiled by Sweetens, with whom the *BEN* had a good relationship, and *Anne Droyd* was currently sitting at Number Two. I was utterly flabbergasted.

On the back of this I mailed out clippings to BBC Greater Manchester Radio and summoned the courage to talk to the *Manchester Evening News*. The result: I was invited onto the Mancunia slot presented by Diane Oxberry, the weather girl on BBC TV's regional programme *Northwest Tonight*. I couldn't believe it when I walked into the BBC building on Oxford Road in Manchester. This was yet another dream come true, going on the radio. I was escorted to the studio, and there she was.

It's Diane Oxberry!

Carol and Mum sat at home with strict instructions on how to record the broadcast. They were hysterical when my voice came on. A piece by Brian Lashley appeared in the *Manchester Evening News* in the same week. Thanks to that, I was spotted by another broadcaster, Becky Want, who invited me back to GMR to be on her Sunday afternoon programme.

It's Becky Want!

By this time *Anne Droyd* had reached Number One in the Bolton chart and was selling healthily at Amazon.co.uk. To my absolute delight, Sweetens manager Stella Morris arranged with Calum for me to do a signing at her shop. Two boys showed particular interest in the book, and one of them, some months later, wrote a fan letter.

Myself and Calum Kerr at the Sweetens book signing
kindly organized by Stella Morris, October 2002.

Thanks to all the media coverage, I was able to get myself a few bookings at primary schools to help promote the novel and motivate children in my locality to reach their potential. If I could do it, they could do it. I performed signings at all the schools and was treated by my young fans as a hero.

One boy had bought the book a few weeks previous and plucked up the courage to approach me. "Mr Hadcroft," he said sheepishly. "I just want to say I've been reading your book every night in bed. And I just want to tell you…" His composure suddenly changed, as if he couldn't contain himself any longer. "It's *fantastic!*" He put a lot of emphasis on the word "fantastic" and his eyes dazzled when he said it. I was deeply touched by his enthusiasm.

I needed to get the novel onto a national footing. Calum gave me his blessing and I began mailing out the book to bigger, more established publishers.

I'd come a long way from my days of feeling useless and inhibited. The negative vibes were still there, the depressions still came and went, and I still had my fits of paranoia. But I was managing it.

I sensed I was on the verge of something.

The Pieces Fall into Place, 2003

On 19 MAY 2003 I started my job at the call centre, my first job in four years. The people were lovely, the atmosphere was professional, and I was getting more and more confident with the work each day. Quite considerably different to my life at the soft drinks factory.

The 4 August 2003 marked mine and Carol's tenth wedding anniversary. We didn't just still love one another, but were still *in* love with one another.

Hey, and what do you know, 2003 was also the year the BBC proudly announced their plans to revive *Doctor Who* as an ongoing television series. The exhibition in Blackpool was remounted shortly after.

But 2003 is important to me for another reason, a more profound reason; for that was the year the pieces of a jigsaw that had been muddled for a lifetime dropped effortlessly into place. I had spent years trying to fit it all together, sometimes forcing the parts to marry up when they didn't quite fit. But now they did, now the picture was crystal clear, now I had answers and reasons. For the first time in my life I could understand where I had come from and where I was headed.

The first piece, the first spark of realization, came in the form of a three-part series entitled *The Fan Gene*, written by onetime *Doctor Who Magazine* editor Gary Gillatt. In the debuting article he considered the behaviour of fans, the way they obsess about the programme, the way they catalogue all the facts and figures and the way they cling to it for security, memorizing dialogue, and so forth. He also discussed the sort of characters one comes across at *Doctor Who* conventions. The geeks, the nerds, the emotionally and socially "challenged" (an awful phrase, that), they're all there, as are what we might consider more accomplished types, writers, journalists, producers, actors and ordinary folk who just love the programme.

I had journeyed with fellow fan Gareth Preston to a convention that very year. When we arrived, one chap, a steward, whose job it was to make sure people knew where they were going, was dressed head to foot in Time Lord robes, complete with elaborate shoulder pads and headdress. He approached Gareth and myself as we stood pretend-mingling in reception. "Hello there," he grinned. He was so cheerful, one couldn't help but feel slightly on edge. "Enjoying the convention?"

Gareth and I nodded. "Er, yes, yes."

The Time Lord, seeming to struggle for something to say, pointed at a large hexagonal Mechanoid robot positioned near the entrance to the conference hall. "Like the car?" he said. "It's the new Mini."

> Oh, I see. I understand now. He's trying to jolly things along. He's trying to be funny. My heart goes out to him.

We took in the Mechanoid, which bore no resemblance to a Mini, or indeed a car of any sort. In fact it just looked like what it was, a huge hexagonal robot. By now I was nodding and grinning and racking my brain for something to come back with. "Oh, right. Yes."

Gareth was much more composed. "It'd have a few problems getting down the stairs in *The Italian Job*." Thankfully, I found myself genuinely amused by his observation and was able to laugh out loud. But the Time Lord was nonplussed. He was grinning, but only out of politeness. "Yes, yes," he said. "Anyway, enjoy the convention."

> Phew, I'm glad I'm not the only one.

This was the sort of thing Gary Gillatt was highlighting in his series *The Fan Gene*. The obsessing, the poor social skills, the misfit factor. Birds of a feather flocking together.

But it was the second article in his series that really struck a chord with me. He described a private conversation he'd had with an actress late one night at the convention bar. He'd asked her what she thought made the distinction between fans and "regular" people, and was more than a little stunned when she said she thought the fans were a bit autistic.

I was stunned too. Thoughts of the film *Rain Man*, starring Dustin Hoffman, swept over me: a man wrapped up in his own little private world, clinging to particular things that make him feel secure, his near-genius qualities hidden beneath his phobias and obsessions, a man who talks to himself and fixates on TV quiz shows. Autistic. Mentally ill.

Stephanie said I'm not mentally ill.

Gary went on to research the subject of autism, and as a result discovered its little known, milder cousin Asperger Syndrome. This is named after a German psychologist called Hans Asperger, who in 1944 analysed a group of youngsters prone to obsession and a tendency to withdraw into fantasy worlds of their own devising. Many were quite gifted on an intellectual level, but were lacking in social skills, some appallingly so. It had taken until 1994, some 50 years, for the condition to be officially recognized by professionals.

Asperger Syndrome.

I found all of this fascinating. It was an interesting theory. I didn't see it as more than that until about a month later when I read an interview with Gary Numan. I had identified very closely with the lyrics of his early hits and had discerned a number of personality traits that we shared. His single-mindedness; his obsessions with the car, the aeroplane, the Vietnam war, the non-existence of God; his awkward, jilted movements on stage, his eccentric "dancing"; sharp observations about the music business and the media, but paradoxically uncomfortable when asked to comment. Living out his fantasies in song, but shy and clumsy in real life.

In the interview he said a friend had suggested that he might have a mild expression of something called Asperger Syndrome.

That phrase again…

As a result Numan researched the subject thoroughly and drew the same conclusion. It explained so much: his problems at school, his obsessive behaviour, his paranoia, his self-motivated determination. I began to wonder if it was why I was drawn to Gary Numan's music, the synthesizers and android imagery aside (although our mutual fascination with such things could be down to the "Aspie" gene. Who knows?). I was also quite taken with the fact that I had seen *Doctor Who* fans at conventions wearing Gary Numan sweaters. Big Finish producer Gary Russell was a Numan fan. He used to put Numan song titles in his reviews of *Doctor Who* merchandise! It was too coincidental, there had to be a connection.

The real clincher came when BBC Two broadcasted a documentary entitled *My Family and Autism*, which explored the day-to-day goings on of a family in Blackpool. The programme was presented by 14-year-old Luke Jackson, a boy who had been diagnosed with Asperger Syndrome. I knew from the advertising trailers that I was going to find it enthralling, and so I videoed it for study. Watching Luke was like going back in time. He talked about being different and feeling like an alien. His raw honesty sometimes created problems for him, he struggled with social cues, and was completely baffled by the "game" of dating members of the opposite sex. His obsession with computers drove his mother bonkers, but he compared it to the national obsession with football, and objected to the differentiation.

"Carol," I said excitedly. "You must look at this."

And look at it she did. "It's like watching a 14-year-old you!"

Anthony agreed. "Even down to the football comment."

Something that made me sit up and take note was the fact that Luke had published an autobiographical book entitled *Freaks, Geeks and Asperger Syndrome*. He was also quite adept at discussing his diagnosis in front of hundreds of people at autism conferences. In fact he told the audience at one that he felt more comfortable talking to them in that official capacity than he did engaging in normal conversation in a social setting.

I bought his book and read it from cover to cover. Then I decided I had better get a professional viewpoint on the subject and ordered Dr Tony Attwood's bestselling book *Asperger Syndrome: A Guide for Parents and Professionals*. The book highlights many facets of the Asperger condition, including academic achievement, depression, anger, anxiety, auditory sensitivity, balance, ball skills, clumsiness, memory (which is detailed with long-term personal history and "special interests", but hopeless with the short term and things which do not interest), dyslexia, eccentricity, empathy, eye contact, fear of failure, preference for bland food (no bits, no seeds, no raisins, no peas, no beans – period!), individualism, special interests, inappropriately vocalizing thoughts, panic attacks, and social phobia. To name a few. There are many others, some of which have never really affected me. But all of the ones in the list above certainly have.

After the book, I rented Tony Attwood's conference video. In it he states that there is a very wide Asperger Syndrome spectrum, ranging from individuals who are severely challenged, to those who have a much more subtle expression of the condition, such as some university professors. Some even think that Albert Einstein probably had a ghosting of Asperger Syndrome. I seem to recall hearing that Einstein had several copies of the same suit so that he didn't have to "waste" mental energy deciding what he should wear when he got up in the morning! Very Aspie indeed.

Dr Attwood also notes the keen interest exhibited by some Asperger people in characters like Mr Spock and Lieutenant Data from the TV series *Star Trek*. Mr Spock is half Vulcan, half human. The Vulcans regard emotion as a weakness and have bred it out of themselves through the generations, preferring to deal only in logic. However, because he is half human, Spock has to juggle how he sometimes feels with the requirement for principled logic and reason. Data, on the other hand, is not human at all. He is an android (a robot that looks like a human). He has no emotional awareness whatsoever, frequently misunderstands social cues and struggles to empathize with the problems of his crew mates. That said, he is forever seeking to become "real" and, although he often gets it wrong, he still mixes with people in an attempt to integrate into society.

Dr Attwood also talks about a teenage patient whose special interest is *Doctor Who*. I nearly fell off my chair when I got to that bit!

Convinced that I had identified what had been "wrong" throughout my life, I set off to see my GP, Dr Tauk once again, to set the ball rolling in my quest for an official diagnosis. It all made perfect sense and I had an overwhelming feeling of completeness and, in a way, a new-found confidence. Stephanie and Suzanne had defined the individual traits and had taught me how to combat them, but no one had ever come up with a satisfactory explanation as to why these problems had existed. But now it was crystal clear.

I regressed myself back through key moments of my life and suddenly all the pieces fell into place. I considered the themes I had explored in my novel *Anne Droyd and Century Lodge*: being different in a world that demands conformity, and Anne Droyd's difficulties in understanding and accepting the things we all take for granted. She is the epitome of the

Asperger child. It slowly dawned on me that I had been writing about Asperger Syndrome without knowing it.

Today I am feeling better than ever. Still at odds with what I see going on around me, still at odds with myself, but better at dealing with it, better at understanding it. The chip has well and truly been knocked off my shoulder (he says humbly!), I have learned to respect people and I always try to see why they think what they think, even if I can't agree with it. I'm getting on with my life. The job, the people skills, they're getting easier by the day. I have friends. I have my best friend. I have my soul mate. I'm looking to the future.

I haven't had a genuinely suicidal thought for well over a decade.

You know, I think I'm going to be all right.

Diagnostic Criteria for Hadcroft Syndrome

1. Social acceptance (intense desire to fit in)

At least two of the following:

- (a) Strong impulse to interact with peers

- (b) A desire to interact with peers

- (c) Very alert to social cues

- (d) Aware of what would be regarded as socially inappropriate behaviour

2. Fashionable interests

At least one of the following:

- (a) Pursues activities deemed fashionable by peer group

- (b) Will only admit to pursuing trendy activities before peer group, with non-trendy activities pursued in secret

- (c) Balanced adherence to activities

3. Speech and language peculiarities

At least one of the following:

(a) Driven to adopt and assimilate speech patterns of peer group. Patterns may change depending on groups. Person will modify own pattern accordingly.

(b) Will utter vulgarities and curse during moments of stress, regardless of how irrelevant or illogical the phrases might be. Some words will have religious or sexual connotations, others might refer to bodily fluids and substances regarded as taboo. These utterances are almost always out of context with the situation or subject matter. The names of religious figures, most notably Jesus Christ, are also employed as expletives. A person might exclaim "Jesus!" or "Jesus wept!" or "For Christ's sake!" Amazingly, the phrase "Oh my God" can denote shock, anger, fear, disgust, grief, surprise, happiness and even excitement. Famous non-religious names, however, such as "Adolf Hitler" and "Diana, Princess of Wales" are never employed in this way.

(c) Will utter curse words merely to be accepted by peer group. For example, the individual starts a new job, but remains fairly quiet until he is sure about the accepted use of expletives.

4. Peer pressure

At least one of the following:

(a) Will buckle under peer pressure and adopt views publicly that are not held privately

(b) Will practise behaviours that are unhealthy or dangerous, out of fear of being perceived as cowardly or different

(c) Will rarely, if ever, make a stand for unpopular beliefs

The author of this work has a mild expression of Hadcroft Syndrome.

Websites Devoted to My "Specialist Subjects"

Television series

Doctor Who

www.bbc.co.uk/cult/doctorwho
The official website devised and maintained by the BBC. Features the original TV series, the spin-off novels, CDs and webcasts, and reports regularly on the programme's latest incarnation.

www.gallifreyone.com
Outpost Gallifrey, edited by America based Shaun Lyon. This is the first port of call for many *Doctor Who* fans. It has forums and a chat room where fans can 'meet' and discuss the programme. News of upcoming conventions is billed, and would-be writers are invited to submit articles and reviews.

The Incredible Hulk

www.incrediblehulktvseries.com
The most comprehensive website devoted to the live action TV series starring Bill Bixby and Lou Ferrigno. Devised and maintained by Mark Rathwell, it carries numerous behind-the-scenes titbits, including an in-depth interview with the man who adapted the Hulk to television, Kenneth Johnson, as well as episode guides and un-filmed scripts.

The Tripods

www.bbc.co.uk/cult/ilove/tv/tripods
A BBC webpage devoted to the television adaptation of John Christopher's classic *Tripods* trilogy *The White Mountains, The City of Gold and Lead* and *The Pool of Fire*, which fell one third short of its proposed run. The pictures and downloadable sequences are great.

www.gnelson.demon.co.uk/tripods
Graham Nelson's very detailed study of the BBC television adaptation, examining the climate within the BBC in the 1980s, details of the production, and the differences between the TV series and the books.

www.thetripods.org
America-based site devised and maintained by Stuart Wyss. Focuses on the television series and reports on fan activity.

The Prisoner

www.the-prisoner-6.freeserve.co.uk
Devoted to Patrick McGoohan's allegorical TV series which addresses the question of us being prisoners of society and, ultimately, of ourselves. Episode guides, news, and how to join the appreciation society.

Religion

www.watchtower.org
The official website sponsored by the legally recognized non-profit making publishing arm of Jehovah's Witnesses. FAQ, articles, as well as a list of available publications. You can also download some of their award-winning video presentations.

www.jw-media.org
The more secular-based website for members of the media and those who are interested in topical issues concerning the organization. News is released regularly and covers all manner of subjects, from announcements about upcoming conventions, to exposing the brutal treatment of persons in countries where the organization is under government ban.

Asperger syndrome

www.lukejackson.info
Website by the author of *Freaks, Geeks and Asperger Syndrome*, published by Jessica Kingsley Publishers, and presenter of the BBC Two documentary *My Family & Autism*.

www.tonyattwood.com.au
World expert and bestselling author of *Asperger Syndrome: A Guide for Parents and Professionals*, published by Jessica Kingsley Publishers.

www.aspergerinformation.net
Loads of information about AS, written by Suz, who herself is diagnosed with the syndrome.

Anne Droyd

www.annedroyd.com
A look at the origins of Will Hadcroft's characters and the setting for *Anne Droyd and Century Lodge*, a 'making of' feature, original art, photographs of the real-life locations, and more.

www.jkp.com
Jessica Kingsley Publishers of London and Philadelphia – home to Anne Droyd and her friends.